Music Is Your Business

The Musician's FourFront Strategy for Success

Third Edition

Christopher Knab
and
Bartley F. Day

Edited by Sue Cook

FourFront Media & Music

Music Is Your Business, Third Edition
A Musician's FourFront Strategy for Success
© 2001, 2003, 2007 by Christopher Knab and Bartley F. Day
First edition 2001
Third edition 2007

FourFront Media and Music
1245 S. 128th St.
Seattle, WA 98168
(206) 282-6116
info@fourfrontmusic.com

ISBN: 978-0-9743420-3-0

Designed by Sue Cook

Printed in the United States of America

A Record Industry Joke

A man is flying in a hot air balloon and realizes he is lost. He reduces his altitude and spots a man down below. He lowers the balloon further and shouts, "Excuse me, can you tell me where I am?"

The man below says, "Yes, you're in a hot air balloon, hovering 30 feet above this field."

"You must work for a record label," says the balloonist.

"I do," replies the man. "How did you know?"

"Well," says the balloonist, "everything you've told me is technically correct, but it's no use to me right now."

The man below says, "You must be a recording artist."

"I am," replies the balloonist, "but how did you know?"

"Well," says the man, "You don't know where you are, or where you're going, but you expect me to be able to help. You're really in the same position you were before we met, but now it's my fault."

Anonymous

Contents

vii Acknowledgements

x Introduction: What This Book Is (and Is Not)

Chapter 1 Welcome to the Four Fronts of Music Marketing

2 How the Music Industry Is Structured Chart

4 What Are the Four Fronts of the Music Business—
and What Do They Have to Do with You?

5 An Overview of the Four Fronts

9 How the Four Fronts Work Together Chart

Chapter 2 The First Front—Artist Development and Product Development

12 Why Artist and Product Development Are Both in the First Front

13 **The First Front, Part One:** What Is Artist Development?

15 Ten Reasons Why Musicians Fail (and How Not To)

35 Con Jobs: Watch Out for the Flim-Flam Man

39 Artist/Band Inventory List

41 The "Creative" You and the "Business" You

44 Songwriter Relationship and Artist Relationship Charts

45 Filing Copyright Applications

48 Trademarking Band Names

53 Starting Your Own Publishing Company: An Eight Point Checklist

57 Eight Types of Publishing Deals: An Overview

63 Artist Management Deals: The Basic Deal Points

66 Artist Development: Questions to Ask Yourself

68 **The First Front, Part Two:** What is Product Development?

70 Who Buys Music?

76 What You Should Know about Your Fans

78 35 Things to Consider When Starting Your Own Record Label

80 Releasing Your Own Record—A 15-Point Legal Checklist

84 Preparing Your Release: Manufacturing and Design Tips

86 Let's Talk about Bar Codes

87 Inside Major and Independent Record Labels

90 Typical Major Label Structure Chart

91 What A&R Reps Do

92 Making Sense of Music Industry Contracts

94 Production Companies

97 Producer Agreements: What's the Deal?

102 Recording Contract Advances

105 Recording Contracts and Recoupables

108 Recording Contracts and the Artist Royalty Rate

111 The "Term" of Recording Contracts

114 Compulsory Mechanical Licenses: The Facts and the Fictions

120 "Profit Split" Deals: An Alternative to the Traditional Record Deal

124 Making Your Record a Priority, or Art vs. Commerce:
A Music Marketplace Dilemma

128 Distribution Setups for Record Labels

129 Distribution and Independent Record Labels

131 Distributors: How to Attract Them and How to Work With Them

136 Getting Your Music to the Customer Chart

138 A FourFront Marketing Plan for Independent Record Releases

140 Sample Marketing Plan for a Band

144 The Distributor One-Sheet

145 Sample Distributor One-Sheet

146 Sample of a Distributor's Letter of Instructions to an Independent Label

148 25 Things to Remember about Traditional Record Distributors

150 What a Record Label Should Know about Music Retailers

156 Music Is Your *Internet* Business

157 Selling Your Music Online—A Reality Check

165 Getting the Most Out of Your Music Website

169 Online E-Music Promotions

171 What is SoundExchange and Why Should You Know about Them?

172 Product Development Questions for Music Sellers

Chapter 3   The Second Front—Promotion

174 Promotion: Getting Airplay for Your Music

175 Radio Station Music Formats

177 Promotion: How Record Labels and Radio Stations Work Together

194 Getting College, Non-Commercial Radio Airplay

197 The Promotion Game: A Day by Day Summary

201 Promotion Front Questions for Radio Stations

Chapter 4   The Third Front—Publicity

204 Publicity: Creating a Buzz in the Media

205 Kits, Kits, and More Kits

206 Ingredients of a Demo/Promo/Press Kit

207 How to Write a Bio and a Fact Sheet

210 Sample Band Bio

211 Sample Fact Sheet

212 Sample Cover Letter

213 The Quote Sheet/Press Clippings

214 Folders and Envelopes

215 Press Kit Photos

218 How to Write a Music Related Press Release

219 Tips for Working with the Press

221 Publicity Front Questions for Magazines, Newspapers and Internet Publications

Chapter 5   The Fourth Front—Performance

224 Performance: Finding Your Audience

225 The Business of Live Performance

229 Selling Your Music at Live Shows

233 Have You Ever Played a House Concert?

237 Sample Band Tour and Work Schedule

242 Performance Front Questions for Working Your Live Shows

Chapter 6   The Future Is Now

244 Changes in the Way Music Is Sold Over the Last 30 Years

248 New Challenges and Chances for Music Marketing

254 Licensing Music for Films, TV, Commercials, and Computer Games

259 Licensing Your Masters Overseas

264 About the Authors

265 Index

 Throughout the book, this symbol indicates legal-oriented chapters written by Bartley F. Day.

The FourFront Marketing System chapters and all other content (except where noted) was written by Christopher Knab.

Acknowledgments

Whoever said that writing a book was a solitary experience never attempted to write a book about the music business. There are many people who helped make this third edition possible. So, I would like to thank the following people for helping me get things right.

To start off I want to give a big thank you to entertainment law attorney Bartley F. Day. Bart, your contributions to past editions of this book gave a clear and concise explanation of some basic legal issues facing any musician who wishes to market, sell, or license their music. So, I'm particularly proud to have you contribute more legal chapters to this edition and truly be a partner and co-author of this third edition. Besides being a good friend and the co-author of the chapter "Contracts and Relationships Between Independent and Major Labels" in the book *The Musician's Business and Legal Guide,* you understand and appreciate all the work that goes into writing a book on the business of music. I appreciate your ongoing support and helpful suggestions that make this edition much more instructive and helpful to developing artists and bands.

For this edition another friend, (and Internet music marketing genius), David Nevue, of www.musicbizacademy.com, contributed the chapter on Internet music marketing. Thank you, David, for taking the time out of your busy schedule promoting your own unique piano music to write this special chapter. The information you provide will go a long way toward helping artists organize and plan their Internet marketing activities. David's book, *How to Promote Your Music Successfully on the Internet,* should be used by all artists and bands who want to make money with their music.

Thank you to John Richards of radio station KEXP 90.3 FM in Seattle, www.kexp.org. Your helpful tips on how artists and bands should submit their music to non-commercial stations is most appreciated. There is nothing like hearing the truth straight from the horse's mouth. And while I'm at it, thanks to Andy Boyd, my producer of the MIYB podcasts, for editing out all my bleeps and glitches and making the podcasts sound so professional.

There never would have been a first edition of this book, let alone this new edition, without the support of my mentor Diane Rapaport, who started the whole idea of helping musicians understand the business of music back in the early '80s with her landmark book *How To Make and Sell Your Own Recording,* now in its fifth edition. Diane, your dedication to helping musicians help themselves continues to inspire me in my work.

My thanks now go to the following cast of characters who were inspirational, informative, and lovingly supportive all the way through this project: Jim Kemp, my first (and only) investor in my company, FourFront Media and Music, and close advisor on everything regarding running successful businesses. Thanks also go to Steve Barsotti and Pam Goad of the Art Institute of Seattle. You both supported the use of my book for the music business courses in the Audio Production Department and for that I am very grateful.

A special thank you goes to Dianne Caron, who took time out from her mega-commute from Bellingham to Seattle to offer invaluable advice, wisdom, and support for this book; and now that I've retired from formal teaching, I'm proud to have you continue the work of teaching the music business courses I used to teach at the Art Institute. Your contributions to the Artist Development section of this third edition are numerous and much appreciated.

I saved my biggest thank-you for last. My editor, my graphic designer, my partner in every sense of the word has been Sue Cook. There would be no third edition, let alone the first two editions without you, Sue. There would only be some hastily written articles that would never have benefited from your eagle eye for creating continuity and catching so many grammatical and other types of writing errors. Sue, you have always believed in the value of this book and put in hundreds of hours to make it become a reality. Ms. Cook, Mr. Knab tips his hat to you, and begs your forgiveness for all the bitching and moaning along the way. It was just my way of admitting that you know better what to do than I do…and yes…you're right all the time.

Christopher Knab

Working on this book has led me to reflect back, gratefully, on the many people from whom I have learned along the way and who have shaped my view of the music industry, and in some instances, the bigger world. It's not possible to list all of them here, but some of the most important are as follows.

Buck Munger, editor of *Two Louies Magazine,* for which I wrote a monthly column on entertainment law from 1986 to 2005. Thanks, Buck, for keeping me on track and churning out those columns, and making me feel that they were beneficial to at least a few people.

Law professor Jules Gerard, whose law school courses I have come to think of in the intervening years as "boot camp for the brain." The mental discipline and analytical skills learned "under fire" in his classes, though hardly enjoyable at the time, have proven invaluable.

Sharal Churchill, CEO of Media Creature Music, and a consummate deal maker, for sharing her vast knowledge of music licensing.

My late parents, Mary and David Day, for (among other things) my mother's love of music, and my father's deep curiosity of the world, and for their teaching the value of striving for excellence.

My friend, former bandmate, and former label executive, Dean MacDougall, for his unique sense of humor, his wisdom and savvy, for the education I received from him early on about the "real world" of the music business, and for all his support and encouragement since then.

Michael Shrieve, of Santana, from whom I learned how much focus, drive, and passion (not to mention talent, of course) it takes to break the mold and create truly innovative art.

My son, Barrett Day, for his idealism and concern for the downtrodden, and for being a far more entertaining and perceptive writer than his dad.

My wife, Pierina Parise, for all of her editorial assistance, and for (diplomatically) letting me know when my legal writing has lapsed into total incomprehensibility, and even more importantly, for all of her belief and support over the years.

And finally, thanks to musicians and artists of every kind everywhere, without whose work and sacrifices our world would be a much smaller and drastically less interesting place.

Bartley F. Day

What This Book Is (and Is Not)

Introduction to the Third Edition

The old saying "The more things change, the more they remain the same," is as true today as it ever was. Even though we see rapid technology developments in the production side of the recording industry, as well as the legal and marketing side (thanks to innovations and new marketing opportunities that abound on the Internet), the "old fashioned" idea of getting down into the trenches and working to promote your own music is more important than ever before; it will always be the foundation that entrepreneurial musicians use to build their success, no matter what technological advances are made in the future.

Today we have many advisors, consultants, and recording industry veterans who each have their own approaches to marketing a record in this new millennium, and this new third edition of *Music Is Your Business* joins a constant stream of books and downloadable articles devoted to the topic of how to market, sell, and protect music. Some of these books and articles are quite good, but many of them lay down a firm plan of action, a "step-by-step" guide to success for you to follow.

We don't see it that way.

If you prefer the step-by-step approach, you'll find some direction along those lines in this book. But we prefer to describe how things work, and how the music marketing industry is set up. We'll suggest that some guerilla marketing ideas work better than others at this time in history, and recommend certain tactics and strategies for you to consider. But we won't, as many books do, tell you to do A, then when A is done, proceed to B, and when you've completed B move on to C, and if you follow those prescribed rules, by the time you get to Z you'll be a star. We can't say that, and nobody else should either. We'll be honest with you; all any industry professional *can* say is that if you have some talent, get serious about protecting and marketing your music, and see it as a real business that needs your undivided attention, you can have a shot at some level of commercial success.

One final note before we dive in. Please note that throughout this book we use the word *record,* when we refer to *record labels, record stores,* and *your record.* Even though the CD and MP3 files are the current standard formats for music releases, the music business doesn't call record labels "CD labels," or record stores "CD stores," nor have they changed "recording studios" to "digital capturing studios" or some other ludicrous term. The recording industry is one hundred twenty-five years old, and out of respect for that past, we'll continue to use words that remind us of where we came from. Records, and the business of selling them, is what the record industry has always been about—is still about today—and (no matter what future devices may be invented) will always be about. Long live records!

Welcome to the
Four Fronts of Music Marketing

The Four Fronts of Music Marketing—

The Development Front

The 1st Front: Artist & Product Development:

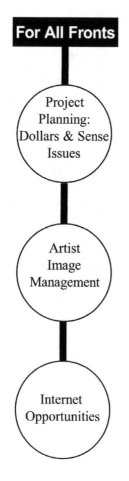

For All Fronts
Project Planning: Dollars & Sense Issues
Artist Image Management
Internet Opportunities

Artist Development	Product Development
Preparing Your Career	*Making and Selling Your Record*
Songwriting Skills	Marketing and Sales Plans
Copyright Issues	Recording: Studios, Producers, Engineers
Music Publishing	
Performing Rights Organizations (ASCAP-BMI-SESAC)	Mastering and Manufacturing
	Graphic Design and Printing
Music Equipment and Instrument Needs	Distributor One-sheets
Band/Musician Issues and Agreements	Distribution and Sales: Research and Contacts
Artist Management	Distributor Options: One Stops Independent Distributors Rackjobbers
Ethical and Moral Issues	
Political Issues	Retail Options: Chain Stores Mass Merchandisers Mom-and-Pop Stores Misc. other Retailers
Record Label Dealings (A&R and misc. other)	
Contracts and Legal Issues (Attorneys)	Live Show Sales
	Internet Sales
Creating Your Image	Mail Order
	Catalog Sales

How the Music Industry is Structured

The Exposure Fronts

The 2nd Front:

Promotion

Getting Airplay for Your Music

Radio Airplay:
  Station Format Selection
Research:
  • Commercial Stations
  • Non-commercial
    Stations
  • Internet Radio Stations

Creating Station Contact
  Lists (Databases)

Promotion Tactics and
  Strategies

Program Director and Music
  Director Relationships

Independent Radio
  Promotion

TV/Video:
  Research and Options
  MTV, VH1, MySpace, etc.

Tracking Airplay on the
  Charts

The 3rd Front:

Publicity

Creating a Buzz in the Media

Print Media Research:
  Magazines, Newspapers,
  Fanzines, E-zines
  Contact Lists

Broadcast Media:
  Radio and TV Interviews,
  Stories, and Features
  Contact Lists

Press Choices:
  Reviews, Articles,
  Interviews, Calendar
    Listings

Publicity and Public
  Relations Plans

Creating Demo, Press,
  and Media Kits:
    Bios, Fact Sheets,
    Photos, Cover Letters,
    Press Clips, Quote
    Sheets, Folders,
    Press Releases

Press Relationships:
  Publishers, Editors and
  Writers

Media Deadlines and
  Timelines

Advertising Options

The 4th Front:

Performance

Finding Your Audience

Live Show Venues:
  Clubs, Halls, Festivals,
  Fairs

Venue Research: Creating
  Venue Contact Lists

Booking Agents and Concert
  Promoters: Roles and
  Relationships

Live Performance:
  Contracts, Lighting, Sound,
  and Equipment Needs

Tours:
  • Planning
  • Tour Coordination
  • Concert Promotions

Road Managers, Roadies, and
  Life on the Road

Touring as Marketing:
  Radio, Press, and Retail
  Opportunities

What Are the Four Fronts of the Music Business—and What Do They Have to Do With You?

If you're a musician and you want to make money from your music, you're in a challenging position. If you're like a lot of musicians, you spend huge amounts of time and money to improve your music and performing skills, but you haven't thought much about the business of music, or how you're actually a part of it. When you combine making music with making money, you become a part of the music business—whether you like it or not. Since most musicians don't know much about the music business, they don't realize how much that ignorance can cost them.

My music business career began in the retail side of the industry in the 1970s. That led me to working in radio broadcasting and running my own independent record label, where I learned about distribution, publicity, and the role the live performance industry plays in making artists and bands successful.

During that time I felt like I was only seeing separate parts of the music business. Then around the early '90s, I finally saw the whole picture, and understood what the entire music industry looked like and how the various aspects of the music business worked together. It was then that I developed what I call the **Four Fronts of Music Marketing.**

I was finally able to describe the structure of the music industry. Since then, I've been using my system to show others what they need to do to work their independent music projects—by using the tactics and techniques that all successful record labels use.

These **"Four Fronts"** I call **Artist and Product Development, Promotion, Publicity,** and **Performance.**

I divide the **First Front into two parts—Artist Development and Product Development**—for a very important reason. **Artist Development** is about developing your music and building a solid business foundation for your career. It's *as* important as **Product Development**, which is about developing a way to record, manufacture, and sell your music. What has or has not been done in Artist Development will either help or hurt the music product you make and intend to sell.

The three remaining Fronts—Promotion, Publicity, and Performance—I call the Exposure Fronts. They include those activities that will get your music heard, talked about and experienced live.

So, let's take a closer look at how the music business is set up, so that you can learn how to protect, promote, publicize, and sell your own independent music.

An Overview of the Four Fronts

The First Front: Artist and Product Development

Artist Development: Preparing Your Career

The Artist Development part of the First Front includes fundamental issues that are the basis of your music career. These are the same issues a professional record label would consider when they're deciding to sign an artist or band. It's your job, more and more these days, to develop your own career creatively and in a professional manner. Artist Development includes such important things as:

- Songwriting skills
- Copyright issues
- Music publishing
- The role of the Performance Rights Organizations (ASCAP, BMI, SESAC)
- Music equipment and instrument needs
- Band/musician issues and agreements
- Artist management
- Ethical and moral issues
- Political issues
- Record label dealings (A&R and misc. other)
- Contracts and legal issues
- Creating your image

Product Development: Making and Selling Your Record

The Product Development part of the First Front includes those areas that are directly involved with recording and selling your music, such as:

- Marketing and sales plans
- Recording studios, producers, engineers
- Mastering and manufacturing
- Graphic design and printing for CDs
- Distributor one-sheets
- Distribution and sales: research and contacts
- Distributor options: one-stops, independent distributors, rackjobbers
- Retail options: chain stores, mass merchandisers, mom-and-pop stores, misc. other retailers
- Live show sales
- Website design
- Internet sales, mail order, and catalog sales

The Second Front: Promotion

Getting Airplay for Your Music

The simplest way to remember it is: Promotion equals airplay. Airplay is how most people hear new music for the first time. It's the business of securing broadcast support for your record. This is the Front that the major record labels rely on to secure a hit record. Radio airplay is still the most effective exposure to get for your music; it's also the most difficult to secure for independent artists. Key Promotion Front issues are:

- Radio airplay: format selection
- Station research: commercial, non-commercial, Internet, and satellite radio stations
- Creating station contact lists
- Promotion tactics and strategies
- Program and music director relationships
- Independent radio promotion
- TV/video: research and options (MTV, VH1, YouTube, etc.)
- Tracking airplay on the charts

The Third Front: Publicity

Creating a Buzz in the Media

If the Promotion Front is about getting airplay for a song, then the Publicity Front is about getting your music talked about in the media. Publicity creates opportunities for music fans to read or see reviews, interviews, and feature stories about your music in print or on the radio, TV, or the Internet. The key issues included in the Publicity Front are:

- Print media research: magazines, newspapers, fanzines, Internet e-zines
- Broadcast media: radio and TV; website interviews and blogs; reviews, interviews, stories, and features
- Creating broadcast, print, and Internet contact lists
- Publicity choices: reviews, articles, interviews, calendar listings
- Program and show research
- Publicity and public relations plans
- Creating demo, press, and electronic promo kits:
    - Bios
    - Fact sheets
    - Photos
    - Press clips and quote sheets
    - Cover letters
    - Folders
    - Press releases

- Press relationships: publisher, editor, and writer issues
- Media deadlines and timelines
- Advertising options and choices (Note: publicity is free, but advertising is paid for.)

The Fourth Front: Performance

Finding Your Audience

For most styles of popular music, the live Performance Front is the foundation for developing a fan base and it's an important part of marketing and selling recorded music. The key areas of the Performance Front are:

- Live show venues: clubs, halls, fairs, festivals, etc.
- Venue research: creating venue contact lists
- Booking agents and concert promoters: roles and relationships
- Live performance contracts
- Lighting, sound, and equipment needs
- Tours: planning, tour coordination, concert promotions
- Road managers, roadies, and life on the road
- Touring as marketing: radio, press, and retail opportunities
- Internet: plans for streaming concerts, downloading concerts, misc. web live music ops.

What All the Fronts Have in Common: Three Essentials

Dollar and Sense Issues: It costs money to develop and promote music. To put it bluntly, it takes more money than talent these days to get your music to the attention of consumers.

Image Development and Management: Developing an honest, yet consistent image is essential for any artist. An image is what people remember about a singer or a band—finding and managing that image is of the utmost importance.

On and Offline Marketing Opportunities: Gone are the days of building your music career without the use of current digital technology. Online sales and downloads are a booming business. Many new Internet radio stations and e-zines can help get your music to an audience. Opportunities for live performance broadcasts are already an everyday occurrence.

Lest you think that the Four Fronts are only for beginning artists and bands, let me tell you this. You may just be getting started and think that all this is a one time deal until you are "discovered." Sorry about that, the truth of the matter is that the more successful you get, the more time you'll spend dealing with the Four Fronts of music marketing. No matter how well-established or famous musicians become, every record they put out is like starting over again. For each new release, even superstars have to devise a marketing plan that is based on the ideas and structure of the Four Fronts.

The Four Fronts are Interrelated

You must realize that the Four Fronts interact and depend on each other. In some ways there's a catch-22. In order for you to get your recording into mass distribution, the distributors and stores will ask you how many sales and downloads your record has had, what kind of radio support your record is getting, how the media is supporting your music, and what the audience response to your live shows has been.

In order for you to get significant airplay, the radio stations want to know why they should play your record; how it's been selling, if you're getting good reviews in the media, and how well your live shows are being received.

In order for the print and broadcast media to be willing to review your music, they want to know why their readers and audience would want to know about you; how your record is selling, what radio airplay you've gotten, and if your live shows are creating excitement.

In order for you to get better live shows and tours, the booking agents, concert promoters, and venue operators want to know that they'll make money from your concert. They may check your retail sales, airplay statistics, and media reviews before they decide to work with you.

So, how does the Internet fit into this formula? The Internet now offers all Four Fronts for marketing purposes (manufacturing websites to place your CD orders, sales opportunities galore, plus web radio stations, web publications, and even the ability to stream or podcast your concerts.) You'll have to work the Four Fronts of music marketing on the Internet as well as in the "real world." So, let me say it again loud and clear: **The Four Fronts of music marketing are interrelated and dependent upon each other!**

No one uses the tools in every Front equally. Many acts, for example, build their careers primarily by playing live as often as possible (the Performance Front). Others have jump-started their careers with college radio airplay (the Promotion Front) or become "critic's darlings" and received a ton of favorable press (the Publicity Front). Others combine *different* elements from the Four Fronts both on and offline. The trick is to pay attention to what works best for you and build on your successes. It's up to you to decide what mix is best for your career.

Where to Start

I believe the safest, most realistic way to develop your music career and market your music is to understand how the music business works and how it applies to you. Use the Artist/Band Inventory List on page 39 as a starting point. This will help you see where you are in your career, what your current resources are, and help you define your goals.

After checking this list, go to the topics you're most interested in. Successful music marketing requires an ability to improvise and be spontaneous. You should be flexible in your business activities. And it can be fun. As you go along you'll meet many frustrations, but the tips and strategies I describe should help you avoid many pitfalls as well. Empower yourself and take control of your music career.

How the Four Fronts Work Together

THE DEVELOPMENT FRONT

1st Front, Part 1
Artist Development
Preparing Your Career

Songwriting Skills
Musicianship Development
Creating an Honest Consistent Image
Copyright / Publishing Concerns
Co-Musician / Band Issues
Equipment Considerations
Artist Management
Ethical & Political Issues
Legal Issues / Contract Negotiations
and….
Artist Image Development Issues

1st Front, Part 2
Product Development
Making & Selling Your Music

DISTRIBUTORS and STORES,
MUSIC BUYERS
Need to Know Your Plans for:
• Selling Your Music
• Promotion Campaign
• Publicity Plans
• Performance Plans

Market Research: Who Is Your Fan?
Recording—Choosing a Studio
Producer and Engineer Issues
Mastering Arrangements
Cover Artwork Design and Printing
Manufacturing CDs

Distribution / Sales Strategies
Retail Plans—Stores & Internet Plans
Live Sales—Mail Order / Catalog Sales

THE EXPOSURE FRONTS

2nd Front, Promotion
Getting Airplay for Your Music

BROADCASTERS
Need to Know Your Plans for:
• Promotion Campaign
• Selling Your Music
• Publicity Plans
• Performance Plans

3rd Front, Publicity
Creating a Buzz in the Media

MEDIA PROFESSIONALS
Need to Know Your Plans for:
• Publicity Campaign
• Selling Your Music
• Promotion Plans
• Performance Plans

4th Front Performance
Finding Your Audience

LIVE MUSIC VENUES
Need to Know Your Plans for:
• Performance
• Publicity Plans
• Selling Your Music
• Promotion Plans

The First Front

Artist Development and Product Development

Why Artist Development and Product Development Are Both in the First Front

There was a time when record labels committed themselves more seriously to developing the careers of their recording artists. Today it's much harder to find a record label committed to this goal. Up until the late 1980s most record labels had a department called Artist Development, and the job of that department was to support their acts' creative side while steadily developing a customer base for them. When sales of records increased with each release, the label stood by their acts, believing that the more the public heard their music, the bigger their popularity might grow, and the greater their popularity, the more records they would sell. Most of the '60s, '70s, and '80s bands that dominate today's classic radio format are examples of the old school version of Artist Development.

By the early '90s, most labels had changed the name of their Artist Development departments to Product Development. In other words, the emphasis changed from nurturing the growth of artists and their music, to developing high-pressure sales tactics and strategies. Product Development today usually means putting the label's energy into creating sales for a new release and doing so quickly. If they had three strikes in the past, they have one strike now, and if they don't get a solid hit, their acts will probably be forgotten in favor of some other act waiting for their one at-bat.

You can still see some cases of major labels that are committed to Artist Development and Product Development when you look at the careers of bands like Radiohead, The White Stripes, or even the Dave Matthews band. This approach is also behind the success of most rap and hip-hop artists, who are truly doing their own street marketing version of Artist and Product Development. Also, today's pop acts that dominate the top of the pop music charts are a result of Artist and Product Development. If a label can get the public to embrace a new release, the labels and the music publishing companies will collect revenues from dozens of new releases over the (potentially) long careers of these acts. (See "The Future Is Now" chapter at the end of the book for all the *new* revenue streams for musicians.)

In today's competitive music business, for the most part, the responsibility for Artist and Product Development has changed hands. Independent labels and entrepreneurial artists have inherited the responsibility of nurturing new talent by fine-tuning their artistic and business development, and by slowly growing their careers over several album releases. Developing a music career for the long haul is all about controlling your own destiny.

Artist and Product Development go hand-in-hand. They should work in combination and coordination with each other. When a balanced approach to developing your music and your business affairs are respected equally, you create a more realistic opportunity for achieving some success with your music. Art and commerce are both important for musicians today.

The First Front: Part 1
What Is Artist Development?

Preparing Your Career

In the music business, everything starts with a song. Without great songs, there *is* no music business. Songwriting isn't just an artistic expression; it's the axis upon which the music business rotates.

So, the first order of business in Artist Development is the music itself. Good songs are not enough when you're preparing to market your music. People only respond to great songs. That means your songs must be of a very high caliber and also have some commercial appeal—if only to a certain music niche—folk, hip-hop, alternative rock, new age, jazz, blues, etc. Finding that niche and learning how to manage your growth is essential to becoming a successful act.

Artist Development is also about protecting your songs by registering them with the copyright office. Songwriters and music publishing companies need to affiliate with the Performance Rights Associations (ASCAP, BMI or SESAC) as well, so that when those songs are played by the broadcasting industry, or in certain public places, they will receive proper payment for the uses of those songs.

Many songwriters have to decide if and when to look for a publishing deal or start their own publishing company. In my opinion, until there's a demand for your songs, (meaning that there are a lot of people who want to hear your songs, or buy them), don't worry too much about getting a publishing deal. Don't get me wrong, the pot of gold at the end of the music rainbow is the income received from the use of songs. The business of music publishing, which is really the business of finding uses for songs, is a very important topic to explore—but only when the time is right.

Choosing a name for your act and filing for a trademark to prevent others from using it are also part of the business of developing your career. As you'll see in upcoming chapters, creating a band agreement is a critically important task that can help define the issues of running your career as a business and how you'll work with the people in your band.

In the beginning, you'll be responsible for managing your own career, with a goal of creating such a buzz about your music that you attract professional management. Many developing acts encounter some resistance to the lyrics or cover art they have created. Be prepared to deal with ethical and moral issues from the fallout of any controversies surrounding your music.

Starting your own business (sole proprietor, partnership, or corporation) will also be a necessity if you want to have control over your career. You'll also have to update any changes in your business operations as they occur, because different city, state, and federal laws affecting businesses are constantly changing and evolving.

As your career develops, you may wish to improve on some of your creative talents by taking voice lessons or master classes from more experienced musicians. Investing in the best equipment and musical instruments is another necessity if you are going to be a professional, working musician. Artists can't perform their best work using mediocre equipment.

One of the most delicate issues involved with Artist Development is the matter of creating and consistently maintaining a clear and honest image. What people hear in your music must be seen in how you dress on-stage. And, your image can help or hurt you when you create promotional materials and artwork for your CDs, etc. **So, be consistent with your chosen image throughout the Four Fronts of music marketing.**

As you become more successful you'll need the services of an entertainment law attorney. Use lawyers who have had experience within the music industry. You'll need them to look over any band agreements, record label contracts, publishing deals, or any other number of legal matters.

If you work hard, your music is great, and you get a few breaks along the way, you'll probably begin to get the attention of the A&R representatives of major and independent labels. Choosing to remain truly independent, or considering a recording contract with any label is certainly another important Artist Development consideration. Choose carefully; your future success depends on clear thinking and number crunching to see what route is the best financial way for you to go.

Artist Development as you can see, is a combination of creative and business issues that must be dealt with to make your music, and the business surrounding your music, run smoothly.

Ten Reasons Why Musicians Fail
(and How Not To)

Why are so many talented singers, songwriters, and musicians unable to make a living from their own music? Let me start by asking a question. How often have you seen or heard successful musicians in the media? Well, the successful ones are the *only* musicians you see. The entertainment industry, which controls everything we see and hear, shows nothing but the glamour and excitement of success. You grew up with music on the radio, on TV, at the movies, and in live concerts. You read about musicians in newspapers and magazines who were already rich and famous (or on the major label–supported road to possible fame and fortune). As for all the other musicians out there—the media spends little time telling us about musicians who aren't famous or on the charts.

So how were you affected by those images of celebrity glorification? Didn't you want to be like the stars you idolized as a kid? Even before you picked up your first instrument, your head was full of ideas about how people become famous musicians, and those ideas probably went something like this:

Choose an instrument, buy some good equipment, take lessons, practice. Start playing with other musicians, play a few gigs, record a demo of your own songs, and you'll be discovered. Someone will whisk you away to the Land of the Superstars, where the drinks are free and the good life is waiting to throw you a party. All you have to do is keep writing and playing your music. You won't have to worry about the business side of things at all; some benevolent record label will recognize your talent and take care of all those bothersome details for you. "Trust me kid. I've got your best interests at heart."

Oversimplified? Maybe. But haven't you thought this way at some time? If you think someone in the recording industry will make you a star and take care of you forever, you're wrong! It's time to wake up. Too often in this business, naive musicians are exploited by industry people who are well informed and well-connected. Even if you get a recording contract and have a "hit," you'll ultimately fail to make a consistent living with your music if you remain uninformed about the changing realities of the business.

I'm willing to bet, however, that if you're willing to re-think your old ideas of how your favorite artists became successful, you'll be able to establish your career on your own, make a respectable living as you develop, and control many aspects of your career. Over the last decade, more and more musicians have come to that conclusion: Loreena McKennitt, Fugazi, Ani DiFranco, Steve Vai, Jurassic 5, Master P, The Arctic Monkeys…the list goes on.

In my career, I've discovered ten major mistakes that prevent musicians from making money with their music. Here they are:

Why Musicians Fail: A Top Ten List

1. You fantasize about being a star instead of working to be a star.
2. You quit because the people you think you need aren't supportive.
3. You have naive concepts and misguided beliefs about the music industry.
4. You're unwilling to get down in the trenches and do grunt work.
5. There's a lack of commitment from fellow musicians in your group.
6. You don't have enough money to record and promote your music.
7. You believe that someone will come along and discover you.
8. You lack the professional skills that make a master musician.
9. Your music is unoriginal and lacks inspired ideas.
10. You refuse to believe that art and commerce are inseparable.

Now I'll go into detail about each reason. There's a lot to think about, so take time to digest each one. They can help you overcome some obstacles that have held you back in your career.

1. You *fantasize* about being a star instead of *working* to be a star.

America loves celebrities. Stars are shown as if their lives were one big party. You've seen the limos, the gorgeous babes, the mansions, and the glamour of celebrity. Of course it looks appealing. Who wouldn't want to live in luxury, meeting other celebrities? Be honest, haven't *you* said to yourself, "My songs are really good… *I* could be on the radio and TV too!" Of course you have.

Remember the scene in *The Wizard of Oz,* where Dorothy and her friends are finally in the inner chamber of the Wizard? They're in awe of the spectacular sights and sounds when Toto pulls back the curtain. The Wizard is nothing but an old, ordinary man who had been pulling strings and pushing buttons to create those sights and sounds. Well, that's what I want you to do. Pull back the curtain of illusion and take a close look at the business of music. If you're going to have any real shot at success, you have to see the entertainment industry for what it is—a multi-billion dollar-a-year business that uses songs as just one of the many ways to get money from millions of consumers. And yes, most of the people behind that curtain are actually old, ordinary looking men and women who have a job to do and do it quite well.

Unfortunately, the media only shows you celebrities; it doesn't offer a course in how to be one. **Your constant exposure to successful artists has had a negative effect on you, whether you're aware of it or not**. The path to success as a musician isn't paved with yellow bricks. Hell, it ain't paved at all. It's a road built with down and dirty, gritty work based on real world realities. The entertainment industry's job is fantasy. Fantasy is what keeps the listeners listening and the viewers viewing. But watch out. Fantasy can be hazardous to your career. Let me tell you about the insidious "starry-itis" disease. It's a disease that affects many musicians each year, but luckily, there are some real cures.

Some of the symptoms of "starry-itis":

- Walking around in celebrity look-alike garb.
- Copping an attitude that a star already uses.
- Writing and recording songs that mimic an established musician.
- Boasting that you're "the next big thing" to everyone you meet.

These symptoms are a sure sign of the disease and are obvious to anyone in the music business. We tend to avoid contact with those who show these symptoms.

Starry-itis can prevent musicians from establishing their careers. Some musicians put together a band, start to play some gigs, make a demo or record a CD, get a website up, and feel pretty good when a few devoted fans start telling them how great they are in e-mails.

But what happens if they can't get their music on the radio, the clubs they want to perform in won't book them, or their demo shopping fails to generate any interest from the labels? Why, the rejection is enough to make a grown man cry.

At this point, bitterness and frustration can lead to a complication of starry-itis. Now, "I could have been a contender-itis" sets in. People at this stage say things like, "If only my bandmates hadn't quit on me," or, "I just picked the wrong guy to be my manager," or, "No one at my booking agency really cared about me." **Their lack of success is always someone else's fault.** They feel unappreciated. It was too much work sending out all those demos anyway, and the clubs don't have a clue what they're missing by not booking them. And those A&R Reps, what do they know? "I'm a great undiscovered artist."

There's a cure for all these maladies. Forget the fantasies. Don't listen to the voices that make excuses for not doing good, old fashioned, in the trenches, hard-ass work. It's not about fantasies; it's about music and your commitment to it. Grab *that* reality and just get down to the business of being a dedicated, practicing and performing musician. That's the secret of it all.

Naiveté is the cause of starry-itis, but the disease is curable, and you, yourself have the cure. The part of you that knew you had to work to get established was right. The error is thinking that after a certain point the work stops and the party begins. Actually, the work never stops. If you thought struggling to make it was rough, imagine the day-to-day reality of maintaining star status. Do you have any idea how much work it takes to tour non-stop for eighteen months? Try that fantasy on for size.

Do what you love because the best success, perhaps the most fantastic sensation of all, is satisfaction. Satisfaction always follows a grounded-in-reality dedication to developing your career. You are a musician, and real musicians never stop playing their music, no matter how frustrating that road may be.

2. You quit because the people you *think* you need aren't supportive.

Creative people often have a strong need for approval. After all, their work is intended for the public eye or ear. But historically, many of the most creative musicians had a drive and passion to express themselves was far stronger than their need for acceptance. In fact, all the real innovators I can think of faced rejection countless times before their "sound" began to break through.

Awhile back a band I'd worked with off-and-on for five years called it quits. They announced their decision in a letter to readers of a local music magazine. They were polite, but lightly scolded the powers-that-be in the local media who hadn't supported them, insinuating that if they had gotten more support they would have been more successful. They'd made it to the finals of a national talent search and been featured at a music industry showcase, but apparently the heartbreak of not being recognized (legitimized?) by the local music media was too much to bear. They went on to say that they would continue to make music as individuals, or in new bands, and then said their fond farewells.

I was ticked off at these guys. They had a small local following and had made some kind of beginning national noise. But they were so discouraged by the lack of *local media support* that their only solution was to stop playing and give up. So, what are they faced with now? Starting from scratch again, with new bands, new names, new fanbases to establish. After five years of working toward their goal, they threw away everything they had worked for.

Five years is nothing! Five years (or more) is behind many bands and artists who were just getting known but not yet on the brink of success. What if U2 had given up back in the 1980s? It took them many years to become the worldwide superstars they are now. And, a newer act like James Hunter, the English R&B singer, got his deal with the great indie label Rounder records after seven or eight years of playing his unique sound. You can't give up! If you want a formula for failure, it's just one word. Quit. That's the one thing that will definitely stop your career cold.

Are you a musician or not? Musicians play music. Period. That's all there is to it. If you're quitting because the people you *think* are important haven't properly recognized your talents, then you have your head on backwards. Look at all the music outcasts who were rejected by the gatekeepers of the industry. The media blasted the Velvet Underground, Frank Zappa, The Sex Pistols, Nine Inch Nails, the Butthole Surfers. Even Lucinda Williams was confined to a small niche audience for almost twenty years. And how about '70s and '80s new wavers like Devo, Pere Ubu, and even punk goddess Patti Smith? They've all received mountains of negative press at some time. Don't think the criticism stops when you become successful. That's when some really scathing reviews will be written by twisted and arrogant music reviewers.

Obviously, there can be legitimate reasons to quit. When inner conflicts within a group prove unbearable, when creative differences within a band become too big, breaking up a band can be the only thing to do. That's not the issue here. We're talking about the strange dependence many musicians have on getting acceptance by gatekeepers as a measurement of their success. Anyone who enters this crazy business to seek acceptance is in for a torturous ride.

I believe the only opinion that matters is the audience's opinion. After many years of listening, I've come to the conclusion that taste is defined by the taster. I get requests all the time to review demos and indie CD releases, and I can hear the disappointment in a person's voice if I don't like their music. So what if I don't like it? I can't like everything I hear, and that goes for everyone in this business. Stop worrying so much about what the industry Reps think of your music. **The public, your fans, will tell you whether or not there's something of value in your music.** If people react positively to your music by coming to see your live shows, or revisiting your website to get new information on your activities, or buying your CDs, then the public has spoken. Their opinions are the only opinions that matter—that and your own belief that your music is truly unique.

If the fan response to your music is good, but the music business doesn't seem to be supporting you with glowing reviews, increased airplay, or gigs in the clubs that matter, then you have to assess what you're doing and what the current trends in music are. You can't pressure or intimidate or criticize the critics. They are who they are. They have their opinions, their own agendas, their own circle of friends, and they'll either support you early on or you'll have to continue on your own until they *have to* report on you, or support you. That can be the sweetest revenge. By not being discouraged, by not giving up, there may come a time when your popularity demands attention. And the very gatekeepers who wouldn't give you the time of day will have to cover your concerts and review your records because the public support demands it.

Think about this; inside the word discouragement is the word courage. Sometimes it's hard to muster up a workable amount of that stuff, but if you don't, you'll have only yourself to blame. Keep on keepin' on. If you're as good as you think you are, start working today to prove it, and never give up.

3. You have naive concepts and misguided beliefs about the music industry.

The history of the music business is filled with stories of musicians being misled or exploited by record labels, managers, attorneys, and other characters. Until the early 1980s, it was difficult to find information about record label contracts, marketing strategies, publishing issues, or anything else about the inner workings of the industry.

That was then, and this is now. Today, musicians who want to learn about the business of music can find dozens of books covering every aspect of it. The Internet also has many wonderful sites to help musicians find their way around the slippery world of the music business. (Wait till you read David Nevue's article on marketing your music online; you won't believe how much help and information is out there for you. See page 157.)

So why do I still meet and get e-mail from so many musicians who don't have a clue that there are more letters in the word "business" than in the word "music"? Once again, I think so much ignorance still exists because of the power of celebrity, the thirst for success, and the escapist fun and honest fulfillment that comes with making music. But most misguided beliefs exist because we're exposed to a never ending flow of music. It's on radio twenty-four hours a day. Television music channels show videos filled with exciting, escapist images. The media interviews your favorite musicians with questions that are as deep as the shallow end of a wading pool. Reviewers write articles about the latest releases and treat musicians like gods or devils, depending on the bias of the writer.

Try out this exercise and make it a new habit…look at all the non-stop entertainment that's coming at you constantly, and see it for what it really is.

Ask yourself some questions! *How* did that song get on the radio, *who* chooses what gets on the music channels, *why* does one CD get reviewed and another doesn't, *what factors* determine who got the opening act gig on the superstar summer tour? How did that act's website get so much attention? It's no surprise that would-be stars see only *what has succeeded,* but rarely understand the inner workings of the business. So, it looks easy. Anyone can do it. That overnight sensation really did happen overnight—it couldn't have been *seven* years in the making. Yeah, right.

Now let me show you some amazing statements I've come across over the years that show how ignorant most musicians and band members can be. They *hear* some things and believe them on faith, when in fact they're hurting themselves by not knowing the business truths of the recording industry.

Here are some misconceptions I keep running across. I've heard these over and over.

"Copyrights? All you have to do is mail yourself a self-addressed, stamped envelope with your lyrics inside and a court of law will accept that as proof of copyright ownership."

"Man, this band I know just got two million dollars for signing with a major label. They're rich!"

"Labels have to give you money to tour, man. It's in every contract."

"Recoup? That just means you have to pay a label back only for what it cost them to make your record."

"Hey, if your band breaks up, you can just leave and go sign with somebody else."

"Once you're signed to a label, they have to put your record out, or pay you a lot of money to break the contract."

The false statements above are just a small sample of the sad things I've heard and read from naive musicians, and really there's no excuse for such ignorance. (You'll find the real answers to these misconceptions as you read along in this book, by the way.) Look at it this way; as a musician, you've invested thousands of dollars in instruments and equipment. You may have paid for lessons and spent money on recording and manufacturing demos. Why not invest in learning about the business of music? Why aren't books, consultations, workshops, seminars, conferences, or music trade magazine subscriptions as necessary to you as your other music related expenses? The fact that you're reading this book shows that you're on the right track.

Check out this fact…the men and women who run the music business got to where they are today because they asked questions and got the answers they needed as they worked their way through their various jobs They learned what they know by attending a different kind of school than the one you may have attended; the School of Hard Knocks. The people who own the labels, record the music, publish the songs, and promote and sell music learned the business by living it. They may have gotten burned in some early deals and lost money along the way, but they took those life lessons to heart and tried not to make the same mistakes again. That's what the School of Hard Knocks is all about…diving into the business, learning as much as you can as you grow along the way, and never forgetting the lessons you learned.

The main reason musicians were exploited in the past was because the industry kept the secrets of the business to themselves. Well, the secrets have been out for a long time now. The only reason you may have naive ideas and misguided beliefs is because you never had a music business education. Today there are many ways for musicians to educate themselves. There are music business degrees given by universities. There are countless conventions, conferences, and workshops for anyone wanting to learn the ropes. If you want to know the truth about recording contracts, publishing deals, management contracts, or anything else, take the time to learn more about the business you are a part of.

What if you start your own label and just *guess* what you're supposed to do? In the past, many successful professionals who helped develop our great musical heritage did just that. But ask them if they had it to do it over—wouldn't they have wanted to know what they know now? Wouldn't they love to have back the money they spent foolishly, the contracts they signed ignorantly, and the deals they made without the proper information? You bet they would.

Get curious. Ask questions when you're not sure about something. Don't believe rumors. Learn from reliable sources because ignorance is not bliss. It's important to educate yourself. (Just don't go to the other extreme and become an information addict who never gets any real work done. I've met some folks like that, and well…don't get me started!)

4. You're unwilling to get down in the trenches and do grunt work.

As a consultant and educator, it's my job to replace your misconceptions about the music business with a dose of business savvy. It's not surprising that so many artists don't have a clue about how much grunt work is required to build the foundation of their career. We consumers see only the surface of the entertainment industry—we see the *results* of the grunt work the record labels have professionally and successfully orchestrated.

But let's get down to it. If you thought writing and rehearsing your songs was tough, that recording them was more work than you expected, that getting the cover art for your CD was difficult, and that finding the right manufacturing plant and the best deal was time consuming, then hold on to your hard drive. It's no coincidence that promoting and selling a record is called "working" the record.

For starters, I'm assuming that you realize it takes money to market your record! Rule of thumb: at least double or triple what you spent on recording your CD, depending on your recording budget. This is recommended for a serious local to regional marketing campaign.

Now, what do you have to do to promote your newly released CD? Unless you want it to remain stacked in your apartment or garage, you have to make industry people and the public aware of your music. You send out free promotional CDs to the music directors at college, commercial, and Internet radio stations, the writers and editors in the press, the booking people at clubs, and the buyers at distributors and stores. You have to stuff envelopes, create and maintain your mailing list data and website. You need mailers, stamps, and a computer with Internet/e-mail access. Then you have to do follow-up phone calls to all those people. You need to schmooz—a lot—on the phone, online, out and about in your local music scene. Get ready for some serious phone bills.

This work is frustrating and time consuming. The reward is the satisfaction of actually hearing your songs on the radio, reading your reviews in the press, landing that first important headliner gig, or walking into a store and seeing your CD in the racks. Think of the grunt work this way. Every record you have in your personal collection had someone doing all those tasks behind the scenes, or you wouldn't have been aware of that music—let alone had the opportunity to purchase it.

I can already hear some moans and groans. You're thinking, "I don't have time to do all that work," or "I'm a musician. I just want to make my music." Well, tough. No one is ever going to care more about your music than you. You must take charge of your own dreams. No one is going to force you to do what it takes to work a record seriously, and no one is going to make you a star, no matter what stories you may have heard. All a record industry person can do is work *with* a committed artist. The message is this: unless *somebody* does the grunt work, your record will remain in the closet, unheard by an audience that might enjoy it. In the beginning, that someone is going to be you.

At a music business conference workshop for developing artists, Tom Silverman, the CEO of Tommy Boy Records once said, "Why did you make your stupid record anyway?!" His point was to wake up the crowd to the realities of this business. No one is waiting for your music. You have to be responsible for building your career in the beginning. The public will judge whether or not your music is great, not you, if and when they get a chance to hear it. Industry gatekeepers and the public have a chance to hear your music *only* if you resolve this grunt work issue.

You have another option. Keep your music as a hobby. Music as a hobby can be very enjoyable. We live in a time when the supply of good music greatly outweighs any demand for it. So, if the grunt work I've outlined is something you want nothing to do with, consider keeping your music as a hobby—there's nothing wrong with that. It may be the best decision you ever made. As your expectations settle down, your music will demand much less of your time and effort. If you make that decision, be clear about it. Be sure you don't harbor secret hopes of being discovered and attaining stardom and commercial success. You can't put in a small amount of effort and expect to get the rewards of a serious, hard-working musical career.

Here's another aspect of grunt work. When you resolve who will do it, and how it will be done, a funny thing begins to happen. You experience what a real record label does. You learn what it's like to compete for exposure. And should you arrive at the negotiating table for that almighty label deal you once knew nothing about, you'll be far more prepared. You'll be on your way to being a respected member of the team, a savvy player who cannot easily be taken advantage of. I recommend this path. If you have the passion to tackle all the work that needs to be done, you'll find yourself with a new sense of pride when you see what you've achieved with your efforts. You can do it.

5. There's a lack of commitment from fellow musicians in your group.

This bugaboo is a make-or-break issue, to be sure. Commitment! Several times in your life you'll have a chance to make a commitment—to getting an education, to a life partner, or to your own business. Your fellow band-mates are your partners in the music business. If you really want a shot at making money with your music, your band is the vehicle to make that happen. If there isn't a commitment within the group to work together toward that goal, you'll join the ranks of could-a-beens. You had the talent but didn't have an agreement to deal with the issues that cause a band to split up.

Entertainment law attorneys have a name for this—it's called **a band agreement or partnership agreement.** It's really proof on paper that there's a commitment within the group to deal with the every day realities of being a professional musical act. How many times have you heard the phrase "money changes everything"? Well, it's true, and it's one of the main reasons that you want to sit down with your fellow band members and work out on paper how you're going to deal with the successes or failures that come your way. I could have called this "Reason #5: You have no band agreement," but would you have stopped reading? Every time I bring up this topic in a class, workshop or consultation, I can feel a restlessness in the room. No one wants to admit that there are personality problems, or business differences, or career goal conflicts within a group. Why rock the boat by bringing up band agreements? Some bands go on for years without a written band agreement and live to regret it.

But hey, if you feel *you* don't need a band agreement, OK, forget about it. Leave everything to an unspoken agreement, to a sense of fairness, to chance. As you read the summary of typical band agreement issues below, say to yourself after reading each point, "Well, that won't be a problem in my group." Perhaps if you chant this enough, you can conjure up a musical genie who'll protect you from the jealousies, egos, and money problems that cause band breakups and lawsuits.

Should you decide you're not immune from these problems, save yourself some attorney fees by discussing these issues beforehand. Write notes on how you'll handle these issues—*before* you sit down to have a legal agreement drawn up by an entertainment law attorney (at a cost of approximately $150 an hour or more). These are the typical issues that should be discussed and resolved in a band agreement.

What form of business will the band take?

You can be a sole proprietorship, a partnership, or a corporation. Do some research and make an appropriate choice. If you start making money with your music, you better realize that you're a business. The IRS and other state and local agencies might just be interested in having you pay some taxes like any other responsible citizen. Besides, choosing the right business form is just the right thing to do. You did say you wanted to make money with your music, right? Well, act like a business and choose a suitable business form.

Who owns the copyrights to your songs? Who is/are the songwriter(s)?

Suffice it to say, there are as many possible answers to this question as there are members in a group. You have to take heed and resolve this issue. The real money in this business will come from the successful exploitation of the copyrights to your songs. Music publishing is a huge issue and there are many good books on the topic. If you want harmony within in your group, then agree on who writes all the songs and come up with a fair system to divide up the songwriting royalties. If you don't do this, when any kind of success comes along you'll be in deep doo-doo about the split of those songwriting royalties with your fellow band-mates.

Share of profit and loss considerations.

You'll have to define how the money (profit or loss) is divided. All band members could be equal partners and divide the profit or loss equally. You could also distribute the profit or debit the loss based upon the percentage owned (i.e. in case you're doing business as a corporation, with each person owning a certain percentage).

How do you make group decisions? How will you vote on band issues?

You have a couple choices; unanimous or majority rules. If you're "All for one and one for all," then choose the Three Musketeers way of voting. All decisions must be made unanimously, with no dissenting votes. If the democratic system is more attractive to you, then agree to a majority vote; the dissenting members of your group will get to hold a grudge and pout for the next month. (Guess which voting mechanism I'm inclined toward? Well, the subject today is commitment isn't it? What kind of commitment is there when contention exists within a group?)

Who owns the name of your group? Or, what about leaving members?

Never thought of that one, huh? Well, you'd better. There have been hundreds, if not thousands of lawsuits by members of groups who split up and then fought over which members could continue to use the band's name. This could be resolved in a band meeting, after a regular rehearsal is over, rather than in a court of law. Consider the following options:

- No one can use the name if the group breaks up, regardless of how many in the band are still performing together.

- A majority of the group members performing together can use the name. For example, if a group of seven people breaks up, then four of them together can use the name.

- Only the lead singer can use the name, regardless of who he/she is performing with.
- Only the songwriter who founded the group and thought of the name, can use the name, regardless of who he/she is performing with.
- Songwriter who founded the group and thought of the name and lead singer can use the name as long as they perform together, but if they don't, no one else can use it.
- If the band doesn't do anything, most likely the band name will be treated the same way as any other business partnership asset—meaning that any of the partners has the nonexclusive right to use it.

How will you fire someone who isn't carrying their load?

What is meant by "carrying your load" in your band? If a band member is showing up late for rehearsals, missing rehearsals with lame excuses, missing or showing up late for sound checks and live gigs, how will you and the other band members deal with that? I suggest you agree to rules for acting like professional musicians. When a rule is broken, your band will have a policy to deal with it. What kind of vote do you use to fire somebody? Choose between majority rules and unanimous.

Ex-members and money—who gets what?

What happens after members are fired or quit? One option: they keep their percentage of money that comes in for past work done with the group. Or, they don't keep their percentage for past work.

Money issues: band member investments and/or loans to the band.

Let's say that someone in your band has more money than the other members. They're the generous type, you know, they say things like "Don't worry about the $200, we're in this together. Some day you'll have money when I don't—it will all work out." Right. Until there are some hard feelings, or the generous donor has some expenses and could really use that dough now. Many unpleasant scenarios can happen when money is spent without a clear understanding of how, or if, it will be repaid. If you have a sugar daddy in your group, discuss in your written band agreement how your business form will deal with that issue.

Spending money and hiring professionals

What kind of vote does it take to approve spending money for the group? What kind of vote do you use to hire a lawyer, agent, or manager, to bring in a new musician? Again, the two basic options are majority or unanimous.

Who does what?

If it's true that musicians often fail in their careers because of a lack of commitment from their fellow musicians, then I find it particularly important for each band member to be responsible for a specific business task. If, for example, someone takes on booking the shows, other members can split the work of getting posters designed, printed, and put up. There are plenty of tasks: getting bills paid, finding rehearsal spaces, sending out press releases. If you're making a recording, someone will be setting up recording sessions and planning for manufacturing, promoting, marketing and selling the CDs. Until a band has established itself as a viable money-making entity—one that is attractive to labels, management companies, booking agencies, publishers, and merchandise companies—somebody has to take on all the jobs of being a real band. And that somebody is everybody in your group.

See pages 51 and 80 for some legal aspects of band agreements.

6. You don't have enough money to record and promote your music.

Many musicians have finally wised up to the idea that they must do more to further their careers than just record a few demos and send them out randomly to a list of A&R reps they found somewhere on the Internet. The smart musician finds a way to record and manufacture a full length CD, and then goes farther than most other wannabees. They actually have money saved up for designing the artwork and manufacturing the CD, and money to do something with the CD. They realize that it takes money to promote and market the danged thing.

We need to look at the basic economic issues of creating and promoting musical product. This subject definitely separates the boys and girls from the men and women. For starters, you must know what the standards of excellence are for recording a CD in your genre of music. By this I mean, whether you're a rocker, a rap or hip-hop act, a potential Top 40 pop artist, a country musician, or a singer/songwriter, the recording quality that's expected of each genre is different. Think of it this way; the more mainstream sounding your music is, the more money you'll be spending on your recording.

I've read many helpful articles and books about raising money for recording projects. They go into detail about the options available. You can save up money from each of the gigs you're playing. (You *are* playing live aren't you... duh 101, please and thank you!) You can borrow money from family or friends. It's a long shot to get a business loan from a bank (good luck— they see it as very high risk and rarely provide such loans). You can do fundraising gigs with other artists. Whatever. Raising the money for an unproven musical talent shouldn't be the responsibility of anyone but the artist. There are thousands of independent records in the musical landscape. The musicians who put out their own music found a way to raise the money. Others have gone before you and gotten the job done. You too can raise the money to record and fund a proper marketing campaign if you're serious about it.

Let me give you some tips on recording expenditures that might save you a few bucks.

- Looking for a studio? Ask around. Talk to other bands and musicians in your neck of the woods. What studios did they use? What was their experience like?
- Call the studios you're interested in and ask for a tour of their facilities. Don't use a studio just because someone else said to, check it out for yourself. If you don't feel comfortable there, how can you do your best recording there?
- Check for deals. Ask about slow times or off-hours when the rent is cheaper.
- What comes with the studio time? An engineer? Is that person right for your music?

- What about a producer? Do you have someone in mind? Does the studio recommend someone? How much will they cost? (Be sure to sign a producer's agreement with any producer too!)
- After you've found the right studio, at the right price, rehearse, rehearse, and rehearse! Many musicians spend precious time in the studio rehearsing. The clock is ticking! Before you waste expensive hours in a recording studio, be sure you've rehearsed your songs until you dream about them at night. In the studio the motto is: Get in, get out.

You've determined a budget for the recording project, and you've stayed to it pretty well. What about the CD cover artwork, design and the manufacturing costs? I usually deal with this topic for several hours in classes and consultations. Think *seriously* about these topics.

You've spent months writing your songs, practicing and recording them. This was the creative stuff. From here on you'll be leaving your comfort zone to enter the world of business. You'll be *making* a product that will represent you for the rest of your life. Your choice of cover design and manufacturer will determine the quality of that product, and once those choices are made, they can't be undone.

Why are distributors now rejecting countless CDs with amateurish cover designs? One reason. Those musicians didn't want to spend money on a cover design for their CD. The *music* is what it's all about, right? What difference can a CD cover make? But think about it. Have you ever purchased a CD just because the cover was so cool you had to buy it? Someday, your CD will be in a store bin filed next to your favorite artist! Will you be proud of it? Will it reflect *your image and your music?* If not, you'll be hurting yourself in the marketplace.

So, you've gotten your music recorded and manufactured, you've spent a lot of money, but you're not done. It's now marketing time! I suggest you budget an amount that doubles, or better yet, triples what you spent on recording, manufacturing, and design. (That's *only* for a local or regional do-it-yourself release.) Here again are some promotion and marketing costs:

- Stamps and mailing envelopes for sending your promo copies to the media.
- Phone bills for the hundreds of follow-up calls you must make to the media after they receive your promo copies.
- Gas money while driving around to put your CD on consignment.
- Internet connection fees, website design, and promotion costs for making a killer-looking site that offers your music for sale using the new methods available.
- Hiring an independent record promoter and their retail counterparts. If you think you can get significant national airplay without hiring someone who has experience and contacts in college and commercial radio, get real. The reason a recording costs so much is because of the hidden costs of promoting and marketing it. And without promotion and marketing your recording has little chance of getting heard. **Budget $400–$1,000 a week for this, for two to three months.**
- Advertising costs. A distributor will presume you have money for this, if you can get a distributor on board these days. For example, the listening-stations you see in stores are not

free; they cost around $100 per station, per store, per month! This practice is changing right now, so check your stores to see what they offer.

- Printing and copying costs for distributor one-sheets, promo packages, response cards, posters, and flyers for live concert sales promotions.
- The unexpected. Other expenses that you cannot predict will surely come your way.

There you have it. An introduction to why you must find a way to properly fund your recording and marketing costs. If you need encouragement after reading this, go down to your local record store and walk up and down the aisles. Look at the thousands of other artists and bands who got their music into the store. *That* is an accomplishment, and if they did it, you can too. Also, don't forget to go online and check out all the CDs that the Internet music sites have for sale.

7. You believe that someone will come along and discover you.

Waiting for someone to discover you is the purgatory of the unimaginative soul. I'm always on the alert for the discover-me musician. Here are some symptoms of these lost individuals:

- They mail outdated cassette demo tapes, instead of CDs, with no contact information. (Tip: stop with the shopping-for-a-deal idea. And when a demo recording is requested, burn it on a CDR.)
- After sending their music to an industry professional, they're never heard from again. The idea of making a follow-up call never enters their minds.
- They scribble an illegible note about having a bunch of "great songs" and want us to "get them played on the radio," or "sign us now!"
- They've been recording songs for several years but never performed for a live audience.
- They send out mass e-mailings to industry people filled with cliché descriptions of their music ("monster songs that will make you rich if you just try to sell my songs for me.")

These unfortunate discover-me addicts have no clue.

How did this come to pass? Why are so many musicians and bands waiting in a self-imposed twilight zone? I blame it on Tin Pan Alley. Yup, since the late 1890s, the income from published songs has been controlled by a coterie of powerful songwriters, publishers, and later, record company executives. These influential people created a system where aspiring songwriters and would-be stars depended on their services and connections. Whether it was access to the vaudeville stages, the budding recording industry, or the wonder of radio broadcasting—if you wanted to "make it," you had to find a way to be discovered by those guys. Only they could open the gates to these opportunities. Hence the term "gatekeepers." "Come on kid. I can make you a star!" was their pitch, and they could do just that.

But this is the beginning of a new millennium and thirty-five-plus years past the birth of the indie revolution, the DIY (Do It Yourself) movement of the late 1970s. Things are different now, but I still encounter hundreds of wannabes at music conferences like the CMJ Marathon, SXSW, SXSE, etc. There they are, an army of discover-me drones passing out those infamous demos with no contact information, and playing the stupid lottery game of "Discover me, I'm really good." Then they go home, only to resurface at some other expensive conference to try once again to make that one really important contact. Let's put an end to this foolishness, whad'ya say?!

Stop dreaming, musicians! Learn the business as you build your own career. The gatekeepers will come, maybe, after you have something substantial to show them; a fan following, a number of CDs sold, some modicum of press recognition. Then you can decide if you actually want the almighty record deal. Or is it actually a series of gigantic financial hurdles that you have to climb in order to earn some lousy $1 to $1.50 per unit sold, after you recouped all the advances?

Now, let me say this. You do need connections. You do need people to help you with your career. The entertainment industry is built on relationships. The best relationships are nurtured over the years and have been built on mutual trust and respect for the different gifts we have as musicians and music business professionals.

As a non-musician, I can honestly speak for myself and other non-musician gatekeepers on this. Music business professionals have found their place by listening to and being inspired by the great music of the past and present. We've developed "ears," a kind of inner radar for what music is "good" by our marketplace definition. We're paid for being able to find the right music for the various companies we represent.

Don't bother us with lame pleas for attention or unprofessional work habits. Prove to us that your music is cool, don't tell us that it's cool. The way you do that is to put yourself in places where we can hear your music, read about it, and pick up the buzz from the excitement of your growing fan base. In this competitive age, you need to do more than just write some songs and send out demos.

You're not the only one who has a dream of being successful, of making money with your music career. Music professionals also want a long career doing what we love to do. Should our paths meet, and should the chemistry work between us, our success could include working to help you succeed.

Industry representatives like to discover new talent, but they like to discover it on their own terms. Build relationships based on a working knowledge of the business you're entering, and cultivate a respect for the business side of things. Draw our attention, but do not demand our attention. The best relationships are those that honor the gifts and talents of the creative person *and* the business professional. When that type of relationship is sought after and established, only then we can say that someone discovered a new act and made someone a star.

8. You lack the professional skills that make a master musician.

Most of the men and women musicians deal with at record labels, booking agencies, radio stations, distributors and stores are not musicians. Frustrated musicians, maybe. Wannabee musicians? Possibly. Appreciators of music? Definitely. In my case, after twelve years of record retailing, ten years of alternative radio work, eight years of running my own record label, and over a decade as a music business consultant, I've listened to countless thousands of hours of recorded and live music. And you know what? After all this, I can tell you straight out that everyone on the business side of music can recognize a competent, incompetent, or master musician. When it comes to auditioning new music, it doesn't take more than ten seconds to judge you in some accurate way.

We can tell when a musician knows their instrument. We can tell if a vocalist has something magic happening or not. We can tell when a drummer can't drum, when a bass player doesn't know a bottom from a hole in the floor. We judge you, perhaps unfairly at times, and our prejudices, tastes, and attitudes toward musicianship can have a profound effect on whether or not you become successful.

You can never go wrong being a master musician. It's no guarantee of success, but it's a big deterrent if you are *not* a master musician on your instrument. Obviously, we can also spot developing talent. We categorize you when we first hear you play. Once I was at a club when a band came on. From their first chord, everyone looked at the stage to catch the amazing performance of the lead vocalist and hear his unique voice. At another showcase, the band started to play and emptied the room. Why? Because they played horribly. The guitar was out of tune with the bass, and the drummer couldn't even keep a steady beat.

In case you haven't noticed, there are a lot of bands out there, more every year…thousands of musicians, and thousands of bands. Buy a clue. Be the best musician you can be. Don't go out too early and practice in front of an audience. A musician is an artist. Artists develop their skills over a lifetime of learning, refining, and perhaps even re-defining. This issue of musicianship is rarely discussed any more, perhaps because "raw" music is fashionable. But as exciting as a raw performance can be, it can get tired very quickly. Please note: there's a big difference between raw and simple. For example, playing simple, straight-forward rock n' roll isn't as easy as it sounds. Simple can sound deceptively easy, from the acoustic blues of Robert Johnson to the "chugglin" of Creedence Clearwater Revival, to AC/DC and the Ramones, up to the Kaiser Chiefs. Believe me, it isn't. Investigate and you'll find that some of the simplest sounding music has been rehearsed for countless hours. That music has lasted and will last.

The business of music demands more than a hobby of music. If you're content jamming with friends and playing occasionally, don't confuse this with the determination you must eat for breakfast if you really want to make your living as a musician. The quality of your musicianship will enable or prevent the promotion and marketing of your music. Music either makes a lasting impression on a listener and becomes part of the fabric of our culture, or becomes a "passing fancy in a midnight dream." However long you take to make your music, it's a blink of the eye compared to the potential life span of a classic that people never get tired of.

Being a master musician simply means being dedicated enough to your profession that you care enough to play your very best, all the time, every time. Do that and you stand a chance of making a lasting impression not only on the industry gatekeepers, but potentially on generations of music fans.

9. Your music is unoriginal and lacks inspired ideas.

If you've ever attended a music business conference and walked into a Demo Listening Session, you may have encountered this: a panel of A&R Reps from major and independent labels evaluate a demo recording that's been submitted to them. The first song is played, and after about ten seconds the Reps are holding their hands over their ears, or waving for the sound technician to "Turn it off!" Another song is cued up, and after twenty seconds the music is stopped and the Reps are muttering. "That really sucks," "I've heard that before," "That sounds like an '80s band," or "Please, Nine Inch Nails already did that." Rude but honest comments are made at such conferences. And in the privacy of their own offices, homes, and cars more crude and rude comments are made about music.

Remember this. *Just because you **can** record your own music, doesn't mean you **should!*** It may sound good to your ears, but may be just crap to the gatekeepers who are paid to evaluate, critique, and sign new talent to their record labels and publishing companies.

When any label puts up the money to record and market any artist, guess what? They want to get that money back and make a profit. It's really that simple. Record labels and music publishers are looking for music that will make money for them. Your music must inspire their business creativity. They must be able to hear your music in the context of the marketplace they're familiar with. Any good promotion or marketing minded person will tell you that when they hear music that turns them on, they begin to think of marketing strategies and tactics to help get that music noticed.

When I'm inspired by a demo that has been sent to me, I find myself thinking, "Oh, this would be perfect for such and such radio station," or "I have to play this for the music reviewer at my local music magazine," or "What a cool song; why don't we do a contest around the title of it?" Music that compels that kind of response is truly inspired for music business professionals. Your music must *excite* the gatekeeper. When that happens, the wheels of the music business begin to turn.

When A&R Reps are asked what they're looking for, they often say, "We don't know what we're looking for, but we'll recognize it when we hear it." Your music must truly stand out in some significant, original, dynamic, and creative way. Ninety-five percent of the demos out there contain regurgitated ideas that were ripped-off from more gifted musicians. Challenge yourself! Talent scouts hear hundreds of wannabees every week and complain about "indistinguishable groups who all sound alike." How does your music stand out from the rest?

Since the late 1970s, the cost of making a recording has gone down each year. Each year, more wannabes have inflicted their unoriginal music on an industry that has grown cynical and jaded about finding new music. Let's face it, there will always be entry-level bands and artists who try to get their music to the ears of an industry they know little about, but expect so much from.

A&R Reps are looking for, but rarely find, was what a Rep at a music conference called "What the f**k was that music!" There's a real clue to what your job is. Your job is to create great music, not just good music, but *great* music. Great music is a lot easier to get people excited about and to market.

Who decides if your music is great? For mass market commercial music, it's the employees of record labels and music publishers who must try to find truly original and outstanding music. And you know what? It's very hard to find. So hard, in fact, that you won't believe this. A Rep who finds as few as three truly great artists (in a lifetime of listening to new music), signs them to his or her company, and jumps over all the bureaucratic hurdles to get the company to commit to developing the artist—that Rep will probably be recognized as one of the great A&R people of all time. (Assuming those artists actually become *commercially* successful!)

So, you may be thinking, if such a high standard is required for getting signed, why is so much crap released these days? Good question. Reps have had to lower their standards because there isn't that much great talent out there. There's huge competition to find the next big thing. I can assure you that there's a sense of desperation among highly pressured Reps to keep their jobs and discover something that might make millions of dollars for their company.

But even though lower standards of originality are accepted these days, many qualities still take precedence when music is being evaluated for its commercial potential.

Songwriting skills: Writing a song that many people like isn't an easy task. Do you really know the basic components of songwriting? If not, challenge yourself to learn the craft of songwriting.

Vocal Abilities: A dynamic, charismatic, individual singing style that is uniquely your own is as close as a musician can get to having a brand. Are the vocal stylings of your singer up to that definition?

Musicianship: Any music business professional can tell instantly if the musicianship in your group is ready for prime time. Amateurism is not acceptable.

Originality: Back to this again. It's a delicate subject, but basically what the labels and publishers are looking for is just one thing about your music that makes it stand out. Remember that the word "origin" is in the word originality. It's OK for your influences to show, but no one is looking for a carbon copy of what's already out there. They look for a sound that is different, but not so dramatically different that it alienates the listener. It could be a band's sound, a vocalist's style, a mix of instrumentation, or simply an attitude your music has that is truly unique.

One last tip about making great music: study the history of popular music. That's it. If you were brought up listening mostly to commercial radio, or watching MTV, you missed out on most of the great music that is our national heritage. Dive in to it. Get immersed in the history of rock, rap, R&B, soul, jazz, folk, blues, country—anything and everything. If that incredible adventure doesn't inspire you, nothing will. There's a world of great music out there. Absorb it. Make it your own. (For starters, give a listen to your local college or alternative music radio station, either on the dial or online.)

10. You refuse to believe that art and commerce are inseparable.

Here's a simple exercise. After you finish reading this, go over to your record collection and look at all the CDs and records you've collected over the years. Go through your collection. As you look at the music that means so much to you, say the following words to yourself: **"I would never have known about or heard all this music I love, if there hadn't been a carefully planned and successfully implemented promotion and marketing campaign for all my favorite bands and artists."**

That's the plain and simple truth. In a capitalist, consumer society like ours, every popular music star is backed by a record label, manager, publishing company, booking agency, attorney and countless others who worked with that artist to help them achieve their hard earned success. This is true for the mega superstars as well as the local and regional artists who found a way through their own efforts to marry the business of music with the art of music making.

When you go into a record store or search for music online, remember this exercise. Say to yourself while searching: "If these artists or their record labels had not dealt with the business side of music, these musicians would not have their CDs for sale here."

The articles you read in music publications, the songs you hear on the radio, the videos you watch on television and www.youtube.com, and the concerts you attend could not have happened for those artists unless someone had successfully dealt with the business of artist and product development.

See what I am driving at? Catch my meaning? Get my drift? Music and the marketplace go hand in hand. There's no other path to success. Someone—*you*, in the beginning—has to take responsibility for making peace with the eternal struggle between art and commerce.

Musicians struggle with this dilemma as much as authors, painters, sculptors, or poets do. It's like a virus that infects many musicians with the notion that money making and music making are enemies. Contracts, marketing plans, budgets and image development are alien to the creative process.

Nevertheless, it's something that must be examined and explored. It's necessary to make peace with that side of us. Funny thing… creativity. On one hand, it wants to be left alone to create. Yet it demands recognition, and rages when society refuses to acknowledge the art that has been created. The creative side feels robbed when it isn't rewarded with enough money to make a living. This conflict tortures many musicians, beginners as well as experienced players. I've observed many frustrated musicians over the last twenty-five years, and I've seen a pattern of ignorance of the rules of the marketplace. I'm not saying there aren't examples of exploitation throughout the history of popular music; there have been outrageous tales of gross mismanagement and outright thievery in recorded music's legacy, but the following observation is also quite true.

Along with a musician's wish for stardom and recognition comes a naiveté that is easy to exploit. I've never bought into the common belief that a recording contract is indentured servitude or slavery. Nonsense. These days, musicians who have been exploited left an opening in their defenses by refusing to take responsibility to educate themselves. That's the cold fact of it. You cannot be exploited unless you've left yourself open to be exploited. See the music business as the protector of your art.

The age of enlightenment has not just recently arrived. The secrets behind the business of music started being revealed almost twenty years ago. In the late 1970s, pioneering music business educator Diane Rapaport came out with her landmark book, *How To Make and Sell Your Own Recording*. That book single-handedly led the way for musicians to learn about the business of music. Today there are countless books and articles available on many different aspects of the music business. I suggest you go to www.amazon.com some time and type in "music business books" to search what's out there.

The future belongs to enterprising musicians who control their own destiny. The downloadable music frontier is here, and never in the history of recorded music has so much potential rested in your hands.

Let's hear the rallying cry by musicians, loud and clear—Educate Thyself! Promote and Market Thyself! **Your music is your business.**

Con Jobs: Watch Out for the Flim-Flam Man

The music business has a bad reputation when it comes to working with musicians. But there are rip-offs and there are RIP-OFFS. If you read about the history of this business you'll find it littered with unscrupulous businessmen who made P.T. Barnum's famous quote their motto: "There's a sucker born every minute and two to take him."

Musicians have been exploited in the past, are being exploited today, and will most likely continue to be exploited in the future, if they allow themselves to remain ignorant of business. Apparently there's something about the very nature of the creative person that exudes the scent of an innocent lamb to hungry wolves. Here are some of the most common ways you can be exploited.

Live Gig Con

There's no one particular rip-off related to playing live but there are a lot of potential ways for a club or venue to weasel out of paying you. The best way to prevent exploitation is to get the deal you agreed upon in writing. However, for new artists and bands that can be easier said than done. Most local scene performers are lucky to get any kind of gig in the beginning and the only contract is an oral agreement made over the phone.

When there is no written contract, the best tip I have is for you to write a letter of agreement to the venue. Be very polite and thank them for the gig. Then just state all the issues that were agreed upon over the phone, mail it to the venue, and keep a copy for yourself. If an argument should arise, pull out your copy of the letter and do your best to fight for what is yours.

Another thing you can do to prevent not being paid properly is to have a friend of the group stand by the door and count with a hand-clicker the number of patrons entering the club. At least that puts the venue on notice that you're an alert and professional musician who won't easily be duped. Over the years I've talked with countless musicians who complain about not getting paid for their gigs from the same venue over and over again! Just because "it's the only place to play, man." Yeah, right. How stupid is that? As your career is developed and you gain a following, written contracts will become the standard operating procedure.

Bogus Compilation Albums

Have you seen ads in your local paper or national music mags that say something like "Your Music Sent To Over 800 Music Industry Contacts...Our Compilation CD Will Put Your Music Into The Hands Of The Right People!" They do that all right. They sell you the idea that for merely $400 to $800 you can have your best song on their CD. They take your money, and along with twenty other gullible artists, you'll get your song on the compilation CD. (Hmmm...20 bands x $800 is $16,000. Not a bad deal when it only costs them $3,000 to

$5,000 to make and mail the CDs.) They usually do manufacture the CD and mail it to the industry list they have. But that's it… it's really nothing.

Any legitimate record label will tell you that making the record is only the beginning of what a record label does. Once the record is finished, the real work begins. "Working" the record is what it's all about. And working a record takes time, a lot of money, great contacts, and patience.

This type of compilation CD is paid for by naive musicians who fork over their money to these sleazy companies. They're happy to take your money, manufacture a limited number of the CDs, and then disappear from your life forever. They may send you a few copies of the record as part of their contract with you, but when you call them to see what's happening to the CDs *after* the mail-out, you'll never be able to reach them. They've moved to a new location, changed their addresses and phone numbers, and you're left wearing the dunce cap.

Shopping for a Record Deal

One of the potentially riskiest endeavors for musicians is when they try to find someone to shop their CD to the labels. The biggest flashing danger signal is the industry person who needs to get your money up-front before they'll begin shopping for you. Listen to me closely: any person who takes up-front money from a musician before they begin to shop that musician's music is a totally unprofessional fraud, a slime ball. This type of exploitation is very prevalent in the business. Any music business professional that demands such an arrangement is preying on the musician's gullibility. Feeding on the dreams of naive musicians is a big business. There are so many wannabes out there waiting to be plucked that the temptation is to take their money and run. So, beware. Real professionals do not ask for your money to begin the shopping process. Remember, legitimate deals are made in writing, and state such things as how long the shopper has to shop the music, and how the shopper will be paid if they're successful in securing a contract. Please consult with your attorney before allowing anyone to shop your music.

Independent Record Promoters

This is an honorable profession. A legitimate independent promoter is someone who has (in most cases) worked for a number of years for a record label promoting records to radio stations. After they've worked with a label and developed their relationships and reputations within the industry, they sometimes go off and start their own independent record promotion companies. This means they have a positive track record of successfully getting songs on the radio. They're usually genre specialists—Top 40, Urban, Alternative, AAA, etc.

When it comes to negotiating with independent record promoters, go slowly—do your research. Ask around about the reputation of the company or person. Meet with them. Ask a lot of questions about what they expect from you and what their rates are. A good independent Rep can cost $400 to $1,000 a week and you'll need their services for at least two or three months. Don't consider hiring an independent radio promotion person without having secured a distribution deal for your release. If a company is willing to take you on and never asks how you're going to sell your record, they're most likely a rip-off company. All good independent promotion companies have some kind of relationship or partnership with a retail and distribution person who is working your release to the music stores while the radio promotion person is working the airwaves.

Songwriting Scams

I can remember reading ads for songwriters in newspapers and entertainment magazines when I was a kid. These companies were looking for songs of any kind and promised a lot of money for the songs you wrote. When you sent off your songs you got this amazing letter back saying what an incredible songwriter you were. For a mere $1,000 you could register your song with them and be on the road to riches because they had "many contacts in the business who know how to make money with great songs like yours."

Today these songwriting scams are still going on. The legitimate publishing business does not work this way. The legitimate songwriting and publishing business is as hard a nut to crack as getting a recording contract.

There are many wonderful songwriting organizations, associations, and clubs that sponsor contests and showcase opportunities. Just remember that even though they're mostly legitimate they're also lotteries in a sense. People do win these contests, but a very small percentage of them go on to long lasting careers as songwriters. Instead of gambling with your talent, build it.

If all you do is write songs, find singers to sing them, develop songwriting partnerships and record a good quality demo. Then search out the legitimate publishing companies who will never ask you for any money up-front before they work with you. If you write and sing your own songs, then form a group and get out there and play as many gigs as you can. If your songs are good, and people are showing up in growing numbers to hear them, believe me it will be a lot easier for the legit companies to find you.

Get it in Writing

So many of the things I've examined could have been avoided if the musician had taken the time to get a promise or an offer down in writing. That's what an entertainment law attorney is there for, to help you protect your best interests. So, find a reputable attorney by asking other musicians and band members who they use. Never sign any contracts without first having an attorney look at them.

There are no shortcuts to success, and there are no formulas for success either. There are, however, a lot of exploiters out there waiting for opportunities to cash in on unsuspecting musicians. To beat the odds, you need to be dedicated, talented, and streetwise. You need to ask questions and even question the answers if you're not satisfied with them.

Possible Internet Scams

Now that the technology of streaming music content and downloadable music opportunities have collided head-on with the plethora of Internet companies eager to exploit any music content the careful musician should be on the lookout for a new generation of exploiters offering deals to good too be true. Watch out for scam A&R Rep websites who are cruising the Internet looking for naive bands and solo artists to lure into their phony record label deals.

To avoid exploiters, you need to be an active participant in building your career, on and off-line, and you need to stop thinking there are shortcuts to success. There aren't any.

Artist/Band Inventory List

There are many things independent artists and bands need to do to put their careers on the right track. Think of this list of topics as an organizational tool for your career. Just like that messy closet at home that needs organizing, your career plans need to be put in order. Use these topics as a way to keep track of your business needs. Make notes under each topic, type or scan them into your computer, use them as categories or rank them by levels of importance. But first, glance through all the topics and see which ones jump out at you. Those are the issues you need to deal with now.

1. Goals and Ambitions
Goals for next 3 years
Longtime career goals
Independent label
  affiliation plans
Major label
  affiliation plans
Self-owned label plans

2. Live Performance Opportunities
House concerts
Clubs
Halls/auditoriums
High schools/colleges
Festivals and fairs
Showcases/conferences
Benefit concerts
Retail stores
Shopping malls

3. Attitude toward Music and Business
Creative philosophy
Business philosophy
Current image
Desired image
Point of view on current
  career status

4. Songwriting Issues / Copyrights
Publishing companies
Personal publishing
  company
Administrative
  publishing company
Trademarks/
  service marks
Performance rights
  organizations (BMI,
  ASCAP, SESAC)

5. Recording Issues
Song selection
Home recording studio
Professional studio
  selection
Producers/engineers
Mixing
Sequencing
Mastering issues

6. Product Design
Graphic needs
  Graphic artist
  Logo
  CD/CDR
  Tray card
  Cover
  Booklet
  Business card
  Stationary letterhead
  Envelopes
  Website artwork
  Press kit folder
  Mailing labels
  Posters
  Flyers
Bar code
Printing contact

7. Manufacturing/ Duplication Options
Manufacturing formats:
  CD
  Mini disc
  Cassette tape
  LP
  EP
  45
Converting files to MP3
CD pressing plant
Tape duplicator
Shipping arrangements
Merchandise (t-shirts etc)

8. Performance

Instruments and
  equipment
Rehearsal space
Sound
Lights
Transportation
Tour itinerary
Per diems
Sound check
  requirements
Equipment insurance
Performance contracts/
  riders
Additional performance
  needs

9. Publicity/Media

Press Kit
  Bio
  Fact sheet
  Cover letter
  Press clippings
  Folder
  CD/CDR
  Photo/photographer
  Photo duplication
  Business card
Broadcast media
  Commercial radio
    connections
  Non-commercial radio
    connections
  Internet radio
    connections
  Satellite radio
    connections
  TV/video connections
Print media connections
  Music industry trades
  National, regional,
    local consumer
    publications
  National, regional,local
    music publications
Online/Internet website
  design and hosting
  issues

10. Sales/Distribution

Live shows
Record store
  consignment
Mail order
Distributors
Rack jobbers
Online/Internet sales
  opportunities
Sales/marketing

11. Administrative/ Business

Record label contacts
Publishing contacts
A&R Representative
  contacts
Entertainment law
  attorney
Band agreements
Management contracts
Record label contracts
Publishing contracts
Merchandising contracts
Video/Film contracts
Advertisement/
  endorsement contracts
Music business
  accountant
Bookkeeper/tax preparer
Artist manager
Business manager
Publicist
Tour manager
Road crew (roadies)
Music equipment store
  contacts
Music instructors/coaches
Music instrument repair
  contacts
Music business
  consultants
Independent promoters
  (radio)
Booking agents
Concert promoters
Venue contacts

12. Other Business Considerations

Bank account/band fund:
  Debt/loans
  Investors
  Business licenses
Monthly music business
  expenses

40

The "Creative" You and the "Business" You

I've been watching and analyzing why some people make it and others don't for a long time, and I've given up trying to discover some magic formula that every musician can follow on the road to so-called success.

Today, more than ever, there are countless advisors like myself who offer tips to developing acts and struggling musicians, and all too often we try to inflict some step-by-step process on musicians to help them become tomorrow's superstar.

I've been asking myself some questions about this phenomenon. Is there a difference between the attitude that successful, well known acts have and the attitude of up-and-coming acts? Why do some musicians make it big, while other equally talented people songwriters and musicians never get their music heard by the masses? What specific skills and/or inherent talents do the successful artists embody that many upstart acts do not?

Is it charisma? That special something that many artists seem to exude the minute they walk into a room? I think that's part of it, but many successful acts have as much charisma as a pitcher of milk, and yet do quite well for themselves.

How about a lot of money? That seems to be the one thing behind so many successful names these days. There are always major labels owned by huge multinational conglomerates behind so many superstars. They can buy their way into the hearts and minds of the public, right?

Wrong.

Money can only push something out to the public for their acceptance or rejection…that's all it can do. Nobody reaches into the public's wallet and forces them to spend their hard earned money on anything unless the public sees some real value in it.

Think about it. Today there's a lot of (what some observers) call "shallow and immature" lyrics and disposable pop music, and yet, no one who bought that music would cop to that criticism. Indeed, the people who buy the latest sounds on the pop charts buy that music because it gives them some kind of pleasure. It means something to them.

I think we should look at what sells and what is successful from this standpoint; *music fulfills the needs, wants, and desires of any group of fans because they identify with it.* Basically they like a song because they can hum it in the shower.

The one thing that all successful acts have in common when they cross over to mass appeal is great songs! This is also true for the more edgy artists who eke out a living from smaller fan-bases…they still write compelling songs that touch the hearts and minds of their fans. I think that's a very significant reason why some musicians succeed and others don't. And this ability puts a pressure on you to have similar creative skills. Being able to create memorable songs in any genre is a rare gift to be respected and nurtured. (Whether or not you personally "like" current popular songs has nothing to do with it. Every day people cough up $10 or more to prove your tastes may not be in tune with what the general public likes.)

Don't bother criticizing what sells in the marketplace. Great artists concentrate on their craft. If you don't like what's currently popular in your genre of music, go out and try to do better, and prove the public wrong. Just get on with your own creativity and concentrate on that!

The title of this chapter hints that there's some kind of balance needed to be successful as an artist. There must be something else besides creativity that separates successful artists from those who don't connect with the public.

What other thing is it that successful artists and bands have that separates them from struggling artists?

My Answer Is Business Savvy.

That's it. Somebody, either the artists themselves took it upon themselves to learn the ropes of this crazy music business, or they found in someone experienced in the business of music to help lead them to some level of success.

My point is that no matter what the creative skills of a particular artist may have be, history has shown that a lot of acts just worked their butts off and found a way to break on through to the other side of the competition. They found a way to get their songs into the ears of the thousands of music fans, and to do that, I can assure you they had a serious business plan that they executed successfully.

There are no short cuts to success, and at the same time there just isn't enough room in this business for everyone who makes music to be able to make a living from their music. But there's a balance that can be obtained in one's life. With the tools available on the Internet, and the technology of downloadable music now an every day reality, no musician who writes great songs should have that much problem realizing modest successes with their music.

I would like to add a word of caution here. Be careful of the "10 Steps To Musical Success" and the "What Every A&R Rep Is Looking For" articles and books. I admit that over the years I have written some articles with similar titles, only because they're my means of getting the attention of an ever growing group of musicians wanting to be stars. Those types of articles, for me at least, are a way to get my reader's attention. Having done that I honestly try to give them proven tactics and strategy tips that are time-tested ways that record labels and industry professionals work.

In Reality, There Are No Ten Steps to Success!

There's only the conscious involvement, and commitment to your songwriting and musicianship, and to actively participating in the business of music. Remember that commercial music is a world of dollars and cents, whether you like it or not. But that doesn't mean that art and commerce cannot walk hand in hand…they must do that.

We live in a capitalist, consumer-driven society. The successful musicians of tomorrow will be those people who either attract dedicated, knowledgeable businessmen and women to do the marketing and promotion for them, or they take that responsibility on themselves and realize that no artist has to sell hundreds of thousands of copies of their music to make some money with their music.

However, you do have to be able to write and perform great songs, and then produce them with the "sound" of your particular genre carefully understood and honored, *and* you have to take the time to find trusted consultants and advisors and also find time to stay on top of this ever changing business.

And, there are no if, ands or buts about it, you also need to do some grunt-work. Call club bookers (over and over), accept the good and bad reviews, put on a great show when you're exhausted or sick, constantly update your website, and tirelessly promote your music. This is where the business professional inside you must step in and handle things.

The business professional is someone who knows that the show must go on. They know that no matter what obstacle is put in front of them, they will persevere. Looking at the work habits of most big stars, I think they all have that business pro inside them. That's what allows them to succeed in all areas of the business. That is what keeps them going during the fifth press interview of the day, and all the other crap that has nothing to do with music and everything to do with the business of music marketing.

When an upcoming artist finally "makes it," the pressure to keep producing sellable music is huge. So you have to be healthy, ready to create and work on demand. You may be asked to hit the road for nine straight months, and then write and record a world class album immediately following a grueling tour. That's what being a successful artist or band can mean.

What it all boils down to is that stars have to be on top of their game, both artistically and business-wise. It's essential to create a balance between music and business early on. First, make sure your psyche is in the right place. You know, screw your head on right! Be honest with yourself regarding what things you are and aren't willing to do to be successful with your music.

Next, make a plan. Think about how you'll improve your skills in both business and in your art. Then, put your plan on paper. Make sure you honor your business commitments and always act professionally. Make sure you keep your artist side healthy and creative. Take days off, take walks in nature, take time to noodle around some new idea for a song that just popped into your head. Those types of habits will keep the artist inside you in good shape and feed your creative juices too.

Being a famous musician isn't a "normal" life. To survive and thrive requires a special set of skills. The good news is those skills can be learned and developed. Every little bit you learn now will benefit your career down the road. Put your hands out. One hand is the creative side and the other hand is the business side…now, put your hands together and get to work!

Songwriter Relationships / Artist Relationships

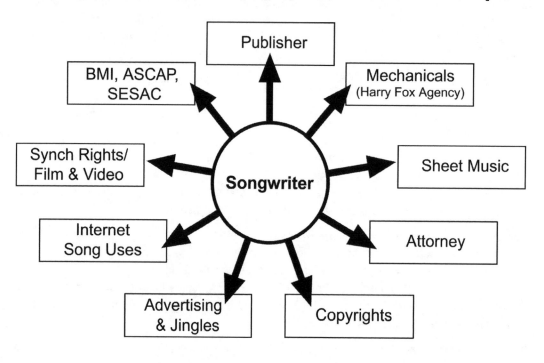

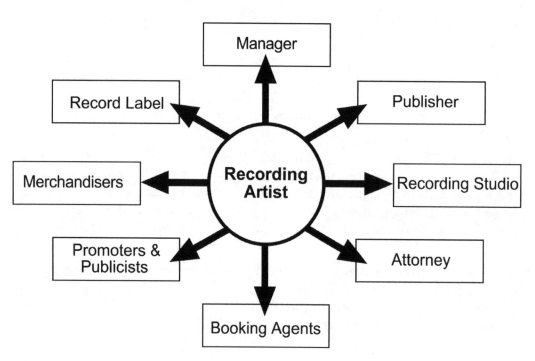

Filing Copyright Applications

The issue often arises: Should you be filing copyright applications with the U.S. Copyright Office for songs you've written or recordings that you've made? The short answer: It's not absolutely necessary, but as discussed below, there are some very good reasons to do so. This is particularly true if you're already performing the material in live performances (or are expecting to do so), or if any of your music is about to appear on a commercially released record or on the Internet.

Whether or not you file any copyright applications, you'll generally have *some* copyright protection—at least theoretically. But there are some very major advantages in registering your copyrights with the Copyright Office.

These advantages really come into play if and when someone steals your material, and a copyright infringement lawsuit becomes necessary. Your copyright registrations can mean the difference between a very weak copyright infringement case and a very strong one.

Incidentally, it's always a good idea to attach a proper copyright notice whenever you sell or distribute any tangible versions of your material (for example, on CDs or in sheet music form). For a song (words and music), it might be © 2007 John Doe Music. For a *particular recorded version* of a song, it might be ℗ (a capital P inside a circle) 2007 John Doe Records. For more information about copyright notices, obtain the Copyright Office's "Circular 3" from the Copyright Office's website, www.copyright.gov .

The Advantages of Copyright Registration

Here are some of the major reasons to file copyright applications for your music:

1. Statutory Damages and Attorney's Fees. If you've registered your copyrights *before* an infringement takes place, and (for "published" works) within three months of the first "publication" of the material, the court can award you from $750 to $150,000 in damages (called "statutory damages") for *each act* of copyright infringement, even if you're unable to prove any *actual* loss of income or profits (called "actual damages") caused by the infringement. (Incidentally, the term "publication," in copyright law terminology, refers to the point in time at which the material is first distributed to the general public *in any form* (*not* just in *printed* form). In the case of a CD, for example, the "publication" would be the date on which the CD is first commercially released. Live performances, though, do not constitute "publication."

However, if you have *not* promptly filed a copyright application, your damages will be limited (with some technical exceptions) to your *actual* loss of income or profits, which are frequently quite difficult and expensive to prove. (This difficulty and expense can be due, for example, to the high cost of inspecting the complex financial records of a large corporation which may have infringed on your copyright.)

Another advantage of filing copyright applications, assuming that you file the applications within the time frame mentioned above, is that the court can make the copyright infringer pay *your* legal fees and costs, which can be very high in copyright infringement cases, particularly when a case goes to trial.

2. Evidence of Validity. The federal copyright statute says, in effect, that if you file a copyright registration with the U.S. Copyright Office within five years of the first "publication" of the work, the registration can be considered evidence of the validity of your copyright, and evidence that all facts stated in your copyright application are true. All of this can be tactically very important in a copyright infringement case, particularly if there's a dispute about whether you wrote a particular musical composition as early as you claim you did.

3. Filing a Lawsuit. The copyright statute requires that before you can start a copyright infringement lawsuit, you must obtain a copyright registration. In many copyright infringement situations, it's important for strategic reasons to be able to move very quickly—for example, to *immediately* seek a court injunction stopping the infringer from continuing to misappropriate your material. But if a copyright registration has not yet been obtained, there will be some "down time" before the Copyright Office processes your application, unless you are willing to pay the very expensive additional fees charged by the Copyright Office to expedite the processing of your application. In the meantime, your legal rights can be seriously prejudiced; hence, the advisability of registering your copyrights ahead of time.

What Forms to File

There are two types of material on a record which can be copyrighted. First, each *underlying musical composition* can be copyrighted. This is typically done using a "Form PA." Then, separately, the master recording itself can be copyrighted, using a Form SR. In other words, you can copyright the musical composition itself, and then separately, your *recorded version* of that same musical composition.

You can file these forms for material *before* it's "published," and then again *after* it's "published." At the bare minimum, you should always file these forms promptly *after* the material is published.

In the case of a musical group not yet signed to a publishing contract or recording contract, the songwriters in the group will ordinarily copyright each of the songs which they have written (using Form PA), and then the group will separately file a copyright application (using Form SR) for the master recording itself.

In certain instances, a "Form SR" can be filed not only for the master recording, but also for the underlying musical compositions contained on the recording. This can be done only if the same people own the musical compositions *and* the master recording. There are certain technical requirements which determine whether a "Form SR" can be filed for both a master recording and the underlying musical compositions contained on that recording. Those technical requirements are explained in the printed instructions which accompany the "Form SR."

Incidentally, it has not been necessary for many years to send in sheet music with copyright applications. The Copyright Office will accept a "phonorecord" (i.e., CD or cassette) in lieu of sheet music.

Registering Collections of Musical Compositions

Songwriters are often concerned, quite reasonably so, about the cost and inconvenience of the copyright registration process. Fortunately there's a way to simplify the process and to keep the cost down. Under certain circumstances (see Copyright Office Circular 50 for the particulars), the Copyright Office will permit you to file one single copyright registration for multiple unpublished separate musical compositions which you have written, so long as all of those musical compositions are registered collectively under one single title.

Registering multiple musical compositions as a collection will allow you to file one copyright application for all of those musical compositions, and pay only one application fee ($45). So, for example, if you were registering 25 musical compositions, you would be avoiding the 24 additional copyright applications, and $1,080 in additional application fees. There are, arguably, some potential technical disadvantages in taking this approach, and I would not recommend this approach for material which is being commercially released.

The "Poor Man's Copyright"

There's one final matter which should be mentioned: the so-called "Poor Man's Copyright," aka the "Mailbox Copyright," where a songwriter mails a tape to himself or herself (rather than filing a copyright application). Based on several court decisions, it's clear that this "Poor Man's Copyright" approach is almost entirely useless. Yet this age old myth still persists today. Suffice it to say, the advantages of a copyright registration make it well worth paying the $45 for a copyright registration and doing it right, rather than relying on the "Poor Man's Copyright."

Obtaining Copyright Info and Forms through the Internet

The Copyright Office now has a website, www.copyright.gov. Copyright forms (with accompanying instructions) can be downloaded from that website. There's also a wide variety of information available on that website, and it's well worth visiting.

The Copyright Office mailing address: U.S. Copyright Office, 101 Independence Ave. S.E., Washington, D.C. 20559. Telephone: (202) 707-3000 and (202) 707-9100.

Trademarking Band Names

I once told this writer a story about how I met the guys in an elevator and found out that we all had the same last name, so we decided to form a band.

— Joey Ramone, The Ramones

Finding the right name for your band can be a tricky process. You not only need to find a name that fits the band well, but also one that isn't already being used by another band. A band's name will often become its most valuable single asset, since a successful band's name will, in itself, sell records and draw live audiences. Unfortunately, many bands fail to take even the most basic and inexpensive steps to legally protect their band's name, and as a result jeopardize their rights to use it and to keep other bands from using the same name.

There are a variety of problems that can arise when a band fails to take the necessary legal precautions. The most common problem, obviously, is adopting a band name that's already being used by another band or entertainment company. A close second would be situations in which one or more members of the band leave the band, or the group splits up, and there's a dispute about who has the right to use the band name.

There are several steps necessary to assure the maximum possible legal protection for your band's name. Some of these steps—such as filing a federal trademark application—can be pricey, and may not be feasible right away due to your limited finances. On the other hand, there are some other steps which are relatively inexpensive, and sometimes even free, but which may possibly help you avoid unpleasant legal repercussions in the future.

In most states, it's very inexpensive to file a state trademark application. Usually the filing fee charged by the state is in the range of $20 to $50, as compared to $300+ that the U.S. Trademark Office charges for *federal* trademark applications. And although a state trademark registration offers far fewer benefits than a *federal* registration, a state trademark registration does offer some benefits, at least on a local level, and will also get your band's name included in the databases of the various trademark database companies that people use for trademark searching purposes. Once your band's name and information is included in such databases, it may discourage some people from adopting it as their own.

Generally speaking, the following steps must be taken in order to seek the maximum possible legal protection of a band's name: (1) When choosing the name, try to be sure that no one else is already using the same name; (2) Once a suitable name is selected, then have a written agreement among the various members of the band as to future legal rights to the name if the band breaks up, or if some of the members leave the band; (3) File the appropriate trademark application forms; and (4) Monitor the entertainment industry to be sure that no one else starts using the same name.

These various steps will be discussed in more detail below. But let's first take a look at a couple of basic principles of trademark law.

Some Trademark Basics

The legal protection of groups' names is available through federal and state *trademark* laws, and *not* as a result of *copyright* law. In other words, your band's name is legally considered a kind of trademark. Often the terms "trademark" and "copyright" are used interchangeably, however they have completely different meanings. Trademark law protects *names* and *logos,* including the names and logos of *bands. Copyright* law, on the other hand, protects such things as artwork and songs. So when we're talking about protecting your group's *name,* we're talking *trademark* law.

Here's another important fact: Legal rights to a band's name, cannot, generally speaking, be obtained merely by sending in a trademark application form. Generally speaking, legal rights to a band name can be created only by active exclusive *use* of the name. There's one exception to this general rule. In certain circumstances, a federal trademark application can be filed even before the name is used, due to major changes in the federal trademark statute in 1989. This is called an "ITU" (intent to use) application.

Before your band starts actually using a particular band name (or files any trademark applications), you should make a serious effort to determine whether the same or a very similar name is already being used by another band. Otherwise, there's the risk that you could spend a lot of time and energy developing public recognition of your band's name, only to find that you have no legal right to use the name. You may also unexpectedly find yourself involved in a very expensive lawsuit.

Now, back to the issue of what steps are necessary to legally protect a band name.

The Difference between Trademarks and Business Names

A trademark is a name or logo that the public, or some significant portion of the public, knows your name by. On the other hand, a business name is a name you do business by, whether the public recognizes that name or not—for example, a company name (Jones, Inc.) or a "dba."

The only reason that I mention this distinction here is that sometimes people file a *"dba" name application* with a state or county governmental agency, mistakenly thinking that they're filing a *trademark* application. Therefore it's important to keep this in mind.

Choosing a Name

Your band name should be relatively unique, since it's much easier to get legal protection for unique names like the "Beatles" than for more generic, descriptive names (like "The Band").

Another consideration is that sometimes you can't even use your own personal name as part of the band's name, since someone else with the same name may already have exclusive trademark rights to it. If, for example, your legal name is Tom Waits and you include that name in your band's name, you can be certain that you'll hear from the attorney for *the* Tom Waits as soon as you reach any degree of recognition in the music business.

Also, as already mentioned, it's EXTREMELY important to avoid band names that are identical to OR confusingly similar to the names of already-existing bands. Another band's name does *not* need to be *identical* to your desired name for it to cause you major trademark problems. As long as there's a *likelihood of confusion* among the public between the two names, you have a big problem. Therefore, it doesn't work to just change the spelling of the name or to make only minor changes in the name.

Therefore, once you've decided on a name you like, you must then determine whether the name (or any very similar name) is already being used by someone else. For example, you should do an intensive Internet search. It's also a good idea to check record store catalogs (*Phonolog,* etc.) and music business directories (like the *Billboard* directories and *Pollstar*). You should also do a search on the U.S. Trademark Office's website, www.uspto.gov, but that database only contains trademarks which have been *federally registered*, so it doesn't contain all the info you really need.

If the name still seems to be available after you've done your research, you should consider, as a final step, having a computerized trademark search done by a trademark research company. The cost for a comprehensive search currently costs around $200–$500. This is often money very well spent. The advantage of obtaining a trademark search report from one of these companies is that they maintain massive databases containing, for example, all business license records of all the states.

You should be aware, though, of a serious problem area in the area of trademark researching: the problem of "below the radar screen" bands. This problem arises from the fact that there are thousands of local bands who've never filed a trademark application, and who've never released a record through an established distributor, and who've never done anything "official," like take out a business license. As a result, these bands will typically not show up on any trademark search reports. Yet they very easily may have established trademark rights to their band name, at least in their own local or regional area. Other than doing as much research as possible, there's really no way to avoid this problem; it's one of several risks inherent in the trademark process.

Trademark Registration

A trademark application can be filed with the *federal* government if the name is being used in interstate or foreign commerce. Also, as mentioned above, under certain circumstances a federal trademark application can be filed even *before* the name is used.

In addition, trademark applications can be filed in any *state* where the band is doing business. If a federal registration has already been obtained, it's generally not *necessary* to also obtain *state* registrations, though it's sometimes a good idea to do so.

As I mentioned above, it's not absolutely necessary to file a trademark application in order to have legal rights to a name. Nonetheless, there are many substantial legal advantages in having a trademark registered, particularly if it's a *federal* registration. As a general rule, any band desiring to protect its name on a national (or even regional) level should file a federal trademark application as soon as it's financially possible to do so. This is because the federal trademark statute says that your filing of a *federal* trademark application is legally considered to give national public notice of your use of the name to anyone not yet using the name. (This is referred to as the "constructive notice" provision of the federal trademark statute.) In some situations, your federal trademark registration may enable you to defeat the future trademark claims of another band using the same name or a very similar name.

In short, the filing of the federal application at the earliest possible time can give you trademark rights which you wouldn't have had otherwise (assuming, of course, that you are issued a federal trademark registration based on your application.) In a number of instances in which a band has obtained a federal trademark registration early in its career and then later confronted a trademark dispute over the band name, the band's early federal trademark registration enabled the band to keep the band name which it otherwise would have lost.

One final comment about the federal trademark application process: The Trademark Office's rules are strict, technical, and unforgiving, and you need to be sure you are dotting every "i" and crossing every "t." Otherwise, you can find that you've either damaged your trademark rights and/or are forfeiting your application fee without any right to a refund.

Agreement among Band Members

It's CRUCIAL that you have a written agreement among the band members regarding who can use the name if the band breaks up, or if *some* of the members leave the band. Experienced entertainment attorneys routinely include such provisions whenever a written partnership agreement or incorporation or limited liability company (LLC) papers are drawn up for a band (most often, these days, it's an LLC agreement). It's *extremely* important, however, that such a provision be drafted *very* carefully, because a *poorly* drafted provision usually creates many more problems than it solves.

Recording Contract Provisions

If you're an artist signed to a recording contract, your contract probably contains a clause saying that, by signing the contract, you're giving the label a warranty that you own all trademark rights in your band name, and that your use of the band name does not now (and will not at any time in the future) infringe on any trademark rights of any third party. Also, the contract may require you to file a federal trademark application, or may allow the label to file such an application in your name (in which case the label will be entitled to deduct any trademarking costs from any artist royalties owed to you in the future).

Further Steps to Protect the Name

Whenever you use your band's name—for example, on posters and record packaging—you should give notice of your trademark rights. If you've obtained a *federal* trademark registration, there should be the symbol ® (an encircled R) next to the band's name in a conspicuous place somewhere on the packaging and in print ads. On the other hand, if a federal registration has *not* been obtained, you can't legally use the symbol ®, but you can use the symbol ™. For example, The Beatles®, or The Jones ™.

It will also be necessary to renew your trademark registrations after a certain period of time—for example, after ten years in the case of *federal* trademark registrations. The renewal requirements for state trademark applications vary from state to state.

In regards to federal trademark registrations, there are also some other documents which must be filed from time to time, even before the end of the ten year removal period, in order to keep the federal trademark registration in effect.

Finally, you should take *immediate* legal action if another group starts using your band's name. Otherwise, you run the risk of losing all legal rights to the name. Names like "aspirin" and "thermos" were once legally protected trademarks, but were later lost because the trademark owners of those names failed to stop other companies from using those same names.

In short, the following steps should be considered whenever a band is trying to protect its band name as much as possible: (1) First, try to be sure no one else is using the desired name: (2) Have a written agreement among the band members as to the members' rights to future use of the name; (3) Obtain federal and state trademark registrations, if possible; (4) Be sure that your trademark registrations are renewed when necessary, and that other necessary documents are filed in a timely manner, and take immediate legal action if someone else starts using *your* band's name as their own.

Starting Your Own Publishing Company: An Eight Point Checklist

I often encounter people who want to set up their own music publishing company but don't know how to go about it. They often assume that the process is much more complicated that it really is. Before laying out the steps involved in starting a music publishing company, it's important to first talk very briefly and basically about what a "music publisher" does, since the term "music publisher" is sometimes misunderstood by people new to the business side of the music business.

Occasionally people think that a music publisher's main function is to print sheet music. This isn't correct. In fact, most music publishers have an outside company handle the sale of their sheet music. Instead, a music publisher's main function is to get a songwriter's material used (for example, on records and movie soundtracks), and then to collect royalties for the songwriter from record sales, etc. The publisher also has other important functions, such as processing copyright applications and various types of contracts.

The formation of a music publishing company isn't nearly as complicated as people often assume. By the same token, it isn't a totally hassle-free proposition. Before starting your own publishing company, you should realistically and carefully evaluate the reasons for doing so. Generally speaking, it only makes sense to consider starting a music publishing company if you're going to make some very serious efforts to market your material, or if your material is on records already commercially released, or is very likely to be so in the near future.

If you decide to start your own music publishing company, you'll need to take various steps, including the following:

1. Choose between ASCAP and BMI. ASCAP and BMI are two separate organizations that serve the same function—namely, collecting royalties from certain users of original material (for example, radio stations and clubs), and then distributing royalties to publishers and songwriters.

No songwriter can be a member of both BMI and ASCAP at the same time, and hence, must choose between the two. In addition, a songwriter and his/her publishing company must belong to the same organization (i.e., BMI or ASCAP). For example, a BMI writer cannot, for example, be signed to an ASCAP-affiliated publisher, but instead can only be signed to a BMI-affiliated publisher.

Since BMI and ASCAP have different procedures for calculating royalties, you may want to obtain informational materials from these organizations before making your choice.

The membership fees charged by these two organizations are also different, and so you'll want to compare the fees which they each charge.

People often wonder which organization will pay them more. In my mind, there isn't an easy answer here. There's one scenario in which it's possible to compare, namely when a commercially successful song has been co-written by an ASCAP-affiliated writer and a BMI-affiliated writer. Yet, I've seen situations in which the ASCAP writer/publisher were paid more, and other situations in which the BMI writer/publisher were paid more.

One technique sometimes used by writers and publishers is to have one co-writer join ASCAP and the other join BMI. Then, whichever writer/publisher is paid less, they go to their organization (i.e., ASCAP or BMI) and seek to have their amount bumped up to the amount paid by the other organization.

Another consideration, aside from who pays more, is who can provide you with more services and assistance. And so you should compare the material in the ASCAP and BMI brochures, as they apply to your particular circumstances and needs.

One valuable opportunity which both organizations can provide is the opportunity to perform at one of their showcases, which are normally well attended by label A&R people and people from major music publishing companies. Taking into consideration the kind of music you play, you might want to ask ASCAP and BMI for specific information about the dates and locations of their various showcases, and also get information about how to be considered for such showcases.

You can obtain more information about these organizations at www.ascap.com and www.bmi.com.

2. Choosing and Clearing the Name. You should choose several alternate names for your publishing company, since your first choice of a name may already be taken by another music publishing company. BMI or ASCAP—whichever one of those you choose to apply to—will require you to submit a list of several different names for this very reason. The best place to start with either ASCAP or BMI is to call them at the numbers listed below and ask them to send you a name clearance form.

You'll also want to obtain the membership application forms. There's one set of forms to join as a *songwriter*, and a separate set of forms to affiliate as a *publisher*. You'll need both if you're a writer *and* are starting your own publishing company. (A songwriter who is acting as his/her own music publisher, is in effect wearing two hats—one hat as the *songwriter*, and the other hat as the *publisher*—for example, Joe Schmoe (the songwriter), and Schmoe Music (the music publisher).

Before sending in the name clearance form to ASCAP or BMI, it's a very good idea to first check the publisher databases on the ASCAP and BMI websites and do some Google searching, to see if there's already a publisher listed who is using the name you want to use. However, this isn't a completely reliable process. For example, one problem I've run into several times is when there's a publisher (most often a foreign publisher) whose publishing company name is a foreign language name, but when translated into English, is the same name as (or is too close to) the English language name my client wants to use. In that situation, neither ASCAP nor BMI will allow you to use the English language equivalent of the other company's foreign language name.

You should also check to be sure that the names you're selecting can be used as a business name in the county and state where you are based, and also that the name does not infringe on any trademarked names.

Incidentally, it's also sometimes advisable to have a comprehensive computer trademark search done to be sure the new publishing company's name is totally clear, especially in situations where there's a substantial financial investment involved.

Also—AND THIS IS CRUCIAL—Allow enough time BEFORE a record release to properly clear the publishing company name, because it can sometimes take awhile to find a name that you like *and* that is available. At least six to eight weeks before your artwork must be finalized is a good rule of thumb. It's also a good idea to send in the documents to ASCAP/BMI by certified mail, return receipt request, and then monitor the status of things. Otherwise, there's a risk that your paperwork will fall into a black hole and you may not realize that that has happened until it's too late.

3. Decide on a Business Structure. You must decide on how your publishing company is going to do business—i.e., whether as a sole proprietorship, limited liability company, corporation, general partnership, limited partnership, etc. Then have the necessary legal paperwork prepared and do all of the same things you would do if you were starting any other type of business—for example, obtain a business license, a federal tax ID number, etc. You'll need to have some of this done by the time you submit your ASCAP or BMI publisher membership application, since the application will require you to provide certain business-related information (e.g., tax ID number) on your application.

Incidentally, if you're a sole proprietorship or partnership, you may need to file an application for a "dba" ("doing business as") name registration. Without a "dba" registration, most banks won't allow you to open a checking account in the name of the publishing company.

4. Miscellaneous Contracts. There are many different types of contracts, which can potentially be involved in operating a music publishing company. If, for example, your music publishing company is going to be handling songs composed by songwriters *other than yourself*, there will need to be appropriate contracts signed between your publishing company and any such songwriters.

Another example: if your publishing company is going to authorize someone to commercially use a song owned by your publishing company—for example, if your publishing company is granting a mechanical license to a band, authorizing the band to record and commercially release one of the songs owned by your company—there will need to be a licensing agreement prepared.

Sometimes people starting a publishing company will initially want to have an array of legal forms prepared, so that they will feel "armed to do business." However, as a practical matter, you should wait to have any such contracts prepared until you have an actual need for them, in order to avoid unwarranted legal costs. Otherwise, those forms may end up collecting dust on a shelf.

5. File Copyright Applications. You should be sure that all necessary copyright applications are filed with the Copyright Office for the songs being handled by your publishing company. There may also need to be "copyright assignments" executed, transferring copyright ownership to your new music publishing company. In certain situations, those documents will need to be filed with the Copyright Office.

6. File "Title Registration" Forms. Whenever a recording of your songs is going to be commercially released or broadcast, you should promptly submit a "title registration form" for each such song with the performing rights organization which you are affiliated with (i.e., ASCAP or BMI). (You can now do this online.) This allows them to monitor the airplay of your song and to pay you royalties accordingly.

7. Consider Possible Affiliations with Other Publishers. You may want to consider entering into an administration agreement with a more experienced music publishing company; that other company handles all your publishing paperwork in exchange for a percentage of your publishing income (typically around ten to twenty percent). However, if you haven't yet had any commercial success, it's normally difficult to find a good solid music publishing company willing to administer your catalog, since they normally won't want to take on all of the work involved unless there's some cash flow from which they can take their commission.

8. File Any Necessary Tax Returns. As for which specific tax returns you'll need to file from time to time, this will depend on the structure of your business (sole proprietorship, corporation, etc.).

Other Steps Possibly Needed

The steps mentioned above are the basic steps involved in setting up a music publishing company. However, for anyone setting up a publishing company, there may be circumstances, specific to their own situation, which may require that other (or even different) legal or business steps be taken.

As you can see, acting as your own music publisher does involve some time and expense. Hopefully, the guidelines suggested above, though not intended to be a comprehensive list of the steps required for every possible scenario, will nonetheless help you to decide whether the benefits of starting your own music publishing company will justify the time and expense involved.

Eight Types Of Publishing Deals:
An Overview

People often speak of "publishing deals" in a generic way, which implies that there's only one kind of publishing deal. In fact, there are a number of different kinds of publishing deals. But first, some historical background.

In the very early days of music publishing, songwriters simply sold their songs to music publishers for a flat amount. Later, as songwriters became more business savvy and gained a little more negotiating leverage, a new kind of contract evolved, consisting of three basic elements: (1) The songwriter would assign all copyright ownership of the songwriter's songs to the publisher; (2) The publisher would have the right to try to get the songs commercially exploited; and (3) The publisher would agree to pay royalties to the songwriter based on income received from third parties from any commercial exploitation of the songs. (As a general rule, a songwriter today receives fifty percent of the total income from his or her songs.)

Although that basic type of deal (which I refer to below as the "traditional publishing deal") still widely exists today, various newer kinds of publishing deals have evolved over the years.

Incidentally, when I use the term "publishing deal" here, I'm using the term very broadly, to refer to any kind of deal whereby some individual or company (other than the songwriter) obtains the right to receive a share of the songwriter's music publishing income (for example, mechanical royalties from the use of songs on records, public performance income from BMI and ASCAP for radio airplay, and synchronization income from the use of songs in films, television shows, computer games, etc.).

This ties into a more general issue, namely the abstract nature of much music publishing terminology. Such terminology is confusing to most people, and also makes it difficult for many people to understand basic music publishing concepts. I've represented many music industry veterans who, almost to a person, say that music publishing is the one and only aspect of the music business that they have trouble comprehending, even after many successful years in the music industry.

In addition, such terminology, if not used carefully and precisely in contracts, can cause major legal disputes. For example, when a contract refers to "music publishing income," it needs to be made clear at the outset, and defined carefully in the contract, whether the term is meant to refer to the *combined* music publisher/songwriter income from music publishing, or only the music publisher's *own share* of that income.

The Different Kinds of Deals

In short, the eight kinds of publishing deals today are: (1) the "Traditional" Publishing Agreement; (2) Single Song Agreements; (3) Co-Publishing Agreements; (4) "Step Deals";

(5) Administration Agreements; (6) Income Participation Agreements; (7) Catalog Representation Agreements; and (8) Sub-Publishing Agreements.

These eight kinds of deals vary from one to the other, but differ most importantly in the following respects:

- What percentage of copyright ownership, if any, is given to the publisher.
- What share of future publishing income the publisher will get.
- What functions the publisher will perform.
- How long the agreement will remain in effect.

For example, the first four kinds of deals mentioned above involve the transfer of at least part of the *copyright ownership* of the songs. Not so, usually, with the last four kinds of deals.

In general, of the eight kinds of deals mentioned, there will usually be one particular kind of deal that will be the most appropriate for a particular situation. By the same token, that same contract will likely be totally *inappropriate* for *other* types of situations. Therefore, I will outline below the situations where each particular kind of deal is appropriate.

Here's a thumbnail sketch of each of the eight kinds of publishing deals.

1. The "Traditional" Publishing Deal

First of all, the term "Traditional Publishing Deal" isn't customarily used in the music industry. I'm only using that term here for purposes of distinguishing this type of deal from the others.

Typical Scenario. This kind of deal dates back to the days of Tin Pan Alley. Today it's used when a songwriter and a publisher want to have a long-term relationship for all of the material that the songwriter will be writing during the duration of the contract. This type of deal is usually not used when the songwriter is signed to a record deal. (See "Co-Publishing Deals" page 60.)

Material Covered by the Deal. This kind of deal will cover material written during the term of the contract, and sometimes may include certain specified songs written before the contract was entered into. Usually the contract will require the songwriter to deliver a certain number of new original songs to the publisher during each year of the contract.

Copyright Transferred. Normally, the writer is assigning (to the publisher) 100% ownership of the copyright of the songs covered by the contract.

Income Sharing. The publisher receives all income from third parties, then pays the writer one-half of that income. (Except for airplay income paid by ASCAP and BMI. Those organizations pay writers *directly* the so-called "Writer's Share" of airplay income.)

The publisher here is getting a larger share of the publishing income than in most of the other types of deals mentioned below. That's because, in the case of this "traditional" kind of publishing deal, the publisher's responsibility is to proactively promote the songs involved and, theoretically at least, it's the publisher's efforts that will cause any future success of the songs. On the other hand, in the case of many of the other types of deals involved, the publisher's role is less promotional and proactive in nature, so the publisher gets a small piece of the pie.

Term. Normally, the agreement will be for an initial one-year period (with the writer obligated to deliver a certain number of songs to the publisher in that one year), then the publisher will have several (in the range of three to six) consecutive one-year options following that initial one year.

Incidentally—and this is very important—the "term" means the period of time during which the songwriter is writing songs for the publisher, and *not* how long the publisher will have rights in those songs. Normally even though the term of the agreement may be only a few years, the publisher will be the *owner* of those songs for a much, much longer period of time, i.e., until they go into public domain many years later. (There's one exception here: if there's a reversion clause in the contract, then copyright ownership may revert to the songwriter at some future specified time.)

Advances. The larger established publishers typically pay a recoupable advance to the songwriter for the first year (payable in installments), often in the range of $25,000 to $50,000. Then an additional advance is paid each following year the publisher exercises its option to continue the contract for another year. Normally the contract will contain somewhat complicated provisions for how the amounts of the advances for the follow-up years will be calculated.

2. The Single Song Agreement

Typical Scenario. This type of agreement basically is based on the same concept and structure as the "traditional" type of deal mentioned above, but involves only one (or several) of the songwriter's songs (i.e., one or several songs already written). Sometimes, a relationship between a songwriter and publisher will start out this way, and later they will enter into the "traditional" type of deal.

Material Covered by the Deal. Even though the title of this kind of deal would imply that it's only for one song, this kind of agreement is sometimes used for *several* songs at the same time.

Copyright Transferred. Same as with the Traditional Deal.

Income Sharing. Same as with the Traditional Deal.

Term. Same as the Traditional Deal, but in the case of the Single Song Agreement, it's much more likely that there will be a reversion clause. Typically the contract will (or, at least, *should*) provide that the copyright ownership will revert to the songwriter if the publisher isn't able to get the song recorded by a signed third party artist or used in a film, television program, etc. within twelve or eighteen months.

Advances. Often the publisher will refuse to pay an advance. However, even when advances are paid, they're usually very small, typically in the range of $200–$500 per song.

3. Co-Publishing Deals (aka "Co-Pub Deals")

Typical Scenario. This type of agreement is typically used for writers who are in groups already signed to a record deal. This type of agreement covers the original material on the group's records. Normally all of the members of the group who are songwriters will be signed to this type of agreement with the same publisher.

Just to be clear here, I'm talking about a publishing deal with a publishing company *not* affiliated with the record company. Today, it's much less likely than it used to be that a record company will demand a publishing deal as part of a record deal, though there are still some indie labels that still do so—for example, many labels in the Christian music market.

Material Covered by the Deal. All of the original songs on the group's first record, then the publisher will have the right to options on the original songs on anywhere from two to four of the follow-up albums, hence for a total of 3 to 5 albums, with the exact number depending on what the parties negotiate.

Copyright Transferred. The songwriter normally transfers one-half of the copyright ownership to the publisher and retains the other one-half ownership. In other words, the song is co-published (and the copyright is co-owned 50–50) by the third party publisher and the writer's own publishing company.

Income Sharing. Normally, the third party publisher will collect all income and then pay to the songwriter and the songwriter's publishing company 75% of all publishing income.

Term. As already mentioned, co-publishing agreements are usually for a certain specified number of albums.

Advances. Advances are almost always paid to the songwriter in the case of co-publishing deals. For groups newly signed to major label record deals, the initial advance from a major music publisher is typically in the $100,000–$500,000 range and sometimes higher, with additional advances being paid if and when the publisher exercises its options for the follow-up albums.

4. "Step Deals"

This type of deal is for situations where the songwriter isn't yet signed to a record deal, but may later enter into a record deal. This contract will provide, in effect, that the deal will be the "Traditional" deal mentioned above, but will automatically transform into a Co-Publishing deal, if and when the songwriter is signed to a record deal.

5. Administration Deals (aka "Admin Deals")

Typical Scenario. This type of deal is used when the songwriter just wants a publisher to collect royalties and handle the various paperwork (for example, the BMI/ASCAP song title registrations, copyright applications, the issuance of licenses, etc.), and where the songwriter doesn't want or need a publisher to proactively promote his or her catalog of song. A good example of a company that does a lot of Administration Deals is Bug Music in Los Angeles.

Material Covered by the Deal. Most often this kind of deal covers all material written by the songwriter, or at least any material that the songwriter has not already committed to other publishers.

Copyright Transferred. No transfer of copyright (usually).

Income Sharing. Typically, the publisher will take 10% to 20% of the income, and the pay the rest to the songwriter and the songwriter's publishing company.

Term. Administration deals are normally in the range of three to five years.

Advances. For catalogs generating a modest amount of income, usually no advance is paid. For more profitable catalogs, usually an advance will be paid, with the amount to be determined on the basis of the income that has been generated in recent years by the catalog.

6. Income Participation Deals

Typical Scenario. This is a "publishing deal" only in the sense that it involves a sharing of future publishing income. Usually this type of deal is used to cut someone in on a share of the publishing income—for example, to serve in effect as a "finder's fee" for having found a record deal for a songwriter. Very often the "income participant" isn't even a publisher.

Material Covered by the Deal. Highly negotiable and varies widely. May only cover, for example, the material on the songwriter's first album.

Copyright Transferred. No share of copyright is transferred. Instead the "income participant" is only entitled to receive a share of income.

Income Sharing. Varies widely, but often is in the range of 10% to 15%.

Term. Again, highly negotiable and varies widely.

Advances. No advance is involved.

7. Catalog Representation Deals

Typical Scenario. This type of deal is used when a songwriter or publisher is primarily interested in getting their material used in films, television programs, etc. and wants to enter into a deal with a company that specializes in doing so and has all the necessary connections. Usually that same type of company will also represent record labels that want to get their *masters* used in films, etc.

Material Covered by the Deal. Typically, as the title "Catalog Representation" would imply, the songwriter or publisher's entire catalog. But sometimes the Catalog Representation company will "cherry-pick" only certain songs for representation.

Copyright Transferred. No copyright is transferred.

Income Sharing. Typically in the range of 25%–50% of the income from any deals secured by the Catalog Representation company.

Term. Often in the range of two to three years, but sometimes longer, sometimes shorter.

Advances. Usually no advance is paid, but there are occasional exceptions.

8. Sub-Publishing Deals

Typical Scenario. This type of deal is between a U.S. publisher (including songwriters who act as their own publisher) and a foreign publisher. For a cut of the income in the applicable foreign territories, the foreign publisher will collect the income in those territories.

U.S publishers enter into this kind of deal in order to receive their money *faster* from foreign territories *and* also to collect more of the income that has been earned in those foreign territories. (Often, for various reasons, only part of the income *earned* in foreign territories is actually *collected*. The money not collected is customarily referred to as "black box money.")

Material Covered by the Deal. Usually the entire catalog.

Copyright Transferred. No copyright is transferred.

Income Sharing. The foreign sub-publisher will normally take in the range of 25% to 35% of the income off the top, then pay the balance to the U.S. publisher. The percentage taken by the sub-publisher is sometime significantly less for large, profitable catalogs.

Term. Usually in the range of three to five years.

Advances. Same situation as with Administration Deals.

Artist Management: The Basic Deal Points

You wonder about people who made (and lost) a fortune, and you always think they drank it up or stuck it up their nose. That's not usually what brings on the decline. It's usually the battle to keep your creative child alive while keeping your business shark alive. You have to develop cunning and shrewdness, and other things that are not well-suited to the arts.

— Joni Mitchell

Keeping one's "creative child" side and "business shark" side alive at the same time is a hard job for anyone, whether you're a successful artist living in a pressure cooker environment, or a struggling new artist facing all the frustrations of trying to get established in the music industry.

A solid manager can greatly help you to balance, in a healthy way, your creative needs with your business needs, not to mention the many other valuable services a good manager performs. Yet, the artist-manager relationship is fraught with many potential problems for you, since there are many ways in which an incompetent or dishonest manager can sabotage your career, intentionally or unintentionally.

When choosing a manager, you should evaluate his or her knowledge of (and connections in) the music business, their personal compatibility with you, and the amount of time they'll be able to devote to you. It's also important to check out the prospective manager's background.

After you and the prospective manager have decided that you want to have an artist-manager relationship, you (or each of your attorneys) should then discuss and negotiate the specific terms of your future relationship; such as how long your relationship is to last, what the manager's compensation will be, and what the manager's specific responsibilities will be.

The outcome of these negotiations will be greatly affected by your relative bargaining power and that of the manager. If, for example, an experienced and well-connected manager is negotiating a management contract with an unknown artist, the manager will obviously have much more leverage than the artist. In fact, sometimes you're facing essentially a "take it or leave it" situation.

Once the most basic terms of the management deal are agreed upon, a detailed written management agreement will then be prepared by one of the parties' attorneys. At that point, there will often be some further negotiations concerning some of the detailed sections of the agreement. If so, then a revised version of the written management agreement will be prepared before you and the manager actually sign the agreement.

There are several aspects of management agreements that are particularly important, namely: the future duration of the artist-manager relationship; the manager's compensation; and if the "artist" is a band, then the possibility of personnel changes in the band.

The Future Duration of the Artist-Manager Relationship. Management contracts typically have an initial term of one to two years, and often give the manager the option to renew the contract once a year for several more years after the initial one or two-year term expires. Sometimes, the management agreement will be based not on a number of years, but instead on a series of "album cycles." An album cycle is the time frame it takes to release an album.

Before you enter into a management contract with a manager, you should carefully evaluate and discuss your expectations of each other. Your management contract should take into consideration your expectations and should contain provisions allowing an early termination of the management contract if the parties' respective expectations are not met. Often, for example, management agreements provide that if a record deal isn't obtained within a certain period of time, or if the artist does not earn a certain amount of income each year, the artist will have the right to terminate the management contract.

A manager's compensation is typically based on a percentage commission of the artist's earnings. Therefore a prospective manager will often push for a *long-term* management contract, so that the manager can participate in the artist's income for as long as possible. You, on the other hand, may not want to get locked into a long-term relationship with a manager, particularly if you don't know how compatible you will be with the manager, or if you aren't sure how much the manager will be able to contribute to your career.

Manager's Compensation. Managers usually receive in the range of fifteen to twenty percent of the artist's gross income. This *manager's* commission is separate from, and in addition to, the commissions paid to *booking agencies* for booking shows.

Management contracts usually contain very complicated clauses pertaining to commissions. Some management contracts, for example, provide for one particular commission percentage for income from record sales, and a different percentage for other types of income. In addition, management contracts will sometimes provide for changes in the manager's commission rate as the artist's income increases.

Incidentally, there's one aspect of management contracts that comes as a surprise to many artists, which is that your financial obligations to the manager don't necessarily end when the management contract expires. This is because many (if not most) management contracts provide than even after the contract expires, the manager will continue to receive income from deals which had been entered into during the term of the management contract. If, for example, you and the manager have signed a three-year management contract, and then sometime during that three years you sign a five-year recording contract with a record company, the manager will normally be entitled to receive a certain specified share of the future record royalties even after the three-year management contract has ended. (These are commonly referred to as "tail-out" commissions.)

By the same token, most management contracts also provide that the manager's percentage share of such income will be *reduced* after the management contract ends, and/or that there will be an outside time limit after which the manager is no longer entitled to share in the artist's income. For example, you and the manager might agree, among other things, that the manager will receive a share of your income and royalties for only one or two years after the expiration of the management contract, even though your recording contract may be generating royalties for years after that.

Personnel Changes. If the "artist" is a band, the management contract should anticipate the likelihood of personnel changes in the band. For example, will the contract give the manager the right to manage the careers of any departing members after they leave the band? And will the addition of new members to the band require the approval of the manager, as some management contracts provide? These types of potential problems need to be covered thoroughly by the management contract.

In short, management contracts can be exceedingly complex, due in large part to the complexity of the music business itself. Yet a carefully drafted contract will substantially reduce the likelihood of future misunderstandings and disputes between you and your manager.

Artist Development: Questions to Ask Yourself

Please take time to answer the following important questions. Thoughtful, honest, and detailed answers to these questions will help you when you write the bios, fact sheets, and press releases necessary for marketing and promoting your music, and will help you evaluate your current career status.

- Name of artist or band? (Include all band members names and instruments played.)
- Is your stage name trademarked?
- Have you registered your songs for copyright protection?
- Have any of your songs been published? (If so, by whom?)
- Have you affiliated with a performance rights organization? (Which one—ASCAP, BMI?)
- What is your background? (Who are you and your band members? Tell your story.)
- Do any band members belong to the Musician's Union?
- Do you have a written band/partnership agreement?
- Why do you want to record and release your own music? (Be very honest.)
- Who is your fan or customer? (Analyze this question thoroughly.)
- Do you write your own songs? (Discuss the songwriting process in detail.)
- Who are your musical influences? (Cite specific examples.)
- How do you describe your music to people? (This isn't a short answer. Discuss it.)
- What image do you think your music conveys? (Do not avoid the image issue!)
- What are your immediate music career goals? (Next one to three years.)
- What are your long-term career goals?
- How would you define the word "success"? (This isn't a short answer. Discuss it.)
- Do you have any personal contacts in the music business?
- Do you have an entertainment law attorney to consult with?
- Are you looking for an independent label deal or a major label deal? (Why?)
- Do you have a demo or press kit, or any promotional materials?
- What live performance experience have you had? (Any industry showcases?)
- How do you rate your live performance ability? (Be very critical. No clichés.)
- Have you recorded any previous CDs or demos? (Which studios? Who was the producer?)
- How did you sell your CDs? (Consignment? Over the Internet? Live sales? Distributor?)
- Have you had any previous print or broadcast media exposure or reviews?
- Are you financially able to fund the costs of establishing your career? (In debt?)
- Do you have a business license? (City, state, federal?)
- What is your current business form? (Sole proprietor? Corporation? Partners?)

- Have you set up a system for tracking your financial activities? (Software system?)
- Are you aware of the tax deductions available for musicians?
- Do you have insurance on your band equipment and vehicles?
- Have you created an exciting, well-designed website? (Aware of new design software?)
- Do you have a presence on the Internet that is active and aggressive? (Looking for new opportunities?)
- Who handles your daily business activities? (Bookings, promotions, etc.)
- Have you created an actual career, marketing, or business plan? (Is it in writing?)

The First Front: Part 2
What is Product Development?

Making and Selling Your Music

Product Development includes those areas that are directly involved with recording and selling your music. Product Development issues become much easier to deal with when all the details addressed in Artist Development have been taken care of. Not all musicians take the time to deal with these responsibilities. They prefer to rush through the songwriting process and move right into the recording studio in their eagerness to get their music out. That's a big mistake.

The first thing a professional label does after signing an act is to start thinking about the marketing or sales plan for the act. That's right, a good record label executive—perhaps the A&R rep who signed you—can already envision how your music will be promoted and sold by the time you enter the recording studio.

Researching the right recording studio, producer, and engineer become key issues in Product Development. Where will your record be recorded? Who will record it? Both of these questions must be considered seriously before you make a final decision.

The choices of what studio to record in and what producer or engineer will be hired to make the record are uppermost in the mind of a label person. Record labels are aware that the music must be recorded in a way that captures the right sound for its genre, otherwise the chances of radio airplay could be hampered and there may be no significant sales of the record. Production choices are part of the Product Development equation when deciding how to market a new artist or band.

Never cut corners when recording your music. Once the recording is finished, you'll have to live with it forever. You never want to say, "Gee, I should have done…." Find the best studios and recording team you can afford. Music production sounds are changing constantly and it's your responsibility to make sure your records sound as contemporary as possible.

Up next is mastering. Mastering isn't something to be passed over lightly. The mastering engineer can enhance or hurt the recording you made. Choose a mastering engineer who understands your genre of music. This is a must.

Who will manufacture your record? Who will design the artwork for your release? These are two more essential questions. Your finances will most likely determine this, as they probably determined production decisions. Take the time to make a record that sounds and looks like something you'd want to buy yourself. Album cover artwork, packaging material design, and printing issues are important because you're creating a product that will be competing for the attention of music fans who have an abundance of music releases to choose from. Is there something about your album cover that will attract a customer to your record?

Once a record has been manufactured and is ready to be sold to the public, Product Development turns its attention to Distribution and Sales arrangements. Many developing acts forget this in their hurry to record their music. But, if you're going to spend thousands of dollars recording your music, don't you think it would be a good idea to find a way to sell it? Well, that's exactly how professional record labels think. They make sure a system is in place to distribute and sell their records to their fans. Many musicians make the mistake of trying to get some radio airplay, or other media attention, before they've found a way for the public to buy it. Make no such mistake. **Product Development, after a record has been recorded, focuses on all the business arrangements involved with selling your music.**

You'll soon learn in this book that the business of distribution, like the business of music retail, is complex and challenging. Welcome to the world of major label distribution companies, independent distributors, rackjobbers, mass marketing retailers, mom-and-pop independent record stores, and the always evolving world of Internet music sales.

Please remember: Product Development is the Front that the other three Fronts of music marketing are aimed at. Radio airplay promotion, publicity efforts, and live performance (the Exposure Fronts), are the methods used by record labels to get the public's attention to recorded music—with the hopes that music fans will either go online or run down to their favorite store to buy the song or CD.

Who Buys Music?

When I first studied marketing, I learned that buyers of consumer products can be placed into three categories: early, middle, and late adopters. Early adopters are the first to buy a new product: middle adopters wait, and late adopters are the last of all. I thought this idea was for other products and had nothing to do with my business, the music business. I was wrong.

Over the years I realized that learning about consumer's buying habits could help me understand what type of person is the first to buy CDs by a new band and what type of person is one of the last. I also noticed that the people who worked in the recording industry were themselves adopters of music products. It could help me in my business dealings with them to know what type of music user they were. So, let's take a look at the habits and lifestyles of early, middle, and late adopters of music products and see if there's some information about their habits that can help you market your music more effectively.

Early Adopters

Early adopters are die-hard fans. Music plays a dominant role in their daily lives. They plan their days around their relationship with music.

Here are some important characteristics of early adopters of music product:

- They know a lot about the history of their favorite music. Early adopters have an encyclopedic knowledge of their favorite bands and artist's music and know when they're recording, touring, or putting out a new record. They will buy releases that contain songs they already have if the release is an import, bootleg, or features songs that were not previously released.

- If they're rock fans, they rarely embrace all styles of rock, but will be knowledgeable about a certain sub-genre of rock, like punk-rock, grunge, or metal. This goes for early adopter fans of all kinds of music—from rap and hip-hop to classical, folk, blues, and even the most eccentric strains of popular music.

- They're fickle fans and they're very critical of musicians. They'll be the first to criticize a band for selling out, or ostracize an act from their circle if a new release doesn't meet their expectations.

- They usually own a large music collection. They collect any and all releases of a favorite band or genre of music. They may have downloaded 20 to 100+ gigabytes of MP3 files to their computer hard drives from file trading and sales sites on the Internet.

- Their social life revolves around the club scene of their city; four to six nights a week you can find them at some local club. When a favorite local or national act comes to town they'll be standing or sitting near the stage. You can count on them to be at every show that's relevant to their musical passions. They seek out new venues on a regular basis.

- They shop for records wherever they can find what they want. They may prefer to shop at independent or mom-and-pop record stores, but they'll also check out the major music retail outlets and scour the Internet for unique or out-of-print music they can't get elsewhere. You'll also find many early adopters at record swap meets.

• They listen to non-commercial or college radio instead of commercial radio. But they'll also tune in to a commercial station's specialty show if it offers the music they want.

• They read print and online music magazines and fanzines. They're insiders who know what's going on in their scene because their grapevine extends from the gossip heard at clubs to the web sites and chat-rooms that proliferate on the Internet. As you know, web-sites on the Internet come and go constantly…here today, gone tomorrow. But, here are a few places to see what's new in music, as of early 2007.

> You Ain't No Picasso: www.youaintnopicasso.com
>
> Fluxblog: www.fluxblog.org
>
> Said the Gramophone: www.saidthegramophone.com
>
> Gorilla vs Bear: http://gorillavsbear.blogspot.com
>
> My Old Kentucky Blog: http://myoldkyhome.blogspot.com
>
> Brooklyn Vegan: www.brooklynvegan.com
>
> So Much Silence: www.somuchsilence.blogspot.com
>
> Stereogum: www.stereogum.com
>
> I Guess I'm Floating:http://iguessimfloating.blogspot.com

How To Market To Early Adopters

Earn their trust. Early adopters are the key to success for new artists and bands. They can ac-tually make or break a new act by either accepting them or rejecting them. When they're ex-cited about your music they'll help spread the word about it.

Encourage them to sign the mailing lists you have posted at your live shows. If they love your act they can become like unpaid employees. The best way to have them help you is to get them involved somehow in your promotion and marketing. For example, early on in your ca-reer they can host house concerts for you. Early adopters often create websites for their favor-ite acts. Linking to those websites from your own homepage and MySpace page are essential.

As your act grows in popularity, your CDs should contain extra goodies. Limited edition re-leases appeal to early adopters. It's a good idea to include bonus cuts or alternative studio takes on some releases.

You should aggressively pursue the new Internet artist promotion opportunities. These Inter-net marketing tools can rapidly speed up the word of mouth promotion that's essential to growing the career of any artist. Also, when your CD is first released it should be put on con-signment at the appropriate local independent and chain record stores, and on Amazon.com's Advantage program, www.amazon.com/advantage. And FOR SURE on CDBaby's website, www.cdbaby.com.

Advertising money should be spent only on those media print and broadcast outlets that directly gain the attention of early adopters. Many small independent record labels waste precious advertising money on media buys that target *late* adopters.

Because of the fickle nature of early adopter's musical taste and their deep psychological investment in music, you have to approach the appropriate media for reviews, interviews and feature stories of your music. Research the musical tastes of the reviewers at magazines, newspapers, and the web. Sending a new CD to the wrong early adopter writer in the music press can put the kibosh on a budding career.

Middle Adopters

Middle adopters of music product are more casual fans. Music is very important to them, but not to the exclusion of everything else—they have other interests or obligations that prevent them from total dedication to a favorite music scene. Here are some of their characteristics:

- They rely on early adopters for much of their musical knowledge. This means they either know early adopters who turn them on to the best of the best, or they read reviews written in the music or pop culture media by early adopter reviewers, or they tune in as often as they can to a hip radio station.
- They might attend one or two concerts or shows a month; early adopters are usually out several nights a week. (Early adopters probably got them to at least one of those shows.)
- They might buy one or two new songs online a week, or two CDs a month because they may be raising a family or want to spend their extra money on other entertainment choices.
- Industry employees often fall into the middle adopter category. In the years before media ownership rules changed the way songs got played on the radio, many music and program directors relied on some early adopter to turn them on to a hot new act. This still happens at commercial radio today; but it's more likely to happen at college stations where so many of the air-staff are early adopters. In this way the playlists of the best college stations can influence commercial radio—when middle adopter program directors and marketing directors read the weekly playlist reports in such music trades as *CMJ* and *Hits*.
- They get the word quickly about a new cool band or song. Often they get an MP3 file or CD from an early adopter and play it at home and office parties and help expose new music to the next type of music consumer—the late adopter.

How to Market to Middle Adopters

This can be a bit tricky. If I were to estimate the number of middle adopters of music in the United States and compare them to the number of early and late adopters, there would be far fewer of them. Marketing to middle adopters is a matter of using the strategies and tactics that have been most effective with early adopters.

If the early adopter is the engine for a train that gets things moving for an act, then the middle adopter is the fuel for that engine so that all the other cars, including the last car, (the caboose, packed with late adopters) come along for the ride. That fuel is really a special energy generated by the early adopter's excitement. It's an infectious energy that carries the enthusiasm of the early adopters to more and more people.

Think about this in your own life. How many times have you taken the advice of a DJ, a record store clerk, or a music reviewer, and bought a record because they told you it was cool—even though none of your friends knew about the record? You trusted a personal recommendation and, if you liked the record, it paid off. You may have told a whole bunch of other people about that music as well.

Marketing to middle adopters can't be done without the help of early adopters. So, if you see any value in getting the attention of this select type of consumer, then go back to your marketing plans for getting the attention of the early adopters and think carefully about how you can best take advantage of the most effective methods to reach them. Actually, **the by-product of a successful early adopter marketing campaign is the capturing of the middle adopter customer**, who simply boosts the efforts of the early adopter by getting the word out about a cool new song or band to more people.

Late Adopters

So, who are these people and why do you want to know something about them? Well, they're everybody else. They're the last to get on board the train. Nevertheless, they're very important. In fact, they're the main target for the mainstream music business because they're the type of music purchaser who make stars into superstars. Late adopters of music product have many other interests in their lives, and put music near the bottom of the list when they decide how to spend their disposable income.

Here are some of the chief characteristics of the late adopter of music:

- They attend very few concerts every year, and when they do it's usually to see a major act or superstar who has had widespread popularity for many years. They don't go out a lot to local clubs. Rarely, if ever, would they attend a house concert (unless they were a relative or a close friend of the performer.)

- They need to hear a song dozens of times before they remember the name of the artist or the song. (Commercial radio's playlists are designed with these people in mind.)

- When they do like an artist they want to hear their music a lot. They may not have a wide interest in music but they are in a sense "brand loyal," meaning they will stay with the act for the long ride.

- They've been accused by early adopters of having no taste, but they apparently get something of value from a mainstream artist. Otherwise they wouldn't buy the artist's CDs or tickets to their concerts, let alone spend all those bucks on merchandise created around mainstream acts (t-shirts, movies, games, etc.).

- They buy few records and usually buy only what are referred to as the "hits." They buy their music at high profile music stores or, more likely, at the record departments of mass merchandisers like Target, Wal-Mart, Best Buy, etc. Online they spend a lot time and money at www.iTunes.com these days. Without the late adopters, the major record labels wouldn't exist because the profits made by acts that can reach the masses cover all the losses of less successful releases by the major labels. The music industry needs to have product that appeals to the masses.

- When they listen to the radio, watch TV, cruise the Internet (www.myspace.com especially), read magazines or newspapers, they usually listen to commercial radio, watch the most popular TV programs, visit the bigger name websites, and read the most popular magazines and newspapers. By the way, one new twist is that all three types of adopters use MySpace. It will be interesting to see how that site changes how adopters choose their favorite music.

How to Market to Late Adopters

There are more late adopters than early or middle adopters. But for music to get the attention of late adopters, it must have the money and business connections necessary to market *to* them. It takes millions of dollars to market to this prized consumer group. It's possible for deep-pocketed independent record labels to get their music to the masses, but most of the music that late adopters support is put out by the major record labels. Major labels have the muscle and money to finance national tours, market to the powerful media exposure outlets, get their songs played on commercial radio and TV stations, and put their records into the mainstream retail stores that cater to late adopters.

Most music releases fail to recoup their initial investment. That's a sad fact of life. But, with a clearer understanding of the buying habits of music consumers, any record that focuses on reaching an early and middle adopter base *first* has a more realistic chance of competing for attention of the mass music buying public.

Unlike a few years ago, today mass marketers of music to Late Adopters have discovered the Internet in a big way. Just go online and cruise around awhile, you'll find tons of major websites with special features on major recording artists (it sure took them long enough).

To Sum It All Up

If you find yourself feeling smug and judgmental about these late adopters, if you smile knowingly when you realize they need to hear a song eighteen times before the song makes an impression on their minds, you're probably an early or middle adopter yourself. I've spent all of my thirty years in this business as an early adopter and did my part in slamming late adopters, accusing them of having no taste, or at least no curiosity about all the great music that has been created. But over the last few years I've realized that I was a late adopter myself when it came to non-music interests. If everybody else was like me, we wouldn't have films to see, gourmet foods to eat, cars to drive, doctors to heal us, athletes to admire, etc. In the game of music marketing, late adopters have an important role to play.

The gatekeepers of the music business, (those people who stand between the artist and the artist's audience), every one of them is either an early, middle, or late adopter themselves. The more you know about how they value music, the more you can prepare your presentations to them, because you'll talk to an early adopter of music in an entirely different way than you would a late adopter.

When you speak with an early adopter of music, always stress the music itself. You should be able to describe your music to them in ways they would describe it to each other. Talk about the influences in your music. Compare it to other past or current acts. Speak knowledgeably and honestly about the music with a genuine excitement about it.

When you speak to a middle adopter of music, talk about how some early adopters have embraced it and what the results were. Talk about the merits of the music itself from your view.

Should you ever have the money and muscle to try and reach the masses, remember this: the late adopter exposure outlets (the media in particular) care less about the artistic merits of the music and more about its accessibility to a wide demographic of listeners, viewers, or readers whom they must cater to. **So, tell late adopters business success stories and give them financial and survey data that prove to them that a wide audience would like your music.**

Now, ask yourself what type of music adopter you are. I hope you're an early adopter because making it in this business is a lot more fun if you're deeply involved in some particular kind of music. If you're a middle adopter, you'd better have some early adopter friends in influential places, because playing this game requires a real passion for music.

Music is an emotional product; it moves people in many wonderful and mysterious ways. Knowing about the different types of music consumers can help you monitor the acceptance of your music by fans and industry people alike and help you find ways to reach them.

What You Should Know about Your Fans

If you're more concerned about getting "a deal" than you are about getting to know your fans, you're on the wrong track. If you understand the lifestyles of your fans, you'll have a passport to making money with your music. Why? Because when you know who your fans are, their habits and lifestyles will show you ways of reaching them that you never imagined.

Study the people who come to your live shows, buy your records and t-shirts, and visit your websites. Besides the great songs you've written, those folks are your most valuable assets.

Customer research is behind many kinds of special promotions. For example, haven't you seen toys for sale at places other than toy stores? You know—toy action figures from some mega movie promotion, free with a hamburger. Or, how about those special deals where you subscribe to a magazine and get a free book or movie discount coupons? To help you get into the mindset of a professional marketer, here are some questions about your fans.

- How old are they? (Determine the widest range of their ages.)
- What gender are they? (If both, what percentage is dominant, or is it even?)
- Are they one specific ethnic background or a mix of backgrounds?
- Do they drive cars to work, carpool, take public transportation, ride bikes, or walk?
- If they're students, what kind of schools do they go to? Grade school, high school, college, business school, university?
- Are they religious, atheists, or free thinkers?
- What political parties do they belong to, and what, if any, causes do they champion?
- What kind of restaurants do they go to—fancy and expensive, ethnic, or fast food?
- Where do they shop for clothes? Thrift stores, Target, Nordstrom?
- What hobbies and interests do they have? Computers, art, hiking, skateboarding, sports?
- What other music do they like? Particularly, what other bands and artists do they spend their money on?
- What movies do they see in theaters, rent online or at video stores?
- Do they get to your gigs by bicycle, motorcycle, car, bus, train?
- What books do they enjoy reading, and where do they buy them?
- What kind of volunteer work might they do—environmental or political causes, fairs and festivals, church or social groups?
- What TV shows do they watch, and what radio stations do they listen to?
- What Internet websites do they visit and download music from?
- Do they subscribe to any blogs or podcasts? Which ones?

OK. How do you find out answers to some of these questions? Well, a client once told me that for two years they had videotaped their live shows to watch at rehearsals, so they could see their stage appearance from the audience's point of view. Great, but I told them that after two years they should turn the video camera around and videotape their audience! A picture is worth a thousand words, right? Studying your audience should give you some big clues to their lifestyles. You see their ages and genders, their hairstyles and clothing, and you can make some pretty good guesses about them.

You'll have to get used to this new habit of studying your fans. Give it time. After awhile your ongoing survey will begin to tell a tale, and before long you'll be thinking like a professional marketer.

For example, what if you see that your audience is mostly male, eighteen to twenty-five, community college or local university students, who buy their clothes at second-hand stores? You can think up fun and exciting promotion and marketing ideas to catch their attention. For instance, concentrate your live shows on house concerts, or play campus venues and blanket the campuses with posters and flyers. Get a campus organization to sponsor one of your shows, get a listing or a story about your act in the college paper. Partner with a local record store to sell your concert tickets and offer a dollar off your CD when fans buy a concert ticket. Make your show a partial benefit for the charity second-hand clothing store. They can promote your show with posters and handouts to their customers, and have a small display at their checkout counter for your CD. (Don't forget to sell your CD and merchandise through your website and at all your shows, and have your mailing list available for new fans.)

If your research shows that you have fans who are older, you'll have to go a different route. Let's say they're females, twenty-five to thirty-nine, who live an alternative lifestyle that includes having friends over for book club discussions, listening to acoustic music, and preferring tea to coffee. Think about doing what I call a "tell a friend" acoustic house concert. You select a fan to host a show at their home and invite their friends to attend for free. You make your money by selling your CDs and other merchandise to an expanding fanbase. See page 233 for info on house concerts.

Promotional ideas for creative self-marketing are endless—when and if you know who your customer is. The best independent labels think this way all the time. That's why you've seen hip-hop CD compilations for sale at shoe stores, or found CD samplers given away at bookstores. Your customer isn't much different from you. Just start paying attention wherever you are, and wherever they are, and watch how other products are being sold and marketed. The customers are out there, but they have a lot to choose from—so get your music to them in fun and creative ways.

Some of these questions can be answered by conducting online questionnaires for your fans. Think up some fun contest or reward them with free CDs or merchandise. You'll be pleasantly surprised how eager your true fans are to help you out by answering your questionnaires. Just keep focusing on the lifestyle and daily habits and hobbies of your fans, and creating fun projects for them to get involved in will reward you in ways you can't imagine.

35 Things to Consider When Starting Your Own Record Label

Deciding to release your own record is only a good idea if you know what you're getting into. As you read through the following questions, mark the ones that you can't answer, and make an effort to find the answers. We answer some of these questions throughout the book. There are, however, some questions that only you can answer, and a few that are outside the scope of this book.

(Answers to any business start-up issues are widely available on the Internet and in many books devoted to that specific topic.)

1. Why are you starting your own label? (What is your motivation?)
2. Why would anyone want to buy your music?
3. Is there currently a market for your kind of music? Prove it!
4. If you're not releasing your own music, have you ever read a recording contract?
5. Are you aware of all the traditional clauses that are in such 75–100 page contracts?
6. Do you know anything about copyright law?
7. What is a mechanical royalty? What is a performance royalty?
8. Have you heard of the Harry Fox Agency, ASCAP, BMI, SESAC? What do they do?
9. What do you want to achieve by starting your own label?
10. What do you know about the day-to-day business of selling music?
11. Will your new company be a sole proprietorship, a partnership, or some type of corporation? (Do you know the pros and cons of each?)
12. Have you trademarked the name of your company to be sure you can use that name?
13. Will you need recording equipment, office equipment, and supplies to run your label?
14. Do you have a recording studio you can work with?
15. Do you know any record producers and/or engineers?
16. How much money will it cost you to start your label, record your records, and market the recordings for the first year? Second year? Third year?
17. How will you raise the money you need to start and run your record label?
18. What local, state, and federal tax responsibilities will your label have?
19. How will you sell your records? (Live shows, Internet sales, mail order, catalog sales, distributors, stores?)
20. What specific distribution and retail sales plans have you arranged so that people can easily find your releases at retail stores?
21. Do you have the money, time, and determination to compete in an industry that releases over 1,000 new records a week?
22 How much will it cost to manufacture your CDs, and/or vinyl?
23. What configurations (CD, vinyl, MP3, etc.), will you need to make and sell your music?
24. How many copies of your releases do you realistically think you can sell?
25. What deals are offered by manufacturers? Will you use their barcode or buy your own?

26. Will you need to make posters, bin cards, or other materials for retailers? If so, how many and how much will that cost?

27. Will you be making special novelty items like t-shirts, baseball caps, etc. and how much will that cost?

28. How did you estimate the number of copies you needed to manufacture?

29. Did you count into your estimation the number of free CDs you'll have to give away for promotions of various kinds?

30. How will you go about finding other acts to sign to your label? Are you the sole artist? Then how many new releases will you have every year or so?

31. How important do you think graphic design is in making your label's logo and cover art work for your releases?

32. Do you know any graphic artists with record design experience?

33. What information should go on the CD cover, back-cover, spine, booklet, and label?

34. What will your website look like? What online marketing news and fan opportunities will there be for your fans to interact with you?

35. Do you know how to write a marketing plan, a distributor one-sheet, and other promo materials?

Plus an extra question:

36. Who are your customers? If you think you know them, then describe them in very specific terms. (Why am I asking you to do that? If you don't remember go back a few pages and re-read the section on how to reach the different types of music adopters.)

Releasing Your Own Record:
A 15-Point Legal Checklist

For artists who are releasing their own record for the first time, without the involvement or assistance of a label, the process can be a little intimidating, and it can be easy to miss some key legal details in the process.

Here's a very basic checklist of issues for you to consider when releasing a record. Bear in mind that your own particular circumstances may dictate that you take certain steps that are different from, or in addition to, the steps mentioned below. Also bear in mind that it's been necessary to greatly oversimplify some of the issues.

1. Agreement among Members of Group. If you are a group (as opposed to a solo artist) releasing the record, and if you haven't already formalized your relationship by way of a partnership agreement, incorporation, or limited liability company ("LLC"), there should at least be a clear and simple written agreement among the group members about how the finances of the recording project will be handled. Also, it's always a good idea to deal with the issue of the ownership of your group's name as early in your career as possible.

2. Investors. If there are investors involved, documents will need to be prepared in order to comply with certain federal and state securities laws. *Be especially careful here.*

3. Distribution and Promotion Strategy. Think ahead about how the record will be distributed, advertised, and promoted, and how much money will be needed to effectively market the record. Sometimes all (or almost all) of the budget for a project is spent on recording and manufacturing costs, and there's little or no money left to effectively advertise or promote the record. This, of course, isn't really a legal issue but is such a common (and often fatal) problem that I feel obliged to mention it here.

4. Mechanical Licenses. For any cover songs appearing on the record, you must obtain a mechanical license from the owner of the song (i.e., the song's publisher), authorizing the song to be recorded and providing for the payment of mechanical royalties.

For many songs, the license can be obtained from the Harry Fox Agency, (212) 370-5330, or www.harryfox.com. By going to the Harry Fox website's "Songfile" search engine, you can determine whether they handle the songs that you need to license. If so, call and ask them to fax or mail you the necessary forms.

Allow six to eight weeks for the Harry Fox Agency licensing process to be completed and the license issued. THERE'S ONE EXCEPTION TO THIS LONG PROCESS: If you're initially pressing 2500 units or less, you can use their online licensing process. That way, the licensing can be wrapped up in a few days. See their website for the details.

For songs not licensable through Harry Fox, you must contact the publisher directly. Usually the easiest way to do so is to obtain the publisher's telephone number info from the "song indexing" departments at ASCAP and BMI.

5. Sampling Clearances. If you're including any samples on your record, you need to obtain sample clearances from the publisher of the musical composition being sampled AND, separately, from the record label that owns the master being sampled. Do this as early as possible; there will be some instances where either the publisher or label won't be willing to issue a license, or the licensing fee they require may not be affordable.

Also, some duplicators require you to sign a form stating that either you haven't used any samples, or that if you have, you've obtained all necessary clearances. If there's any obvious sampling done, the duplicator may require you to show them the clearance documentation.

6. "Work for Hire" Agreements. For any session people, engineers, etc. you're hiring, it's wise to have them sign a short and simple "work for hire" agreement, to preclude any possible future claims by them that they're owed royalties or that they have ownership rights in the masters. Do this BEFORE you go into the studio.

7. Producer Agreement. If you're using an outside producer, you need to have a producer agreement signed, defining (among other things) how the costs of the recording sessions will be handled, what advances (if any) and producer royalties will be paid to the producer. Just as in the case of the Work for Hire agreements mentioned above, do this BEFORE you go into the studio.

8. Production Credits. Make sure that the production credits listed in the liner notes—for session people, producers, and others—conform to any contractual requirements. For example, the producer agreement will often be very specific about how the producer's credits are to be listed. For musicians performing on the record who are signed to a label, they will normally need to be credited as appearing "Courtesy of" their label.

9. Liability Releases/Permission Forms. You need to consider the possible necessity of getting a liability release or permission form signed in any of these scenarios: (a) if a photograph and/or artistic image of an individual outside the group is included in the artwork; (b) if any of the artwork you're going to use is owned by a third party; or (c) if any logos or trademarks owned by third parties appear in your artwork. There can be some tricky legal issues in this area, so be very careful here.

10. Copyright Notices for Songs. Be sure that the liner notes contain the correct copyright notices for all of the songs on the record, i.e., both for your original songs and any cover songs that you're using. Information about copyright notices can be obtained at www.copyright.com. Also, make sure that the song credits are correctly stated for each song; the name of the song's publisher and the publisher's performing rights society (i.e., ASCAP, BMI, etc.).

A non-legal side-note: At the same time you're working on the artwork and the copyright notices, etc., double-check to make sure that your artwork meets all technical specs of whoever will be printing the artwork. Also, if you'll be distributing the record through a record distributor, make sure that your artwork conforms to the distributor's specs.

11. Copyrighting Your Original Material. Certain copyright applications need to be filed promptly for your recordings and for your own original songs. Use "Form SR" for copyrighting the masters of the songs, "Form PA" for each of your original songs on the record, and "Form VA" for the artwork (if you own the artwork and want to copyright it). You can download copyright forms from the copyright website link mentioned earlier.

In some instances, it's possible to file an SR form to cover both the musical composition and your particular recording of that musical composition. The instructions for Form SR discuss when and how you can do this.

12. Registering Your Original Songs with BMI/ASCAP. Assuming that the record contains one or more songs that you have written, and assuming that you're affiliated with ASCAP or BMI, or are in the course of becoming affiliated, you'll need to file "title registration" forms for each of your original songs appearing on the record. This will enable your rights society (i.e., ASCAP or BMI) to monitor any airplay of your material.

13. Trademark Notices/Registrations. Be very sure that you have the legal right to use the group name and label name that you've chosen, and consider the advantages of filing trademark applications for those names. Generally speaking, it's a very good idea to file a federal trademark application for those names as soon as possible.

Also, make sure that your liner notes contain a proper trademark notice for the name of your group, and (if applicable) the name of your label. Information about trademark notices can be obtained at www.uspto.gov/.

14. Obtaining a Bar Code. For bar code information, check out www.gsone.org or call them at (937) 435-3870. Also, many CD duplicators will, as part of their service and at no additional charge, provide you with a bar code for your record. Ask about this when getting quotes from duplicators. For the reason mentioned in the next paragraph, you may want to make sure that any bar code you obtain from a duplicator will identify your particular record, not someone else's record.

15. Registering with SoundScan. If you anticipate significant sales and want to come to the attention of record labels, it's a good idea to register your record with SoundScan, a private company. SoundScan compiles record sales data based on the scanning of bar codes from sales at retail stores and then sells that information to its subscribers, which include all of the major record companies. SoundScan has an application form you can get online at www.soundscan.com.

If you plan on submitting a SoundScan application, be sure that you obtain a bar code specifically for your own record. If, instead, you "borrow" someone else's bar code (or use your duplicator's general bar code), your sales will be credited to them and not to you.

The Value of Careful Planning

Hopefully this checklist will help reduce some of the stress and strain of putting out your own records. The key is to think ahead as much as possible. Some of the steps, such as obtaining sampling clearances and mechanical licenses, can take time. A lack of planning can increase your costs and/or delay the release date.

Make sure you have all of your "ducks in a row" before you schedule any record release event. It's not an enjoyable experience to be locked into a record release date, only to find out at the last minute that you aren't going to be receiving your CDs from the duplicator by the time of the event, or that there are legal or technical problems with either the CD or the CD artwork.

By thinking ahead, the odds are much better that your record release will proceed smoothly and that, after the record release, you'll be able to spend your time and budget effectively promoting the record, rather than having to spend time doing damage repair.

Preparing Your Release: Manufacturing and Design Tips

There's more to making a record than just recording it. Here are a few things to think about before you manufacture your release and prepare it for the marketplace. How many CDs will you manufacture? What will the cover (and booklet) design and artwork look like? If you know the answers to these questions, you'll increase your chances of selling your music.

Let's get into some manufacturing basics. The cost of making CDs has gone down since the CD debuted in 1982. Manufacturing plants offer dozens of "package deals" to make it easier for artists to release their own music. In fact, when I ask a new client why they pressed up 1,000 copies of their first CD, they usually answer, "Well, I called this company I saw advertising in a music magazine and they had this great deal on pressing up 1,000 CDs."

OK—but please stop and ask yourself these questions before you order:

- Do I have 1,000 potential customers?
- Do I have a good shot at selling *more* than a thousand records? Or, have I underestimated?
- Will I send promo copies (freebies) of my record to radio stations, newspapers and magazines? How many do I need locally, regionally, and nationally? How many will I give away to family and friends?
- If I'm going to work with a legitimate distributor, how many copies will they need?

Answers to these questions will help you determine the number of records you actually need to make. And that will affect how much money you need for manufacturing. Also, are CDs the only configuration you need to make? Think about it.

The cover design of your release is also a crucial issue. What's your package going to look like? The time you spend designing your CD cover will pay off in the future—in many ways. The image you select, the graphic artist you choose to design the cover, the colors and fonts you use, all play a huge role in creating or maintaining your image.

A well-designed, attractive cover and CD package can either help you sell your CD or hurt sales. Go through the following questions and evaluate the design, images, text, and colors used for your record. Critique your artwork and make some suggestions to make it more appealing. Do the graphics reflect the music inside the package?

Graphic Design Tips for an Effective Introduction to Your Music

Front Cover Is the name of the artist clearly visible?
      Is the name written with a *unique* logo design?
      Is the name of the artist in the *top third* of the cover?
      Is the title of the release distinguishable from the artist's name?
      Is the genre of music reflected by the cover art?

Back Cover	What specific information is included on the back cover?
	(Label name, catalog number, bar code, song titles/ times, contact info, production credits, e-mail address, website URL, more?)
	Are the graphic images and text and colors used clear and readable?
Label	Is the artist's name (logo?) present and clearly visible?
	What specific information is on the disc itself?
	(Many artists leave the disc blank for "artistic" reasons. Do you want to make such a statement, or do you want to list the songs and times again, or repeat other written information from the back cover or booklet?)
Booklet	Describe the type of booklet/tray card used in your packaging.
	What specific images and text information are included?
	(More credits, thank-yous, lyrics, pictures, etc.)
	Is the booklet artwork and design consistent with the artwork and design on the front and back covers?
Spine	What specific information is on the spine of the CD?
	(Label name/logo, catalog number, artist name, release name?)
	Will you invest in the plastic tear-off strips that most CDs have now?

Musicians aren't usually sensitive to graphics. They create in a world of sound. When they get to the point of choosing the graphics for their records, they tend to rush this important stage in the manufacturing process. Don't overlook the importance of graphic design! Professionals in the Four Fronts and shoppers at record stores will usually have a *visual* impression of your music before they hear it. After you've approved the graphics and sent your CD to the manufacturer/printer, it will be too late to change anything. When you see it in a record store someday, will it stand out? Will you still be proud of your cover design ten years from now?

Here's an exercise for you. Go to your favorite record store and give yourself one solid hour of browsing through the bins. Look at other artist's covers. Pay attention to how they look. How many truly great covers can you find in one hour? How many bad ones? What made the great covers great, and the bad covers bad? At the end of that hour you'll be far more aware of your competition. Which pile will some future Music Director, distributor, or store buyer put your CD in…the "great" pile or the "bad" pile?

I want you to realize that you'll be sending your record to people who see more records in a week (between 800–1,000 CDs!) than you'll see in a year. Your cover makes an impression that will last a lifetime. That's right—a lifetime. That's how long you'll have to live with your decision. Preparing your record for manufacturing takes as much thought and consideration as writing and recording your songs.

Let's Talk About Bar Codes

If you've ever wondered what a bar code is all about, according to http://gsone.com, a bar code is "a precise arrangement of parallel lines (bars) and spaces that vary in width to represent data." Specifically, they represent a unique 12-digit number, sometimes called a Universal Product Code number. When placed on a product, these bars can be scanned by lasers so that stores can digitally record what products they have sold. You've probably seen how much time they save cashiers at supermarkets. So, do you really need one?

You don't, unless you plan on selling your CD in a store that requires you to have one. This would include all retail chains and online stores. If you're just selling CDs at your gigs and in little mom and pop stores, then you don't need one.

Now don't freak out, but if you want to be a real record label you must buy your own barcode. Unfortunately, for most independent musicians the high cost of obtaining your own barcode can be prohibitive at first. The cost has been going up every year, so check the above website for the current cost.

Now…there's an alternative way to go, and here's how it works. When you buy a bar code, what you're actually doing is buying a unique six-digit number for your company or band, let's say it's 123456. But what you're really getting is a range of numbers from 12345600000 to 12345699999 (plus one more number known as the check digit, but let's move on). So you can buy one UPC number and assign it to your first ten thousand releases. Now, while you might not need your own bar code right away because you won't be producing ten of thousands of albums, a CD manufacturer like Disc Makers or Oasis (and even CDBaby.com) offer good deals for you. They've purchased many six-digit numbers and have been giving out all the possible 12-digit combinations to their clients. This is perfectly legal and there's nothing wrong with doing that, in the short run. It's common practice. Major labels even do this for some of their newer bands.

If you want Neilsen/SoundScan to be able to track sales of your CD, you need to register your bar code number with them, as I mentioned earlier, so they know to attribute any sales to you, rather than your CD manufacturer. So, if you haven't done this yet, get to it. You simply download the Soundscan application form, fill out the information, and fax it back to them. You can also download the SoundScan form from Discmaker, www.discmakers.com. For your own barcode, GSOne can be reached at http:// www.gsone.org

If you have a manufacturer's bar code, you should put the manufacturer's name down on the form as your parent label. That doesn't mean anything technically, it merely lets SoundScan know where you got the number from. If you're on a label, put that down as your "sub label."

Once you get your bar code, your CD manufacturer will make sure it gets printed on your CD. If you're supplying your own design, make sure you leave a 1.25″ x .5″ space where you want the bar code to appear and they'll insert it for you.

Inside Major and Independent Record Labels

Signing, recording, promoting, publicizing, and selling music is a lot of work. As you'll see, the larger record labels have the luxury of having many different departments and dozens of employees to run the label. The smaller companies have the same responsibilities to manage and they have to be creative and energetic to get all that work done.

Inside a Major Label

What are the key departments at a record label, and what are those departments responsible for? The CEO of a major label will generally oversee the business affairs of all the affiliated labels under their corporate umbrella. Each major label will have its own **President** who is responsible for all the label activities. For example, at Warner Brothers, there's a president for Warner Brothers Records, as well as a president for Reprise Records, a president of Atlantic Records, etc. Each department at a major label is run by a **Senior Vice President.** Each of the following areas has a Senior Vice president in charge:

The **Business Affairs Department** takes care of label finances; bookkeeping, payroll, etc.

The **Legal Department** handles all contractual issues and other legal responsibilities.

The **A&R (Artists and Repertoire) Department** locates and signs new talent. They work with the artist in song selection, choice of producers and recording studio selection. They communicate with the label's Business Affairs Department to make sure all the paperwork and accounting issues involved with the actual recording of an act's record are set up properly. In short, the A&R Department can serve as a liaison between an artist and all the other departments at the label.

The **Art Department** supervises all product design jobs, (CD, vinyl cover art, etc.), trade and consumer press advertising, retail sales posters and flats, and other print projects.

The **Marketing Department** is responsible for creating the overall marketing plan for every record the label is releasing. They're also involved in coordinating all the promotion, publicity, and sales campaigns that the label is committed to.

The **Publicity Department** arranges for feature stories, interviews, or record reviews in local and national newspapers, magazines, web-zines, as well as the broadcast opportunities for coverage on radio stations and television. They may also coordinate any of these publicity opportunities with an artist's own publicist.

The **New Media Department** creates the websites and produces the music videos for the label's artists. This department also oversees all the promotions and marketing opportunities on the Internet that use the audio and video technologies to stream or offer downloads of your songs.

The **Artist Development Department** usually oversees the career planning of artists signed to the label. This department coordinates a consistent marketing and promotion presence for an artist throughout their career with the record label. Remember, the Artist Development Department has changed over the last decade. Many labels no longer have such a department. Others have changed the name to Product Development and concentrate more on "breaking," or promoting artists quickly in order to try to speed up the return on their financial investment. The pressure to return a profit to shareholders has changed the face of the music business dramatically in recent years, so the emphasis has been more on Product Development and securing a hit as fast as possible.

The **Sales Department** oversees all the retail activities of the label and concentrates on building relationships with key record store chains and other music and mass merchandise retailers. At some labels online sales may be handled by the New Media Department, but if so, they'll work closely with this department. The Sales staff coordinates their efforts with the major label's distribution company, and communicates regularly with the Promotion and Publicity departments at the label.

In the last few years some of the Major labels have delegated their manufacturing and distribution business to outside the label companies. Nevertheless, a **Label Liaison** is the person who coordinates the business of the major label's plans for manufacturing and distribution with the needs of their parent record labels. Street dates, (the date that a new release goes on sale at music retailers or when it can be sold online), must be approved by the label's distribution company in cooperation with the label.

The primary goal of the **Promotion Department** is to secure radio airplay for their company's new releases. These days radio is more than AM/FM stations. There are satellite stations and key Internet broadcasters to deal with, and in 2006, High Definition Radio made its debut, giving the Promotion personnel more than a handful of work to do. Their ability to get songs played is central to the success of the whole company. The Promotion department is closely connected to, and constantly communicating with, other departments within the label to make sure that all strategies being used to market and sell an artist's record are working together properly. Soliciting videos to MTV, VH1, BET and other music oriented television networks and Internet programs may also be the responsibility of this department. At some labels this job is a separate department, or part of the New Media department.

Every department at a record label plays an essential role in the success or failure of the company. They're team members, working together toward the goal of selling their music as one lean, mean, machine.

Inside an Independent Record Label

Independent record labels come in all sizes and shapes. The large well-funded Indie labels are organized into departments similar to the major label structure described above. The more money a label has, the more people they can hire to handle the various responsibilities of a label. Smaller, grass roots or "garage" labels organize the work of promoting, selling, and publicizing their releases by having their staff wear as many different hats as possible.

These smaller labels have an awesome task marketing their records. There may be only two or three employees, including the label owner, doing the A&R scouting, calling all the different types of radio stations about airplay, working with a distributor (if they even have one), checking with the brick-and-mortar as well as online music retailers, and coordinating the publicity efforts—as well as dealing directly with their artists and bands to help them find gigs and put tours together.

Running a record label is a very expensive and time-consuming job. Few independent labels successfully manage the issues I've just outlined. It takes a lot of money and a lot of time to operate a legitimate record label. The more research and planning a young label can do before jumping into the world of music marketing, the higher the likelihood that they'll survive and prosper in this competitive business.

Typical Major Label Structure

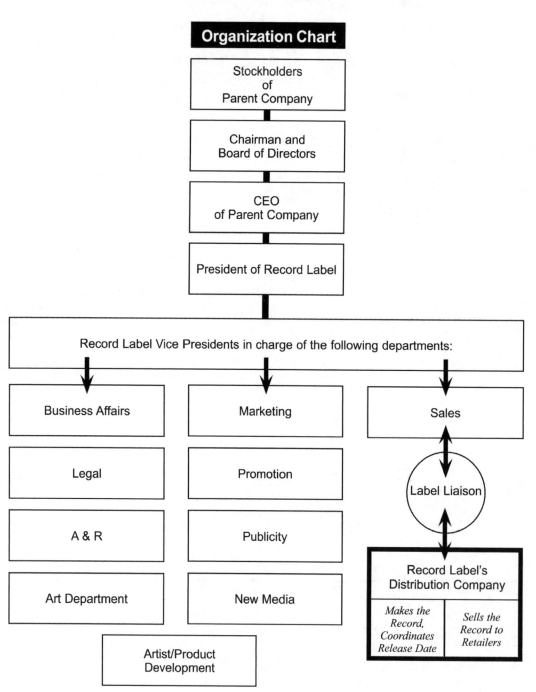

What A&R Reps Do

The A&R Reps Primary Job

To Find Talent By:

- Auditioning demos, solicited and unsolicited, depending on the record label's policy.

- Attending live shows at clubs, showcases, concerts, and other venues.

- Looking for leads on new talent by checking with industry insiders (managers, agents, attorneys, concert promoters, label Promo Reps, retail contacts, trade and consumer press tips, regional scenes, websites, or other sources).

- Looking for a buzz of excitement about an act that's been created by the efforts of the artists themselves.

- Watching for talent on other labels to see whose contracts are expiring.

Other Responsibilities

- Evaluating a new act's potential for writing hit songs and determining how well their songs match current marketplace trends.

- Signing talent to their record label (with the label executives' approval) and making sure the best possible record is made.

- Planning the recording budget with the business affairs department.

- Finding the best producer for the act's recording session.

- Providing creative input and direction on artist's material. (From the perspective that the material selected for the recording is commercially viable.)

- Advising on proper website development and online relationship opportunities.

- Monitoring the recording session to ensure a professional standard that will meet the requirements of the marketplace.

- Searching for songs by other songwriters that might be appropriate for the acts they've signed.

- Establishing and maintaining relationships with key personnel at their own label to ensure their acts get the marketing attention they deserve when their record is released.

Making Sense of Music Industry Contracts

It's common knowledge that music industry contracts are complex, legalistic, and full of gobbledygook. This is particularly true with recording contracts and music publishing agreements. Regardless of the kind of contract involved, there will sometimes be *more* to the contract than meets the eye. Other times, there will be *less*. Hence the need to examine any contracts you're signing very carefully. Contracts are much easier to analyze and understand if you keep in mind the following points:

Pay attention to the definitions contained in the contract. Many music industry contracts contain a section defining the various terms used in the contract. For example, most recording contracts define in great detail such terms as "recording costs," "advance," "retail list price," and other terms.

Contract definitions sometimes give such terms a meaning either much broader, or much *narrower*, than the common sense meaning. Consequently, these contract definitions must be kept in mind while reading the entire contract; otherwise, you'll almost certainly misinterpret the practical effect of the contract.

Look out for what might be missing in the contract. If you're not accustomed to examining contracts, it's very easy to get fixated on what's *in* the contract and not think about what might be *missing*. In many, if not most, situations, you're just as likely to be hurt by what's *not* in a contract, as by what's in it. It's always a good idea to step back from the contract and think about what clauses are needed in order for you to be as protected as possible.

It's also a good idea to compare the contract you have with similar contracts and see if there are any basic clauses which are missing, but which would have given you some protection if they had been in the contract. You can find a sample version of many music industry contracts in books such as *This Business of Music* and *The Musician's Business and Legal Guide*. (Both are available through online book retailers and in many bookstores.)

Be aware that there may be governmental regulations or statutes, or court decisions that affect the legal consequences of the contract, even if they're not mentioned in the contract. Whether or not a contract refers to any particular government regulation or statute, there are often regulations and statutes which do in fact apply, and which will preempt the provisions of the contract.

A good example of this would be the California labor regulations and statutes which regulate the length of time a California recording contract can remain in effect. As a result, even if a California recording contract purports to be for a longer duration than is allowed by statute, the contract won't actually be enforceable beyond the legal time limit allowed by the statute.

Another example would be the statutes of various states regulating the signature of contracts by minors, and *invalidating* in some situations contracts which have been signed by minors.

Also, there are some past court cases which will affect how a particular contractual clause is to be interpreted, and sometimes the court's interpretation will be different that what the common sense interpretation would be.

Be wary about references in the contract to other contracts, or to federal or state laws. Often a music industry contract will refer to other contracts (such as related publishing and production contracts), and to certain specific sections of certain statutes—most often, the federal copyright statute. Once you actually look at those other documents or statutory sections, the meaning of the contract can suddenly become significantly different. Therefore, it's important to review to those other contracts and statutes when interpreting the contract.

Be sure that any necessary prior oral agreements are repeated in the written contract. Many contracts provide that the *written* contract will cancel out any *prior oral agreements* between the parties to the contract. Therefore, if there are any prior *oral* agreements which are important to you, those oral agreements should be restated in the written contract.

Look out for the clause that says which state's laws will apply to the interpretation and enforcement of the contract. Many music industry contracts provide that if there's a contract dispute, the contract will be interpreted under the laws of a particular state (usually California, Tennessee, or New York), and that any breach of contract lawsuit must be brought in that state. This type of provision, though seemingly harmless, can have major consequences. For example, the laws of California are in some respects more favorable to recording artists than the laws of New York. For this reason, and for other reasons as well, record companies often want to have the contract provide that the laws of New York will be applied in the case of a dispute.

In recording contracts, look out for clauses that have the effect of reducing the basic royalty rate. For example, recording contracts generally provide for a specific base royalty rate to be paid to a band. Generally this base royalty is stated as a certain specified *percentage* of the *retail price* of each record sold.

However, most recording contracts go on to provide that various deductions, such as "packaging deductions" of ten to twenty-five percent of the retail price, will be deducted from the sale price when the band's royalties are being computed. Also, most recording contracts contain provisions for reduced royalty percentage rates for record sales outside the U.S., for CD sales, for record club sales, etc.

As a result, the *actual* royalties paid to a band are almost always *significantly* less than the base royalty rate would suggest. What the first page giveth, the fiftieth page taketh away. The same applies to other music industry contracts, such as music publishing contracts.

Because of the significant financial impact of these various deductions and reduced royalty rates, it's extremely important that, before the contract negotiations are finalized, you crunch the numbers and make sure you understand what the actual royalty per record will be in dollars and cents.

Production Companies

In recent years, there's been an increasing frequency of so-called "production deals"—in other words, deals between record companies, on the one hand, and production companies, on the other hand. There are a number of reasons for this development, but it's largely due to the increasing clout of established producers over the years, as well as the business savvy of some of those producers.

Some Basic Terminology

Before we go too far, first, a word about terminology. When I use the term "production deal," I'll be talking about deals between production companies and *record companies*, and not deals with "for hire" record producers. (See page 97.) It's important to make this distinction here, because the latter kind of deal is also occasionally referred to as a "production deal." But they're two completely different animals.

Production Deals: The Basic Points

Production companies, sometimes referred to as "imprints," are companies which find and sign talent and produce records. Many are owned by producers who have reputations for turning out commercial hits. Others are vanity labels owned by successful recording artists who have been rewarded by their labels with production deals.

Usually the scenario with production deals is this: The production company signs artists to a recording contract and agrees to pay royalties at a specified royalty percentage rate. The production company also signs, separately, a production agreement with the major label. This provides for a higher royalty rate to be paid by the major label to the production company, than the royalty rate which the production company label has agreed to pay to the artist. The production company's profit, then, is based on the difference between the royalty rate it receives from the major label and the (lower) royalty rate which it's obligated to pay its artists.

Under the terms of the usual production deal, the production company delivers master recordings to the major label, which then presses, distributes, markets and promotes the records directly or through its subsidiaries.

Often these production companies have a company name and logo which make them look like a record company, and the production company's name and logo will appear on records next to the major label's name and logo. This can sometimes give the mistaken impression that the production company is a stand-alone record company.

Incidentally, in the case of production companies owned by major producers and artists, sometimes the deal between them and a major label is different than the type of deal discussed here. Often, for example, it will be a joint venture deal, where the established producer or artist is setting up a joint venture with a major label. In that situation, the major label isn't paying the production company a royalty, but is instead sharing *net profits* with the production company. In short, though, joint venture deals are very different from "production deals" (as that term is usually used).

Term of Agreement

A production deal will typically have an initial term of two or three years, with the major label having options for an additional one to three (or more) years.

Signing of Artists

These contracts typically limit the total number of artists the production company may sign over the entire term of the agreement and/or for each year during the term. The more established and successful the production company is, the more artists it will be entitled to sign.

The contract will specify the total number of albums the production company will be required to supply for each artist. The production company (and its artists) will be obligated to ultimately deliver that number of albums, even if the term of the production agreement expires before that happens.

Most production agreements are "first look" agreements, giving the major label the first rights to a record delivered by the production company, but the major label will not be *obligated* to commercially release all albums delivered by the production company. For example, the major label might reject an album or artist that the label considers to lack significant commercial potential. As a result, the production agreement should allow the production company the right to offer any rejected artists or masters to another label.

Royalties

Production deals provide for the major label to pay royalties to the production company, based on a percentage of the retail price. The typical range is 16% to 18%, less the same packaging deductions and the other kinds of deductions that are standard in most artist recording agreements.

Advances

The major label may advance monies for administration costs and other overhead costs not necessarily attributed to any specific recording project; and/or it may advance the recording costs for each album produced. It will have the right to recoup those costs before it pays any royalties. Recording budgets for each album project are specified in detail in the contract.

From a production company's perspective, recording costs should be recouped only on an artist-by-artist basis; the production company should avoid any cross-collateralization clause that allows the major label's recoupment of recording costs for all artists from the total amount of royalties owing for all artists. Otherwise, the monies paid by the major label to the production company may not be sufficient for the production company to be able to cover its royalty obligations to those artists whose records have been commercially successful.

Ownership of Masters

Typically, the major label, not the production company, owns the masters of any recordings released and sold. Because the production company isn't acquiring any equity interest in the masters, unlike the situation with joint venture agreements, production deals are sometimes referred to as "the poor man's joint venture."

Some production companies, however, have been successful in negotiating for a reversion of that ownership to occur sometime after the end of the term of the agreement (for example, seven to ten years after the end of the term).

Producer Agreements: What's the Deal?

Under the terms of the typical record producer agreement, the producer is paid a cash advance by the record label, unless the label is very small and can't afford to pay producer advances.

The record label will also pay royalties on future record sales to the producer, subject to certain conditions (described below). However, the record label will be entitled to first recoup (deduct) from those royalties the amount of the advance originally paid to the producer. Any remaining amount will then be paid to the producer.

For example, if the advance is $25,000 and the producer's royalties eventually add up to $60,000, then the producer will receive an additional $35,000 (i.e. $60,000 minus the original $25,000 advance).

Record Producer Agreements: Who Signs the Deal?

Depending on the terms of the artist's recording contract with a record company, it may be either the record company who contracts with the record producer, or it may be the artist who does so.

If the Record Company Is Signing the Deal. If the producer agreement is between the producer and the *record company*, the record company will generally require a "Letter of Direction" from the *artist*, authorizing the record company to pay a certain designated advance and royalty directly to the producer.

Depending on what approval rights are contained in the recording agreement between the artist and the record company, the record company may be contractually required to obtain the artist's written approval as to the selection of the producer, as well as the terms of the producer agreement. From an artist's perspective, it's very important to have this right of approval, since a "sweetheart deal" between a record company and a producer can sometimes have very negative financial repercussions for the artist.

If the Artist Is Signing the Deal. If the producer agreement is between the producer and the *artist*, the record company will often (but not always) have the right to approve or reject the producer.

Also, the record company will typically require the producer to sign a side agreement directly with the record company (sometimes called a "Producer Declaration"). This document will say that if there's any conflict between the terms of the agreement between the artist and producer, and the recording agreement between the artist and the label, the terms of the *recording agreement* will supersede and preempt the producer agreement. This permits the record company to, in effect, override any provisions in the producer agreement which are contrary to the label's normal policies, and to avoid any contractual obligations not already contained in the artist's recording contract with the label.

Record Business 101: If you're a producer, you want to do everything possible *before* you start producing a record, to try to get the record company to agree in writing to pay your producer royalties to you DIRECTLY, rather than you having to collect your producer royalties from the artist.

First of all, the artist may very possibly not have the money to pay you when your producer royalties become due. Secondly, even if the artist "directs" the record company to pay you directly, such directions are not *binding* on the record company and so the record company may refuse to do so.

Getting a record company to pay you directly will require not only a "Letter of Direction" signed by the artist, but also a document signed by the record company agreeing to pay you directly.

Record Producer Agreements: The Basics

The basic provisions of record producer agreements are as follows:

Payment of Recording Costs and Ownership of Masters. The record company pays the approved recording costs. Often there's an itemized recording budget attached to the producer agreement. The record company will own all masters and will normally have approval rights over the masters. This gives the label the right to reject any masters which are not technically or commercially satisfactory.

If the producer owns the studio where the project is going to be produced, the producer will usually submit a recording budget for the estimated studio fees and the miscellaneous recording costs (e.g., session musicians). These expenses will usually be referred to in the producer agreement but generally will not be considered as part of the *advance* to the producer.

Payment of an Advance to the Producer. The agreement will provide for the producer to be paid a certain cash advance. This advance will be recoupable from the producer's future royalties, as shown in the example above. Sometimes the advance is paid on a "per track" basis and can be in the range of $1,000 to $25,000 and even more for top producers.

Producer Royalties. Usually the producer royalty is in the range of 3% to 4% of the retail price of records sold. For hot producers, the royalty is often higher.

In most instances, the band's recording agreement with the record company will provide for an "all-in" artist plus producer royalty. For example, if there's an "all-in" artist/producer combined royalty of 14% of the retail price of records sold, then if the producer royalty is 3%, the artist will receive the remaining 11%. This remaining percentage payable to the artist is usually called the "Net Artist Rate." (Incidentally, sometimes, particularly in the case of country music recording agreements, the royalty rate provided for in the recording contract is an "artist only" royalty, and not an "all in" (artist plus producer) royalty rate. In that situation, the artist's royalty rate isn't affected by what the producer's royalty rate is.)

Producer agreements and recording agreements usually provide that no royalties will be paid to the producer until all recording costs have been recouped at the so-called "Net Artist Rate." Using the example from above, if the producer royalty is 3% and the "all in" artist plus producer royalty is 14%, then the "Net Artist Rate" is 11%. Once the amount of artist royalties, (calculated at the "Net Artist Rate"), equal the total recording costs, the producer will be entitled to be paid royalties. The "artist royalties calculated at the net artist rate" will not *actually* be paid to the artist; this calculation is merely an accounting process and is only done to determine the point at which *producer* royalties must be paid.

Example: Let's say, to make it simple, that the total recording costs are $125,000 and that the 11% "Net Artist Rate" equals $1 for each record sold. Once 125,000 records are sold, the recording costs will have been recouped by the record company (at the Net Artist Rate of $1 per each record sold). Producer royalties will then be owed to the producer at that point. Under the terms of most record producer agreements, those producer royalties will be calculated on a "record one" basis.

"Record One." The term "record one" is often used with producer agreements. It means that once the recording costs are recouped at the Net Artist Rate, the producer will be paid for all records sold, *beginning with the very first record sold*. Again, this is referred to as being paid "from record one."

This concept has very important ramifications for both the artist and producer. In short, *producers* are typically paid from "record one," but *artists* are not. So, using the above example, once 125,000 records are sold, the producer is paid for all records back to the very first record, but under the terms of the typical record deal, the artist would be paid artist royalties on only those records sold *after* those first 125,000 records. In other words, the artist, using the sample numbers listed above, would not be paid artist royalties on those first 125,000 records. Therefore, as a practical matter, the producer typically gets a bigger piece of the total artist/producer royalty pie than their respective royalty rates would suggest.

Here's a (somewhat oversimplified) example how all this works: Let's say a producer is paid a $20,000 advance, and that the producer's royalty rate equates to 25 cents for each record sold. If, using the sample numbers above, 125,000 records are sold (such that the $125,000 in recording costs are recouped at the $1/record "Net Artist Rate"), the producer is owed $31,250 (125,000 multiplied by 25 cents for each record) for those 125,000 records. But since the record company is entitled to recoup the original $20,000 producer advance from the producer's royalties, the record company must pay the producer only another $11,250 for those 125,000 records (the $31,250 in total producer royalties up to that date, minus the producer's original $20,000 advance).

For all records sold *after* those first 125,000 records, the producer will continue to receive additional producer royalties at the rate of 25 cents for each such record sold.

"Pass Through" Clause. Most producer agreements contain a clause, often referred to as the "pass through clause," which provides that the *producer's* royalties will be calculated on the same terms as the *artist's* royalties. For example, if the artist's recording agreement with the label says that the *artist* will not be paid on "free goods" and will be paid a lower royalty rate on foreign sales, then the *producer's* royalty will be adjusted in the same way. This kind of clause can have very negative consequences for a producer who is producing an artist who has signed a sub-standard record deal.

Tricky Issues Concerning Recoupment. There can be some fairly tricky issues in terms of how the recoupment provisions are written. For example, the producer will want to make sure that the definition of "recording costs" in the producer agreement excludes any *cash advances* paid to the artist.

In general, the producer will want to have the term "recording costs" defined as narrowly as possible. All things being equal, the narrower the definition of "recording costs," the lower the total dollar amount of recoupable recording costs there will be. And the lower the recording costs, the sooner those costs will be recouped by the record company, and therefore, the sooner the producer royalties must be paid.

"A-Side Protection." This term relates to the producer royalties payable on "singles," and means that the producer's royalty is based on the entire retail price of a single, and not *prorated* if a different producer produced the "B side."

Incidentally, when I refer to "singles" here, I'm referring to "singles" in the traditional sense—i.e. physical records containing two songs. With the onset of the digital distribution age, the sale of single songs is once again becoming popular, but the new downloadable digital single is, of course, not typically sold as a two song set (as was traditionally the case). Therefore, even though "singles" are standard practice in the digital world, the traditional two-song single—as well as the related concept of "A-Side protection"—is essentially obsolete in regards to record releases today.

The Producer's Audit Rights. If the producer agreement is between the producer and recording company, the producer will normally have the right to audit the record company's books.

However, if the producer agreement is between the producer and *artist,* the producer will not have the right to audit the record label's books. Therefore the producer will often request a clause in the producer-artist agreement allowing the producer to compel the artist to audit the label's books on behalf of the artist and producer jointly.

Producer Credits. Usually the producer agreement will state, sometimes very specifically, how the producer credit will read on record artwork and in any print ads.

"Re-Recording Restriction." Generally the producer agreement will prohibit the producer from using any song from the project in *another* project within a specific period of time, usually two or three years.

The Financial Realities of Record Company Recoupment

As mentioned above, producer royalties become payable once the record company has recouped the recording costs at the "Net Artist Rate." As a practical matter, these calculations are "Hollywood accounting" and have little or nothing to do with the financial realities of the situation. In many (if not most) instances, the record company will have "broken even" from sales of the record long before it has, for *accounting purposes*, "recouped recording costs at the "Net Artist Rate."

Recording Contract Advances

One of the most frequently discussed and hyped aspects of recording contracts is the issue of advances. Generally speaking, advances are designed to cover recording costs and also (at least in major label situations) to provide money to cover some of the band's miscellaneous other expenses. The record company pays a separate advance for each album that the band records for them.

Recording contract advances are often mega-hyped in press reports. For example, it's not unusual for a record deal for a new band to be hyped as a "million dollar deal"; whereas that "million dollars" has to cover, for example, the recording budgets for four albums at $250,000 per album, all of which will be recoupable from the band's future royalties.

A relatively small portion of that money will go into the band's pockets as cash advances, and even that portion will be further reduced by deductions for management commissions, taxes, and so on, with the balance then usually spent soon thereafter for living expenses, new equipment, etc. And, like advances for recording costs, any such cash advances will be entirely recoupable by the record company from the band's future royalties.

Recording Budgets and Recording Funds

There are two different ways recording contracts can deal with the issue of advances: by providing for *"recording budgets,"* or by providing for a *"recording fund"* for each album. In other words, the typical recording contract will be structured either on a "recording budget" basis, or on a "recording fund" basis.

"Recording Budgets." In the case of recording contracts based on *"recording budgets,"* the record company pays the recording costs directly to third parties, such as recording studios, based on recording budgets to be approved by the record company. The record company holds on to the money until the costs are incurred, and then pays for those costs directly to those third parties (such as recording studios).

The record company may also advance your band, separately, a specified amount of money for your anticipated living expenses during the recording project and sometimes for other expenses as well.

"Recording Fund." In the case of the *"recording fund"* deal structure, on the other hand, the record company pays a specified lump-sum amount of money—a "recording fund"—*directly* to the *band* on an album-by-album basis, which the *band* then uses to pay for recording costs, etc. If anything is left over, your band will pocket the balance. Theoretically this is designed, among other reasons, to give you an incentive to record your albums as cost effectively as possible, since the band gets to keep whatever money you don't spend on recording costs. As a practical matter, however, even bands paid on this "recording fund" basis frequently run over budget.

Even in the case of this "recording fund" structure, there will often still be a recording budget drawn up so that the record company will have some assurance that your band won't be trying to record the album too cheaply *or* too expensively. Under many contracts for new bands, you won't be entitled to start recording an album until the record company approves the budget.

Typically, part of the recording fund will be paid at the beginning of the recording project (often one-half), with the balance to be paid upon the band's delivery of the masters to the record company.

Advances Are Not Gifts

Advances are, in effect, merely loans to your band, which will be deducted by the record company from your record sales royalties, but only from those royalties.

So if the recording costs for an album (and related cash advances to your band) are $200,000 and the album generates $300,000 in royalties payable to you, the record company will reimburse itself (recoup) from royalties the first $200,000 (in order to reimburse itself for the $200,000 advanced) then pay you the remaining $100,000.

The record company's right to reimbursement is carried forward from album to album. Let's take, for example, an extreme (and admittedly unrealistic) situation, which I'm exaggerating here to make a point.

Let's say that you receive $200,000 for the first album, and (to make it simple), let's also say your record sells zero units and therefore generates absolutely no royalties. Then you record a second album for $250,000, and that record also generates no royalties. So, when starting the third album (assuming that your band hasn't already been dropped from the label at that point, which obviously is a very questionable assumption), you're going into the third album already $450,000 in the hole. (In reality, the band in that scenario would likely be even further in the hole, due to the record company's recoupable advances to make music videos, etc.)

If your band then gets an advance for the third album of another $250,000, then you're already $700,000 in the hole when the third album is released. As a result, you will see absolutely no record royalties from the third album until the total royalties from album sales exceed the amount of $700,000. In short, the record company has the right to recoup from an album's royalties not only the advance for that album, but also any past advances for earlier albums which have not yet been recouped.

There's also the "rolling accounting" problem to consider. Often, once royalties are starting to be earned on a prior record, the recording company is just starting to pay the costs of the *next* record, and deducting the new costs from the royalties about to be paid.

If your total royalties ultimately end up being *less* than the total advance(s) paid to you, the record company will, under the terms of the usual recording contract, have to "eat" the shortfall, since the record company will only be entitled to be repaid from the band's *record sales royalties*. Your band members will *not* be *personally* responsible for repaying the advance;

hence such advances are generally referred to in recording contract legalese as "recoupable *but non-returnable* advances." Any band should be sure that its recording contract contains similar wording.

Cross-collateralization

Incidentally, and this is extremely important, you should be absolutely sure, *before signing a recording contract,* that the contract allows the record company to recoup advances from only your band's *artist royalties,* and *not* also from your *publishing* royalties from record sales (i.e., the "mechanicals"). In recording contract parlance, the record company should be contractually barred from "cross collateralizing" against mechanicals.

Minimums and Maximums

Recording contracts usually specify that a certain dollar-amount of advance will be paid separately for each album under the contract, and will state the minimum and maximum amounts for each such album advance.

The structure for these minimums and maximums is usually as follows: The contract will specify a certain set amount for the first album's advance. For albums after the first album, the contract will specify (for each album) a minimum dollar-amount advance (called "the floor"), but will also provide in effect that if the album sells well, the advance for the next album will be computed at 60% to 70% (typically, two-thirds) of the royalties earned to date by you from the prior album (or sometimes, the average royalties earned from the prior two albums), but only up to a certain specified maximum amount (called the "ceiling").Typically, these minimum and maximums will increase from album to album. For example, the minimum amount for the second album might be $200,000 with the maximum at $300,000, whereas for the third album the minimum might be $250,000, and the maximum at $350,000.

Given all of these various factors, it's easy to see why seemingly successful bands sometimes receive more modest levels of income than you would otherwise expect, and why it's so important for you to structure your record deal in the most favorable way possible.

Recording Contracts and Recoupables

As mentioned previously, the typical recording contract will allow the record company to reimburse itself (recoup) certain specified costs from your future royalties, before any artist's royalties are actually paid to you.

For example, if you are due $100,000 in royalties, and at the same time $80,000 of recoupable expenses have accumulated, the record company will reimburse itself the $80,000 off the top, and pay you the remaining $20,000 (i.e., the $100,000 *minus* the $80,000).

If, on the other hand, your future royalties are $30,000, and the total recoupable expenses are $80,000, then the record company customarily will have to eat the $50,000 shortfall (i.e., the $80,000 minus the $30,000), and will not be entitled to go after you personally to collect any part of the shortfall.

When negotiating a recording contract, it is of course in your best interests to limit as much as possible the costs which the record company can later recoup from your royalties. The outcome of such negotiations on the issue of recoupable expenses will depend in part on your negotiating clout and on the particular record company involved. Even so, there are some customary parameters on what can be negotiated on the various issues relating to recoupables and there are customary limits beyond which record companies will generally not negotiate.

The most common recoupables are as follows:

Recording Costs. The most common traditional recoupable item is recording costs. This usually includes not only the recording studio's time charges and recording materials (such as tape and outboard gear), but also rehearsal studio expenses, session fees paid to session musicians, the cost of transporting equipment, and miscellaneous other recording-related expenses. However, "mastering" is *not* generally considered a recoupable expense.

In some situations, the producer's fees will also be treated as a recoupable expense, depending on how the deal is structured.

Personal Cash Advances. Major labels often pay cash advances to artists above and beyond the actual recording costs. For example, the advance for an album might be $150,000, with $125,000 of that amount allocated to the estimated out-of-pocket recording costs, and the remaining $25,000 to be considered a cash advance to you, to be used by you for living expenses, etc. These personal advances are almost always recoupable from future royalties, at least for new artists. However, if you have substantial negotiating clout, some or all of the cash advance may be treated as a non-recoupable signing bonus.

Production Costs of Music Videos. Typically, one-half (50%) of the cost of producing music videos will be recoupable from your future *record sales* royalties. Recording contracts often also provide that the other one-half of the video production costs are recoupable from video-related monies potentially payable by the record company to you—for example, royalties payable to you from across-the-counter music videos sales (though as a practical matter such royalties are rarely generated in any significant amounts, except in the case of very successful artists).

Independent Promotion. If the record company hires outside (*"independent"*) promotion people to promote a record to radio stations, usually one-half (and sometimes *all*) of the "*independent promotion*" costs will be recoupable. The exact percentage will depend on your negotiating leverage. If you have any negotiating clout at all, recoupability can usually be kept to 50%, and if possible, independent promotion costs should be totally non-recoupable. It should also be mentioned that typically *none* of the costs of the record company's own *in-house* normal promotional efforts should ever be considered recoupable.

Special Promotion. Some contracts will provide that "*special* promotion" expenses (but not "*normal*" promotion expenses) will be recoupable. It's very important that the term "special promotion" be *specifically* defined in the contract. Otherwise, there are likely to later be disagreements between the artist and record company as to whether particular expenses should in fact be considered "special promotion" expenses (as opposed to "normal" promotion expenses), and hence recoupable.

Tour Support. Years ago, tour support for concert tours was almost always totally *non*-recoupable. Today, however, tour support is often one hundred percent (100%) recoupable.

The 100% recoupability of tour support for *concert tours* is to be distinguished from tour support for so-called "*talk tours*," where the record company sets up tours at its own expense for press interviews, radio station visits, "meets and greets," in different locations, not involving any concert performances. Due to the high cost of performance touring, these "talk tours" have become increasingly common in recent years for certain genres of artists. The cost of such "talk tours" is generally *not* recoupable from your future royalties.

Artwork. Artwork costs are generally not recoupable. However, many recording contracts provide that if the label incurs extra and unusual expenses due to the fact that you have requested or approved "special" artwork or packaging, the label will be entitled to recoup the additional and non-standard costs involved.

Red Flag Issues

Sometimes you'll encounter an independent label contract providing that the record company will be entitled to recoup not only the various expenses mentioned above, but also *in-house* promotion expenses and even sometimes the cost of *mastering* and (in extreme cases) the cost of *manufacturing* records.

These types of costs (particularly *manufacturing* costs) should, of course, never be recoupable. If they are, it's extremely likely that you will never earn a significant amount of royalties, if any at all. In effect, what the record company is doing here is making you shoulder the large bulk of the total costs from your relatively small share of the total record sales income.

No reputable record company will try to recoup manufacturing costs and in-house promotion costs from your royalties.

The comment just made assumes, however, that the contract involved is an *artist-record company recording agreement*, which typically gives you a royalty of somewhere between twelve percent (12%) and fifteen percent (15%) of the list price of records sold. However, there are *other* types of common agreements in the music business, such as "artist-producer development agreements," artist-label "profit split" deals (see page 120), joint venture agreements," and "pressing/distribution ("P & D") agreements," which *do* allow the recoupment of costs not normally recoupable under the traditional *recording contract*. However, these other types of contracts are structured very differently than the typical artist-record company recording contract, and the royalty percentage paid to you, as the artist, is usually much higher under those other types of agreements.

Therefore, when determining what is reasonable and what isn't reasonable in terms of recoupable costs, it's extremely important to know exactly what *kind* of contract you're looking at, since the appropriate percentages will vary dramatically from one kind of contract to the next. You'll just need to "crunch the numbers" and on that basis determine whether the deal makes economic sense for you or not.

Also, it's *extremely* important to remember that any recoupable expenses are normally recoupable only from *"artist royalties"* and not from *"mechanical royalties"* (i.e., those royalties paid by a label to band members because they've written songs on the band's records). As a result, band members who wrote material on the band's records will typically start receiving *mechanical royalties* before they receive any *artist royalties*. These *"mechanical royalties"* should never be affected by a label's recoupment rights.

Recoupables and Royalty Accountings

It's important for you (and/or your manager or accountant) to *very* carefully review all royalty statements received from the record company, since record companies sometimes try to recoup expenses which aren't properly recoupable under the terms of the recording contract.

Also, a review of a royalty statement will sometimes indicate that the record company is attempting to recoup an expense of *questionable* recoupability. In other words, the recording contract may not be particularly clear about whether or not that particular expense may properly be recouped by the record company under the terms of the recording contract. In this situation, the issue will need to be negotiated and resolved with the label.

Recording Contracts and the Artist Royalty Rate

You have many issues to consider when deciding whether a particular recording contract is acceptable. One of the issues is always what the artist royalty rate is. (The typical recording contract provides for the recording artist to be paid royalties at a certain specified percentage royalty rate.)

Before going further, it's important to note that in many instances very little in artist royalties is actually ever paid, even when a record has sold well. In the typical recording contract, the record company is entitled to deduct from the artist royalties any recording costs paid by the record company, as well as other costs, such as part of the video production costs, and typically part of any independent marketing and promotion costs. (See page 105, "Recoupables.")

Because of this right to deduct such costs from royalties before they're paid, there are often situations where the record company pays little, if any, artist royalties to the artist. There are numerous records which have sold platinum, yet minimal (or no) artist royalties were paid, because of the huge costs incurred by the label to promote sales to that level.

However, there's a different kind of royalty which is also provided for in recording contracts—*"mechanical royalties"*—which must be paid to the people who *wrote the songs* on the record. Unlike the situation with *"artist royalties,"* the record company is normally not entitled to deduct any of its costs before paying *mechanical royalties*. Therefore an artist who is a songwriter is much more likely to make money from mechanical royalties than from artist royalties.

It's still important to discuss here the *artist royalty* rate situation, because these artist royalties can potentially become a major source of revenue.

Generally, when people say that a particular recording contract is paying a particular artist royalty rate (let's say 12%), they're actually referring (knowingly or unknowingly) to the so-called "base royalty rate." This is the royalty rate which applies to the sale of records sold at or near *full list price* in the *United States* through *normal retail channels* (i.e., record stores). In recording contract parlance, this rate is usually referred to as the "USNRC" rate (standing for "United States Normal Retail Channels").

Typically, this royalty rate is an *"all-in"* royalty rate (i.e., a combined royalty rate for the artist *and* producer). For a new artist (and their producer), the USNRC "all-in" rate will most often be in the range of twelve to fifteen percent of the retail list price. For example, a recording contract might provide for a USNRC royalty rate of twelve percent ("twelve points"), with you as the artist receiving approximately nine of those twelve points, and the producer receiving approximately three points. To the extent that you and/or the producer have some real bargaining power, these percentages will be somewhat higher.

Sometimes the stated royalty percentage rate is significantly higher than twelve to fourteen percent, but the higher royalty rate may not actually result in more money for the band or producer. This is often because of the fact that even though the recording contract provides for a higher royalty rate, various royalty adjustment clauses have been inserted elsewhere in the contract which reduce or eliminate the ostensible benefit of the higher royalty rate. More often than not, this is a way for a record company to make a band feel that the contract is wonderful (and to give the band some bragging rights), without actually having to pay you any more money per record sold (and perhaps pay you even *less* money).

So, you have to be very careful and not just look at the royalty rate by itself. The only real way to evaluate the real financial consequences of the royalty clauses in the contract is to calculate the numbers and determine the exact amount (in *dollars and cents*) which will be paid per record sold, after including all of the various royalty adjustment clauses in the contract.

Non-USNRC Sales

I mentioned that the USNRC rate applies only to sales in the *United States* at or near *full price* through *normal retail channels*. A *lesser* royalty rate is customarily paid for records sold at significantly less than the full list price, and for records *not* sold through so-called "normal retail channels," and for sales made *outside* the United States.

Some common examples of how royalties are typically paid for different types of sales:

Budget Records and Mid-Priced Records. For so-called "mid-priced" records (often defined in recording contracts as records selling at between sixty-six percent and eighty percent of the full list price), the royalty will be seventy-five percent of the USNRC rate. To make it simple, if the USNRC royalty rate were ten percent, the royalty paid for *mid-priced* records will be 7.5 (seven and one-half) percent of the list price (i.e., seventy-five percent of the ten percent USNRC royalty rate).

For "budget" records, often defined as records sold at between fifty percent and sixty-six percent of the full list price, the royalty rate will be fifty percent of the USNRC rate. (Or, again using the example above, fifty percent of ten percent, hence a royalty rate of five percent.)

Cutouts/Deletes. Usually the contract will provide that no royalties will be paid for records sold as cutouts, etc.

Promotional Records. No royalties are paid on records given away for promotional purposes, such as records given to radio stations, etc.

"Free Goods." If a record company sells records to a record store, the record store might get ten percent in "free goods." In other words, the record store would get 110 records, but pay for only 100. No royalties are paid to the artist on those ten records which are, at least for accounting purposes, given to the retailer as "free goods."

Typically, in recording contract negotiations, the artist will want to put some type of limit in the contract on the percentage of records sold which can be given away as "free goods."

Record Club Sales. For record club sales, the royalty rate is usually one-half of the record company's net receipts from the record club. For records *given* away as *bonus* records under record club programs, usually *no* royalties are paid.

As a general rule, the band will try to insert certain clauses in the recording contract concerning how record club sales will be handled, since record club sales can drastically reduce the band's future income from record sales.

Foreign Sales. Typically a reduced royalty rate is usually paid for records sold outside the United States. The exact royalty rate is typically a bone of contention during recording contract negotiations. Often a record company's first draft of the recording contract will provide that the artist will be paid only fifty percent of the USNRC royalty rate for any records sold outside the United States. (Again, using the example mentioned above, we're talking about fifty percent of ten percent, hence five percent of the list price.)

Almost always the foreign royalty rates can be negotiated substantially upwards. Typically the royalties paid for *Canada* can be negotiated to anywhere between two-thirds and one hundred percent of the USNRC royalty rate, and for major territories (Europe, Australia and Japan), typically sixty-six percent to eighty-five percent, and then typically fifty percent of the USNRC base royalty rate for all *other* countries, referred to in recording contract jargon as "ROW" (the rest of the world).

Artist Royalties: The Three Main Points to Remember

Although the issue of royalty clauses is complicated, there are some important things to remember. Number one, the royalty rate will vary, depending on the circumstances of sale. Number two; there are contractual provisions which can be negotiated that will significantly reduce the negative financial impact on the artist of these reduced royalty rate provisions.

And there's a third thing to consider: the greatest royalty rate in the world will be meaningless if the record company is cooking the books. So try to choose a record company with a relatively decent record for *not* cooking the books. In particular, some independent labels have a reputation for a pathological aversion to paying royalties. By the same token, few major labels are likely to be nominated for sainthood when it comes to honestly paying all royalties due. I've had numerous royalty accountants tell me in the past that in every royalty audit for a successful major label group they've ever done, they've always found at least enough accounting discrepancies to justify the cost of the audit, and that usually there are accounting discrepancies substantially in excess of the audit costs. Not exactly an encouraging thought, but something to consider if you have the luxury of choosing between multiple label offers.

The "Term" of Recording Contracts

Recording contract negotiations always address one issue: how long the contract will last—or in recording contract jargon, the "Term" of the contract. In the somewhat distant past, the typical recording contract would be for an initial one-year period (in which the artist would do one to two albums), followed by four to seven consecutive one-year option periods. In each of those option periods, the artist would be required to do one or two albums (with the exact number of albums depending on the terms of the particular contract involved). In short, recording contracts in the *past* were generally structured in terms of how many *years* the contract would be in effect.

This situation changed, starting in the mid-1970s. Today the conceptual focus of recording contracts isn't on how many *years* the contract will be in effect, but instead, how many *albums* the contract will be for.

The Olivia Newton-John Case

This change occurred because of the problems record companies encountered with the old type of contract, particularly in situations where an artist failed to record one or more of the required albums.

This problem came to a head in the late 1970s in a lawsuit between MCA Records and Olivia Newton-John (your favorite and mine), in which Newton-John asked that her contract with MCA be terminated. Her contract with MCA had been for an initial two-year term, with three one-year options following that. In other words, the contract was for a total of five years.

During the term of the contract, Olivia Newton-John had failed to record some of the required albums. Nonetheless, she argued in her lawsuit that she should be entitled to terminate the contract at the end of the five years, even through she hadn't yet recorded all of the albums required by the contract. In response MCA argued that it should be allowed by the court to extend the term of the contract past the end of the 5-year contract period, for a period of time equal to the recording delays caused by Olivia Newton-John during the five-year term of her contract.

The court decided against MCA and in favor of Olivia Newton-John. The court held, in effect, that even though Olivia Newton-John had failed to timely record all of the albums required under the contract, the contract expired at the end of the five years anyway. The net effect was that MCA would never receive the total number of albums from Olivia Newton-John which the contract had originally provided for.

Largely as a result of that lawsuit, record companies quickly changed their recording contracts to base them upon the number of *albums* to be recorded, rather than on the number of *years*.

Recording Contracts Today

The typical recording contract today obligates your band to record a specified number of *albums*. This is a *one-way* street, though, because the *record company* will customarily have the right to ultimately decide *unilaterally* the total number of albums the band will eventually be permitted to actually record. In the recording contract, it will say that the record company will have a certain number of *"options,"* each option being for one (or sometimes two) albums.

Typically, the record company will want to have "options" for as many albums as possible, so that if your early albums are very successful, you'll be obligated to record for the record company for a longer time.

On the other hand, you, as the *artist,* will typically want to negotiate for as *few* albums under the contract as possible, so that if your early albums are successful, you'll be more easily able to renegotiate the contract sooner (on terms more favorable to you), or to sign another record deal with another record company.

It should be mentioned, though, that there's some middle ground at which the self-interests of the record company and the artist do converge. For example, unless a major label is guaranteed the right to do a reasonable number of albums with a new artist, it won't make sense for the label to spend large sums of money on recording and promoting your early albums and developing your career.

The main point to remember here, is that once the contract is signed, the *record company* (and not you) will control how many albums you'll eventually record for the record company. So if you're committing yourself to a large number of albums, this doesn't mean that you'll actually be doing that number of albums for the record company, but only that you'll be obligated to record that number of albums *if* the *record company* so chooses.

Incidentally, it's essential that if at all possible, you obtain the label's guarantee of a specified monetary amount of promotional funding for each record. Though obtaining such guarantees is certainly not a sure-fire solution, it increases at least a little the odds of some success with the label. In the final analysis, however, each deal with a label (particularly a major label) is almost always a crap shoot. The deal can often be either vastly successful, or vastly *un*successful, for a wide array of possible reasons (such as label hirings and firings) which have nothing to do with the terms of the recording contract itself.

"Firm" Albums

I've talked above about the *maximum* number of albums a band will be obligated to record. But, what about the *minimum* number of albums the *record company* will be obligated to *finance?* These are often referred to as "firm records," as in "The deal is for two records firm."

For a new band with little or no clout or negotiating leverage, the recording contract will often obligate the record company to finance the recording of only *one* album. In other words, the band could be dropped after one album. But in the case of a band with at least some bargaining leverage, the record company will very often commit in the recording contract to finance the recording of two albums, and sometimes three albums.

There's one particular point which should be made here concerning these so-called "firm records." Just because a deal is for, let's say, "two records firm," the contract will typically not guarantee that two records will *actually be made*. Instead, the recording contract in that situation will more likely say that if the label chooses not to make either or both of those two records, the label will be required to pay the band a sum of money and the exact amount of money to be paid will be based on a formula set forth in the contract. Oftentimes, especially in the first draft of the contract, the contract will say that if a "firm record" isn't made, the label will be required to pay the band only the minimum AFM union scale for that album. More often, the contract will say that the label will be required to pay the band the cash advance which would have been required to have been paid to the band under the terms of the contract for that "firm album" if that "firm album" had in fact been made. There are other formulae which are also used sometimes, but the two formulae above are the ones most commonly used in connection with so-called "firm albums."

"Contract Periods"

As already mentioned, most recording contracts today are structured in terms of how many albums the artist will be obligated to record for the label. Even so, such contracts include time frames. Most current recording contracts are based on the concept of "Contract Periods." Each "Contract Period" begins a certain number of days or months after the release of the record done in the prior Contract Period. Once the Contract Period begins, the recording process must begin within a certain period of time. Then the masters must be delivered to the label in another specified period of time, and finally the record must be commercially released within a certain period of time from when the masters were delivered.

Recording contracts typically proceed for a series of consecutive "Option Periods" or "Contract Periods," during each of which the artist will be required to record a certain number of albums (usually one or two). So, instead of requiring that a certain number of albums will be recorded in each *year*, as used to be the case, most contracts today provide that a certain number of albums will be recorded in each "*Contract Period.*"

At the end of the "Initial Contract Period" the record company may choose to exercise its option to move on to the next Contract Period. The artist will then be obligated to record the number of albums specified in the recording contract for the next Contract Period.

This cycle will then repeat itself from one Contract Period to the next, for as many Contract Periods as are allowed by the recording contract, assuming of course that the record company continues to exercise its options to move from one Contract Period to the next.

Compulsory Mechanical Licenses:
The Facts and the Fictions

Q: "Please review this document. Do you know what a fax is?"
A: "Yeah, I do, man. It's when you tell the truth, man, tell it like it is. That is what the facts is."

—Excerpt from a trial transcript, from *Uncle John's Great Big Reader*

When it comes to compulsory licenses, here's "what the facts is." Before you put out a record containing your cover versions of songs written by somebody else, you're required by the federal copyright statute to first obtain a "mechanical license," which typically comes in the form of a two or three page document.

This "mechanical license" document will allow you to record and sell your cover version, and in exchange, require you to pay a "mechanical royalty" at the so-called "statutory rate," which currently is 9.1 cents per song per record. However, if you're obtaining the mechanical license *directly from the music publisher* (copyright owner) of the song, you can sometimes negotiate a lower rate (for example, 75% of the "statutory rate").

There are three possible ways to obtain the mechanical license that you must have in order sell records containing your cover version. These three ways are: (1) directly from the music publisher(s) (i.e., copyright owners of the song); *or* (2) from the Harry Fox Agency in New York; *or* (3) through a formal "Notice of Use" procedure set forth in the federal copyright statute and in the Copyright Office's Regulations.

People who are recording cover versions sometimes get into problems in two ways. First, by assuming either that the music publishers (copyright owners) of songs are always obligated to let you record a cover version; or second, that if you obtain a "compulsory mechanical license," there are no restrictions on what you can then do with your cover recording. These assumptions are erroneous. And often, unfortunately, the problem isn't discovered by the artist/label that released the record, until sometime *after* a large quantity of records have been manufactured, or even worse, after the records containing the unauthorized cover version have already been put into record distribution channels.

In short, you're entitled to a mechanical license only if the song you are covering meets certain legal requirements. And even if you obtain a compulsory license, there are certain legal restrictions on what you can do with your cover recording.

Some questions that commonly arise in connection with compulsory mechanical licenses:

What is "compulsory" about compulsory licenses?

If you meet the legal requirements for being entitled to record a cover version, you can in effect force a music publisher to allow you to record your cover version by going through the Notice of Use procedure in the Copyright Office. The only reason that the Harry Fox Agency and music publishers routinely issue mechanical licenses is because they know that if they don't do so, the person or company seeking the mechanical license can use the Copyright Office procedure, which involves complications for everyone involved. So, most music publishers prefer to issue mechanical licenses directly to the party recording a cover version or have the Harry Fox Agency issue mechanical licenses on their behalf.

If you go through the Copyright Office's procedure, it's referred to as a "Compulsory Mechanical License." On the other hand, the licenses that you obtain from the Harry Fox Agency or directly from the music publisher are sometimes referred to as "Consensual Mechanical Licenses." But most often they're referred to generically as "Mechanical Licenses."

When are you entitled to be issued a "compulsory mechanical license"?

You're entitled to a compulsory mechanical license to sell records containing your cover version, but only if all of the following requirements are met: (1) the song you're covering was written by *someone else* and was *previously released* as an *audio-only* recording; (2) your record will be an *audio-only* record and won't contain anything other than music; and (3) the primary purpose of your record is to sell it to the general public and for private use. Therefore, if the primary purpose is *not* for *private* use—for example, if you're making the recording for the primary purpose of broadcast usage or a Muzak-type system—you're *not* entitled to a compulsory license. It is then completely up to the music publisher to decide whether to allow you to cover the song and the publisher sets the fees and royalties that you must pay to them.

What if a song has never previously been on a commercially released record, or if for some other legal reason you don't qualify for a compulsory license?

In that situation, the copyright owner of the song has no obligation whatsoever to issue a mechanical license to you and the copyright owner is free to deny a license to you, even if they're doing so for no good reason.

Incidentally, if the publisher is willing to issue a mechanical license for a song that was never before on a record, it's called a "First Use License."

What's the logic and policy justification for the compulsory license procedure?

Congress has attempted to balance the intellectual property rights of composers with the rights of members of the public who want to record cover versions. Essentially, it's been the policy of Congress to give composers and music publishers the right to put certain conditions on their ability to completely control the use of their song (for example, to be able to unilaterally and sometimes arbitrarily refuse to allow lyrics to be changed in cover recordings), while at the same time allowing artists to record cover versions, subject to certain limitations.

How do you get a compulsory license?

There are three ways: (1) directly from the music publisher (i.e., the copyright owner) of the song; (2) from the Harry Fox Agency in New York; (3) through a formal "notice of use" procedure set forth in the Copyright Office's Regulations.

Most people use one of the first two procedures because there are a number of disadvantages with the Copyright Office's procedure. For example, you have to pay mechanical royalties every month rather than the usual every three months. You also have to submit to the music publisher of the song an annual audit certified by a CPA, which isn't ordinarily required with the first two procedures.

When does it make sense to seek a compulsory license from the Harry Fox Agency?

First of all, the Harry Fox Agency can only issue licenses for the songs of those publishers who have authorized the Harry Fox Agency to do so. Most large music publishers use the Harry Fox Agency, however it doesn't represent many medium-sized and smaller publishers. If the Harry Fox Agency doesn't represent a publisher, it cannot issue mechanical licenses on their behalf.

You can determine whether the Harry Fox Agency handles a particular song by going to their website, www.nmpa.org. If they do, you can use their online licensing process, as long as you're manufacturing 2,500 units or less.

Also, if you need rights that are somewhat out of the ordinary—for example, if you want to make changes in the lyrics or music or use several songs in a medley, the Harry Fox Agency will not issue licenses allowing you to do so. In those instances, it's better to seek a license directly from the music publisher (whether or not the music publisher is already represented by the Harry Fox Agency). And any music publisher can issue a license *directly* to you, *whether or not* the Harry Fox Agency already represents them.

As mentioned previously, you can sometimes negotiate a lower rate directly with the music publisher than with the Harry Fox Agency, since the Harry Fox Agency will not, as a general rule, negotiate the compulsory license rate lower than the so-called "statutory rate" set forth in the Copyright Office's Regulations. (The current "statutory rate," as already mentioned, is 9.1 cents per song per record sold, but the rate is slightly increased every couple of years.)

In any event, it's wise to obtain the necessary mechanical licenses before you record the cover song. And bottom line, you absolutely need to obtain those mechanical licenses BEFORE you *commercially release* your record.

What if the music publisher of a song you want to cover hasn't registered the song in the Copyright Office?

You're entitled under certain conditions to "royalty free" use of a song until the copyright owner registers the copyright with the Copyright Office. But if, sometime after you release your record, the music publisher obtains a copyright registration for that song, then at that point you're obligated to obtain a mechanical license (through one of the three procedures described above). If you don't do so, your continued selling of your record will constitute copyright infringement. Therefore, it's safer to just secure the necessary mechanical licenses before releasing your record, even when it's not legally required.

Does a mechanical license entitle you to use part or all of someone else's sound recording on your own record?

No, a mechanical license only allows you to record a cover version of the song. It doesn't allow you any rights to use any part of anyone else's recording.

What rights do you have to make changes in the song you're covering?

The copyright law provides that you may create and use a musical arrangement of a song "to the extent necessary to conform it to the style or manner of interpretation of the performance involved, but the arrangement shall not change the basic melody or fundamental character" of the song.

This language is admittedly vague, though there are some things that this provision of the copyright law clearly allows you to do, and other things that are clearly NOT allowed.

For example, you're clearly entitled to change the speed of a song, use whatever instrumentation that you want to use, or change vocal phrasings. On the other hand, you are clearly NOT entitled to change any lyrics or melody lines, unless your cover version is a parody.

If your cover version in fact meets the legal requirements for being considered a "parody," it won't be necessary for you obtain a mechanical license at all or pay mechanical royalties, since parodies are considered "fair use," thereby exempting you under the terms of the federal copyright law from any requirement to obtain a mechanical license. There are various rather technical guidelines about when a song will legally be considered a "parody." The main thing is to NOT assume that just because a song has humorous features, that therefore it's legally a "parody." There are many humorous cover versions that do not meet the requirements to be considered a parody. If you ever get into this situation, you should take whatever steps are necessary to determine, as a legal matter, whether your particular song is entitled to be considered a parody.

If you can obtain a compulsory license, what kind of projects can you use it for?

In audio-only releases, but not in audio-visual projects (e.g., DVDs and karaoke machines with a video screen. (Factoid: the word "karaoke," literally translated from Japanese, means "empty orchestra.")

What if the song you want to cover is co-owned by two or more music publishers?

If that's the situation, under copyright law any one of those publishers can issue a non-exclusive mechanical license for the song, on behalf of all of the music publishers who own the song. However, if they receive mechanical royalties, they have to account to their co-owners of the song and share the mechanical royalties in portions proportionate to each publisher's percentage ownership of the song.

As a practical matter, co-publishers often have an agreement between themselves, providing that each co-publisher will issue a separate mechanical license for its fractional share of any song covered by the agreement.

This leads into another issue; the importance of having the mechanical license agreement contain a clause, whereby the publisher represents and warrants that they are legally entitled to issue a license to you and that no one else's consent is required, and also stating that the publisher will reimburse you for all expense if it turns out that these representations were false and you are sued by some third party for your use of the song.

If I obtain a compulsory license in order to record my own cover version, what countries can I sell records in?

Mechanical licenses generally apply only to sales in the *U.S. and/or Canada.* For all *other countries,* there's a different system (discussed later).

Many U.S.-originated compulsory licenses, including all Harry Fox licenses and all licenses obtained through the U.S. Copyright Office, cover sales in the *United States only,* and do not extend to Canada. So in some instances, you'll need a separate mechanical license covering Canada.

If you determine that you need a mechanical license for Canada and you aren't able to obtain one from a U.S. publisher, then you'll need to contact the Canadian Musical Reproduction Rights Agency (or "CMRRA"), the Canadian equivalent of the Harry Fox Agency. The web address for CMRRA is www.cmrra.ca.

There's one exception to this. In some instances, the U.S. *distributor* for a label will handle the mechanical royalty payments due for Canadian sales. If you have a distributor distributing your records to Canada, you should check to see what its mechanical royalty practices are with respect to Canada, (unless it's already spelled out in your distribution agreement).

In general, the mechanical license documents and procedures for the United States and Canada are very similar.

And now, for the rest of the world.

Very rarely will a mechanical license originating in the U.S. or Canada cover sales in *any other countries.* This is because the mechanical licensing procedures for all other countries are significantly different; music publishers in those countries do not issue mechanical licenses *directly* to labels or groups. Instead, there is a formal agreement negotiated between the main trade organization for record companies in that country and the trade organization for music publishers in that country. In short, the trade organization for the labels pays mechanical royalties directly to the "mechanical rights society" in that territory. Then the mechanical rights society pays out to its music publisher members their share of the mechanical royalties received, based on how many records they sold.

In most countries, there's only one mechanical rights society, and it's quite often an official government-related organization. Also, in many countries, there's one organization that collects both mechanical royalties *and performance income* (for example, income due to publishers based on the airplay of their songs), unlike the situation in the U.S.

For songwriters/publishers who are selling a significant number of records in foreign countries, it's often a good idea to have sub-publishing agreements with music publishers in those countries. If you're not affiliated with music publishers in those countries, there are very high odds that the money to which you are entitled will go into "black box" accounts held by the music publisher associations in those countries, in which case your money will be retained by those organizations and their members, and never paid to you.

Incidentally, if you are manufacturing records in the U.S., then *exporting* those records to foreign countries, you are technically required to pay a mechanical royalty in the U.S. (because you manufactured the record in the U.S.); then your foreign distributors will be required to pay an additional mechanical royalty to the mechanical rights organizations in those countries where your records are distributed.

Does the catalog number that you designate for your record have any relevance to mechanical licenses?

Most mechanical licenses are issued for a particular recording, as designated by the record company's catalog number for that record. Therefore, even if you've obtained a mechanical license to cover a song that you use on one record, you usually have to get another mechanical license for any later records that you might want to put that same cover version on.

What if my records are being rented to consumers in foreign countries?

In some countries, such as Japan, there are record rental stores. This is due to the fact that the retail list price of records in those countries is significantly higher than the list price in the U.S. There are some 3,700 record rental stores in Japan. In those countries, there are particular arrangements for how royalties will be calculated for record rentals.

"Profit Split" Deals:
An Alternative to the Traditional Record Deal

One of the recent changes in the music business, particularly in the last few years, is the increasing use of so-called "profit split" deals as an alternative to the traditional record deal. This is particularly true in the case of indie label deals (as opposed to *major label* deals). That isn't to say that major labels aren't doing "profit split" deals, but most often they're only done with very established artists.

With these profit split deals, which are basically a kind of joint venture, the basic idea is that the net profits will be split (in most deals, 50–50) after all expenses are paid. Compare this to the traditional record deal where you, as the artist, are paid on a royalty basis, with the typical royalty being in the range of 12 to 15% (of the retail price).

Profit split deals can be attractive to *labels* because the label doesn't have to pay you anything (including, usually, mechanical royalties) until *all* costs have been recouped from record sales by the label. This is usually not the case with the traditional type of record deal.

Profit split deals can also be attractive to *artists,* but for different reasons. For one thing, if record sales are quite substantial and the costs involved are reasonable in comparison, you may well come out significantly better on total sales with a profit split deal than the traditional record deal. Also, the idea of a 50–50 split of net profits seems inherently fairer and more comprehensible than the voodoo economics of the traditional record deal. Plus, some artists prefer the general feel of a profit split situation which can feel more like a partnering arrangement and a more collaborative relationship with the label than is typically the case with the traditional artist-label relationship.

All of that having been said, there are some subtle financial issues under the surface with these profit split deals. As a result, it isn't always easy to determine in advance whether a profit split deal will in fact be more or less advantageous to a particular artist or label than a traditional record deal.

The Basic Financial Structure of Profit Split Deals

Under the terms of the typical profit split deal, the record company advances all costs (overhead costs, recording, manufacturing and marketing costs). The artist and the record company then share the net profits from record sales. To compute the net profits, the record company typically deducts off the top all actual out-of-pocket costs incurred by the record company for recording, manufacturing, promotion, marketing, etc., plus often a so-called "overhead fee" of 10 to 15% of the gross record sales income. After the record company deducts *all* of those costs and fees from the gross record sales income, the label pays you a share of the profits in whatever proportions their contract says (usually 50–50).

Although this percentage is obviously much larger than the 12 to 15% royalty range for traditional record deals, the artist in a profit split deal is only getting 50% of the income for records sold *after all expenses are paid*, whereas in the case of the traditional record deal, you start receiving artist royalties after the record company recoups the recording costs (and certain other costs, typically) from the artist royalties. (See page 105, "Recoupables.")

In short, comparing the economics of profit split deals to traditional record deals is complicated, and to a large extent, comparing "apples and oranges." The only way to determine which arrangement will likely be better is to look at the numbers and do a spreadsheet analysis based on projected sales levels and projected recording, marketing, and promotion costs.

The "Territory"
The typical profit split deal will either cover record sales worldwide, or if you have significant negotiating clout, will apply to the sale of recordings in only certain territories (e.g., North America), in which case only you will have the right to make other deals for other countries. Even then, the contract will often provide that you'll have to pay the label a percentage of your income from foreign deals.

The "Term"
Sometimes the profit split deal is for just one record (a "one off"), or for one initial record with the record company having options to do a certain number of follow-up records.

From the artist's point of view, it's crucial that the agreement contain clearly defined termination provisions in case the deal is unproductive or if the label fails to perform its contractual obligations. The contract should specify what your rights will be if the record doesn't get released, or if it goes out of print, or if the label ceases to have bona fide national distribution, or if it defaults on other obligations, for example, if the label fails to spend the amount of money on marketing and promotion that it had guaranteed in the contract that it would spend.

Cash Advances
In most cases, since a lot of profit split deals are done between newer artists and very small labels, there often is no cash advance paid. However, there are certainly situations in which you have some negotiating clout and the label has sufficient financing, and in those situations there are often cash advances.

Ownership of Masters
The master recordings will be owned either by you and the label jointly, or far more commonly, by the record company alone. (Usually the ownership will continue for the full life of the copyrights of the masters, i.e., a very long time, and long after the parties are no longer actively working together.)

Miscellaneous Contract Issues
Despite the differences between profit split deals and traditional record deals, there's a certain amount of overlap between them because many of the same issues need to be dealt with in

both—for example, when will you be obligated to deliver masters to the label, what approval rights will you have, who will have the right to maintain your "Official Website," and so on.

Song Ownership and Music Publishing Income

Usually, with these kinds of deals you retain all ownership of your original songs, as is also usually the case with traditional record deals (at least in modern times).

But, there are a couple of wrinkles with profit split deals. First of all, profit split deals often provide that your share of record sales income will cover both your artist royalties AND *songwriter* (mechanical) royalties. This is different from the traditional record deal situation, in which the artist/songwriter is entitled to receive mechanical royalties on all record sales on a regular basis once the record is released, and most often this is an important source of cash flow for the artist. But with profit split deals, if you aren't entitled under the contract to receive mechanical royalties, as is often the case, you don't have the cash flow benefit of receiving mechanical royalties on a regular basis during the term of the deal.

Secondly, it's important to mention that the initial contract proposal from the label may propose that the label will share in all music publishing income (for example, airplay income paid by ASCAP/BMI), and sometimes will even provide for the label to share in merchandise and touring income as well. In most instances, though, by the end of contract negotiations the label won't be entitled to share in those kinds of income.

Marketing and Promotion Issues

Depending on your bargaining power, you may be able to obtain the right to approve (or at least be consulted about) major marketing and promotion decisions, and to have the contract guarantee that the label will spend up to a certain specified amount of money each year for marketing and promotion.

In many such agreements, if the label fails to make the guaranteed "spends," you will either be entitled to terminate the agreement and/or the label will at least not be entitled to exercise any options for follow-up records.

Accountings

Usually the agreement requires the label to regularly provide (usually semi-annually) an itemized accounting for all income received from record sales and for all expenses incurred.

Advantages and Disadvantages for Artists

There are several potential advantages and disadvantages for you with these kinds of deals. In terms of advantages, as mentioned above, there are situations where, if sales are very substantial, you will receive a much larger share of total record sales income with a profit split deal than with a traditional record deal. It's often hard to determine which is the best option, because it's often difficult to predict what the actual record sales income and expenses will add up to. The only way to thoroughly analyze a situation like this is to "spreadsheet it," based on a range of projections about what the total expenses will be and what the sales levels will be. As in any kind of contract situation, it's crucial to "crunch the numbers."

One real *disadvantage* of "profit split" deals is that, unlike traditional artist recording agreements, which usually provide for mechanical royalties to be paid to the artist/songwriter on top of artist royalties, "profit split" deals often provide that the artist/songwriter will not be entitled to receive mechanical royalty payments during the course of the deal. The contract will usually say that your share of the net profits will be deemed to *include* not only *artist* royalties, but also any mechanical royalty payment due to you as *songwriter*.

One problem with this is that in the case of these profit split kinds of deals, the label is usually spending money faster than it comes in, so it may take quite awhile (if ever) before there's any net profit for you to get a share of. And if there are *zero* net profits from record sales, you'll be getting zero money from the deal, whereas in the case of the traditional record deal, you would at least have received mechanical royalties (assuming, of course, that you have your own original songs on the record).

Another potential disadvantage is that it's more difficult and cumbersome to do a royalty audit with profit split deals than it is with traditional record deals. That's because the only way you can know whether you were paid the proper amount is by verifying all income and *all* expenses that the label incurred. On the other hand, with the traditional record deal, you only need to verify the income received and *certain kinds* of expenses (for example, recording costs), but not *all* expenses.

That isn't to say the traditional royalty audit is a piece of cake, but instead, that the profit split audit is even more cumbersome, expensive, and complicated than a traditional record deal audit. Even a traditional record deal audit, particularly in the case of major label deals, can easily cost in the $15,000–20,000 range and in some instances much more.

In short, it's wise for you to have the contract provide strong audit rights, and if possible, to provide that if the label's accounting statements are off by a certain percentage, that the label will be responsible for reimbursing you for any audit costs incurred.

Advantages and Disadvantages for the Label

The main disadvantage of profit split deals for labels is on the back end; that is, if the records are successful and the costs are relatively small in comparison. In that scenario, the deal will be less profitable for the label than would be the case with a traditional record deal.

Negotiating Profit Split Deals

Profit split deals have become common only recently. There aren't yet any clear industry standards for their exact terms; there's still a lot of improvising being done. If you're considering entering into a profit split deal, particularly if you're comparing a profit split deal offer from one label and a traditional deal offer from another label, it's imperative that you carefully think through the financial and logistical issues lurking under the surface.

Making Your Record a Priority at a Record Label, or, Art vs. Commerce: A Music Marketplace Dilemma

Just because you get signed to a record label doesn't automatically mean that you'll be treated well by your label. Once a record has been scheduled for release, a number of factors will determine if it becomes a priority at the label. The term "priority" is used to designate which releases will get the most promotion and marketing attention—out of the hundreds of records a label may put out each year.

The reasons why one artist's new release may be more important than another to a label are varied and often hard to understand. The major labels—and many independent record labels—juggle a lot of apples and oranges when they go about the business of trying to sell records. There are a number of circumstances that contribute to the (sometimes irrational) decisions about which records will or will not be made a priority. Some of these reasons reflect cold, hard, business realities. Others are emotional and complex. The biggest factor is this: music, after it's been recorded, becomes a product.

At this point, art enters the world of commerce. When a product containing an artistic creation becomes something people can buy, art meets commerce and the two worlds collide. In today's music business environment the party that pays for the production and manufacture of the artistic product usually wins any arguments about how the art contained within the product will be marketed.

Music is an emotional product, and because of that there will always be issues that come up; during the recording of the songs, the marketing of the record, or in the personal relationships that are developed, that can deeply affect the success or failure of the project.

Music isn't the same kind of product as a shoe. You don't *sell* a shoe the same way you sell a CD. If you want to sell a shoe, the shoe itself won't object too much about how you sell it. Not so with music. The artists and bands that make music have an emotional investment in their creation. As artists, they concentrate more on the creative side of music. Rarely are they well-versed in the intricacies of the business world. So, as creative creatures they can easily develop strong opinions on how their art should be marketed.

Songwriters usually write a song as a creative expression; musicians and singers interpret and record the song. But a record label pays the bills for making the recording and then has to sell the recording. (Devising a plan to sell the recording is called marketing.) Business people usually know more about commerce than art, so the tensions that exist because of this dynamic can lead to misunderstandings, and misunderstandings can lead to disappointments for everyone involved.

Many musicians get themselves into trouble with record label executives because they think the only thing that's important is the music itself, while the record label executives and their teams of Promo Reps have very little emotional investment in the songs they promote. From the label's point of view, it's the responsibility of the record label to find a way to sell the recording they invested in. The label may try to preserve the emotional investment their acts have in their songs as best they can, but they will stop at nothing when, for example, a promotional opportunity comes up that may be at odds with the image or ethics that the artist holds. If the label executives see a potential profit coming from some controversial promotion campaign, they will usually do what they can to take advantage of that marketing opportunity. At the same time, if the artist is creating such a nuisance to them that they sense a threat to their investment or even their egos, they may decide to cancel a promotion campaign at a moment's notice. Take my word for it, if you're perceived as a troublemaker by the label executives, or if they decide that your record shows no signs of being accepted at radio or by music retailers, then your recording contract may be about as valuable as a sheet of Kleenex.

It would take another book to fully explain the strange dynamic between the fragile emotions of aspiring musicians and the egos of materialistic record company executives, but let's take a look at some fairly common situations that come up in the complex world of record labels, marketplace realities, and artist relations.

Factors That Determine Priority Releases

Major labels often find that they've over-extended themselves by signing too many acts within a short period of time, and scheduling too many releases to come out at the same time. So, when they discuss which scheduled records have the best chance of success in the marketplace, they may simply push a release back six months to a year. (Unfortunately, depending on an act's actual contract, there may be no guarantees that a label has to ever release their record.)

Another situation is this. If a label signs an act because they play a genre of music that is currently hot on the charts, but the negotiations for signing the deal or the recording process took too much time, they may have missed their opportunity to cash in on a current popular music trend. Realizing that, they may decide not to make the record a priority release but to sit on it and wait to see if another time of year would be more opportune for releasing the record.

To complicate matters even more, a label executive may sign an act only to stop a competing record label executive from signing them. When the record is released, any interest in promoting it takes second place to the executive's personal satisfaction of having one-upped a competitor—and the act is left out in the cold.

But the ego issue can also work positively for a recording artist. An artist may have a manager who also manages another act that is currently hot. The label executive may sign the lesser known artist with hopes of getting the manager to sign the other band to their label some day. So, when the record of the lesser-known artist comes out, the label executive may pull out all the stops promotionally, to show the manager what a great job the label can do. If the label shows it can do a good job with a newer artist on that manager's roster, perhaps the manager will send one of his established stars over to the label when the existing recording contract with the established artist runs out.

Here's another reason why a record might become a priority at a label. We're constantly hearing about downsizing—companies reducing their staff with every new merger or corporate buyout. Many major labels are merging with other large labels and increasing the workload for the remaining staff. A decade ago there were six major labels, and today we're down to four, with the possibility that in 2007, there will be just three major label corporate groups.

It can be important for a label executive to demonstrate to the shareholders of the corporation and the staff at the label that the downsizing issue isn't a concern. A particular act's new release is given a stronger push to impress all concerned parties.

There's a flip side, however. When downsizing occurs, an artist's record may be shifted to a different priority level. Key personnel who were excited about and instrumental in "breaking" a new label act may be fired or asked to take early retirement. When it comes time to release the new record, a different person may be assigned to work the act; someone who may not care much about or even *like* the music of the artist. Will that record remain a priority? There are no guarantees that the new employee will be excited about the act's music. They may have their own pet projects to put ahead of any previous arrangements.

"Bidding wars" also affect priority status. Bidding wars occur when a new band is the hot topic of the industry grapevine. One label makes an offer to sign the band, another label hears about it and ups the bid, a third label offers even more money. The winner of this bidding war will probably be forced to make that act's initial release a priority. The label will need a sizeable return in sales dollars from the new band's recording to recoup their large investment. Interestingly, no band or act signed from any bidding war has ever gone on to major stardom.

Music trends come and go. In the early and mid '90s grunge came and went. What followed in the late '90s were young boy vocal-groups, and blond ingénue solo-artists. Today R&B, hip-hop, and rap acts have become more mainstream than ever.

When a hot new music style comes on the scene, any act that's signed to take advantage of a new popular music trend will usually become a priority at the record label that signed them. By the way, new releases by superstar acts are usually automatic priority records because of their star status, and the simple fact that they sell a lot of product consistently.

So, take heed. Many people think signing a recording contract with a record label means automatic stardom. That's not the case. You'd do well to research a label's track record and reputation for making their releases priorities before signing a recording contract with any label.

These issues have come up often enough to contribute to a change in the attitude many musicians have toward working with record labels. Over the last three decades more and more musicians have taken charge of their own business careers. The list of artists and bands releasing their own records and marketing them themselves grows longer every day. Perhaps the level of success these entrepreneurial musicians reach may not equal the success of major superstars, but at least when they wrestle with the dynamics of art meeting commerce they're wrestling with themselves. And they are the acts that become interesting to the major labels for business affiliations.

Distribution Setups for Record Labels

When we look at the way major labels and professionally run independent labels organize their operations, we find that *before* they start their promotion campaign to secure radio airplay for a release, they've already set up a way to distribute and sell it. This is where independent artists and small record labels commonly go wrong. They haven't thought ahead about how people will find their recording to be able to buy it. Distribution is the process of getting records into retail stores. It's a key element in the marketing plan of a label. Here's a brief introduction to the way labels—big and small—set up their distribution systems.

Distribution and Major Record Labels

Major labels are called "major" because of their large share of sales in the music marketplace. These large record companies control over 80% of all records sold in the U.S. To be clear: The major labels have their own distribution arrangements, and those distribution companies are in charge of shipping and marketing their music product to retail. For example, WEA is the distributor for Warner Music Group of labels. They market and sell all WMG products.

(Recently WEA and other majors sold their manufacturing divisions to a Canadian company, Cinram. Cinram is like Diskmakers for the major labels. They make the actual goods and "distribute" them back to WEA, to one-stop distributors and rack jobbers, and to retailers, based on the orders and sales created by the labels.)

There used to be six major label groups a decade ago, but after a slew of mergers and consolidation, the "Big Four" record label groups, **as defined by their distribution companies,** currently are:

SONY/BMG: distributes Columbia, Epic, and other affiliated labels; plus labels from BMG (Bertlesmann Music Group) such as RCA, Arista, Jive, and others.

WEA (Warner, Elektra, Atlantic): distributes Warner Brothers, Elektra, Atlantic, Reprise, and many other affiliated labels.

UMG (Universal Music Group): distributes Interscope, Geffen, MCA, and other labels affiliated with it.

EMM (EMI Music Marketing): distributes Capitol, Virgin, Blue Note, and other affiliates.

Distribution and Independent Record Labels

Record labels that have no distribution companies of their own are commonly known as independent labels. In most major markets throughout the country, you can find independent distributors who handle the wholesaling of CDs, tapes, and vinyl releases for these labels. Independent labels are often thought of as being small companies, but that's not always the case. An independent label can be a small label owned by a garage band or solo musician, or one with multi-millions of dollars behind it. Basically, "independent" is simply the name given to any label that doesn't have a business affiliation with one of the major labels, and so must use alternative distribution systems to get their releases into the marketplace (retail stores).

To complicate matters, several independent distributor alliances have formed over the last decade and some so-called independent distributors are actually owned whole or in-part by one of the majors. The Alternative Distribution Alliance, co-owned by Warner is one such "independent distributor." In fact almost all of the major labels have their own so-called "independent" distributors these days.

How Record Sales are Monitored

Monitoring the sales of records is one of the most important tasks a record label must do. Since the goal of radio airplay is sales, labels must constantly check with music retailers to see if the airplay is turning into actual sales. Since the early 1990s record sales have been monitored by SoundScan. This company (now known as Neilsen/SoundScan, as they were purchased by the Neilsen media research company years ago) changed the way sales data was collected by using the bar code on the back of all records, tapes, and vinyl recordings to more closely monitor the sales from music and other retailers. The SoundScan summary reports published every week in the music industry trade magazine *Billboard* reflect the actual number of purchases made by music fans at record stores and other retail outlets, and show a record's weekly progress on the sales charts: up, down, or the same.

The information in *Billboard's* "Hot 200" and other chart reports are just the tip of the iceberg when it comes to the information SoundScan makes available to its subscribers. Record labels pay SoundScan for weekly in-depth reports that break down sales data into great detail. Labels can see how well each of their releases are doing; regionally, in specific cities, even at particular stores within a city. The more data a label can study, the more accurately they can find the strengths or weaknesses in their marketing strategies. If, for example, a new release is doing poorly on the West Coast, but has strong sales in the Midwest, a label can react to that information by adjusting their promotion and marketing plans accordingly.

Record labels are not the only ones who benefit from studying the SoundScan reports. Radio stations also subscribe to their reports, as do many artist management agencies and booking agencies. The SoundScan reports can influence everyone who has an investment in the success of a recording artist. A radio station's decision to add a song to their playlist or increase the amount of play a song gets can easily be determined by positive sales reports. When artist's managers keep track of record sales they can better analyze what career moves their clients should make. Booking agents can make more informed decisions on where to get gigs for their clients if they can track what specific regions of the country are reacting favorably to an act's latest release.

For the last few years now, SoundScan also reports any and all digital music sales, (as long as they come from legitimate sites that charge for downloading songs, like iTunes for example). SoundScan data can also tip off a label to a hot selling independent artist. So, artists and bands interested in attracting the attention of record labels should register with them!

Distributors: How to Attract Them and How to Work with Them

The purpose of making a record is to sell it. The job of a distributor is to get records into retail stores, the job of a record label is to get customers into retail stores, and both use promotion and marketing tactics. Today more music product is manufactured, promoted, and distributed than ever before, (11,331 new releases were put out in 2005), and the distributor is increasingly important to independent labels who want to get their records into stores nationally.

What does it take to gain the respect and attention of distributors, and how do they work? Independent labels and artists who are releasing their own records need to understand the role of distributors and the relationships between record labels, distributors, and retail stores.

A distribution company is a "middle man" between a record label and the retail stores. It isn't possible for an independent label to get into the many record stores across the country without a distributor. Although they can "consign" their records to stores on a store-by-store basis, the independent label can only get national retail coverage through a distributor.

Basically, the *buyers* for the distribution company buy music "product" (CDs, vinyl records, etc.) from a record label. The sales staff for the distribution company sells the label's product to their retail store accounts. Thus, **the primary job of a distributor is to get CDs, vinyl records, and an ever-decreasing stock of cassette tapes into brick-and-mortar retail outlets; as well as the plethora of online music sellers.** They do this by working closely with their clients—the record labels—to promote and market the label's product.

Different Kinds of Distributors in the United States

One-Stop Distributors carry a wide selection of major label and select independent label product, and sell to independent (mom-and-pop) stores and other retail outlets that sell recorded music.

Rack jobbers are companies that rent or lease space in large department-type stores and other mass marketing retail outlets. They usually carry only the best-selling commercial product available; they concentrate on major label product but also carry some independent label product with a strong regional presence.

Independent Distributors are distributors of independent label product, either on a regional basis, or more likely, as national distributors. The 1990s gave birth to alliances between many regional and national distributors and prominent independent labels. By forming an alliance, independent distributors combine forces to form a stronger entity, representing many independent labels, and offering retailers a wider variety of product from one source.

A primary job for a new record label is to attract the attention of a distributor. The label does this by achieving some success on its own; by having sold product on consignment, at live shows, through mail order and direct sales. So, make sure there's a market for your style of music. Prove it to distributors by showing them how many records you've sold through live sales, Internet sales, and other alternative methods.

After a distributor accepts your product, you must work closely with them, providing information on successful airplay, print media support, and live performance successes. Keep the distributor updated on any and all promotion and marketing plans and results, as they develop. Create a relationship that is a true partnership between your label and the distributor.

What a Distributor Wants to Know about a Label's Release

- Has the artist had any success with established mainstream labels?
- Does the artist have a following, if so, how well known are they?
- If the artist is unknown, what sales/promotion ideas does the label have?
- Are any well known "guest" musicians on the recording?
- Does the recording and artwork meet the standards of the musical genre?
- Is there any current airplay on commercial or non-commercial radio?
- Will there be independent promotion of the release to retail and to radio?
- Has the artist hired a publicist, and/or what is the publicity campaign?
- What kind of Internet presence do the label and the act have?
- Will the artist be touring in support of the release?
- Does the label have the financial resources to provide "co-op" ads?
- Does the label have the financial resources to press additional product?
- Does the label have a "back catalog" of proven sellers?
- How much product from the label is already out in the stores?
- Does the label have other distributors selling the same product?
- What are the next releases from the label, and when are they coming out?

What a Traditional "'Brick-and-Mortar" Distributor Requires

The CD is the preferred format in most cases, with vinyl records and cassette tapes appropriate for certain "niche" musical genre. Obviously, the music should be professionally recorded. A way to determine if your record sounds professionally recorded is to match the sound quality of the recording with that of the material played on the radio.

In most cases distributors make the following requirements of record labels:

- The label must have been in business at for least three years or have at least three previous releases that have sold 10,000–30,000 copies. Most distributors will not take on a first release product. Note: an exception is the newer breed of "boutique" distributors like Nail which specialize in alternative rock labels.
- The label must have its own trademarked name.

- Catalog numbers must be on each release (usually a three letter abbreviation followed by the numbers; for example, CJK415).
- Each release must have a Universal Product Code, the bar code on the back of the product, because most retail sales are now tracked through SoundScan technology that monitors retail sales.

There are many "store programs" that labels can buy into. You must pay for any distribution or retail promotions. These programs can get a release into the "listening stations" in the chain store. Prices for a month-long program can range from $2,000 to $5,000 per chain store. They can arrange for "co-op" advertising, where the costs of media ads are split between the record label and a retailer for specific new releases. The record labels also provide the distributor with "P.O.P.s" (point-of-purchase) items, such as posters, flyers, and cardboard stand-ups that can be used for in-store display. Your record label needs to be well financed. It's a big mistake to try to work with distributors without a realistic budget for participating in promotional opportunities.

Be able to furnish the distributor with hundreds of "distributor one-sheets." These are summary sheets that describe your promotion and marketing plans for your album. They include a bar code, list price, small photo of the album cover, release date, and catalog number of your product.

Distributors expect to receive a negotiated number of "free goods" to use as incentives for retailers to carry the product. Distributors may ask for hundreds of free promotional copies of your release. They need "promo" copies to use in-house, as well as to give away to contacts in the media and at retail stores. All promotional product should have the bar code "punched, clipped, or drilled," and should not be shrink wrapped. This is to make sure that they are not returned to the distributor as "cleans." Cleans are the regular product sold in stores. Many people who receive promos have friends in retail or at distributors who can exchange cleans for other CDs.

Labels sell their CDs to distributors for approximately 40–50% of the list price of the release. For example, a $15.98 list CD might be sold to the distributor for $8. **Online music retailers have their own price structures for buying independent CD releases, and I suggest you associate with www.cdbaby.com and consult the site for their amazing list of all their affiliated online music retailers.** By the way, the recently announced their first relationship with a brick-and-mortar distributor, so check their site for information on how that can work for you.

If you work with a traditional distributor, when an invoice comes due for payment, the distributor may not necessarily pay that invoice in full. For example, let's say a label has billed a distributor for a total of $5,000 worth of product. Let's assume that $1,500 of this product is still in the distributor's warehouse. This means that $3,500 worth of product is out in the stores, and some of it's probably still on the store's shelves, unsold. The distributor is responsible for paying the $3,500 worth of product placed *less a reserve of 15% to 20% for that por-*

tion of the label's product which may be returned to the distributor by the stores. The distributor would, hopefully, send a check to the label for about $2,800 to $3,000.

Distributors accept product on a negotiable billing schedule of between 60 to 180 days per invoice. Don't expect a distributor to pay your invoices in full or on time. You'll always be owed something because of the delay between orders sent, invoices received, time payment schedules (50-120 days per invoice) and whether or not your product has sold through or returns are pending.

Most national distributors require an "exclusive" arrangement, making them the sole distributor of a label's product. Also, expect the distributor to request that you remove any product you have on consignment in stores so that they can be the only one to service retailers. Be prepared to sign a written contract with your distributor, because there are no "handshake" deals any more.

Before You Sign With a Distributor

Investigate the distributor's financial status. Many labels have closed down in recent years and you can't afford to get attached to a distributor that may not be able to pay you. Read the trades, especially *Billboard*, for weekly news on the health of the industry and/or the status of your distributor.

When searching for a distributor, find out which labels they represent. Then talk to someone at those labels to find out how well the distributor got their records into retail and online stores. Ask if the distributor has a sales staff and how large it is. Get to know the Sales Reps.

Find out what commitment the distributor will make to help get your records into stores. Is the distributor truly a national distributor, or only a regional distributor with ambitions to be an national distributor? Many large chain stores will only work with national distributors. Make sure that your distributor has the ability to help you set up retail promotions, such as co-op advertising, (where you must be prepared to pay the costs of media ads for select retailers), in-store artist appearances, in-store listening station programs, and P.O.P.s (point of purchase posters and other promotional items).

How Co-op Advertising Works

Co-op advertising is a way for record labels to use their product to pay for media advertising space, and it's an effective way for them to use their inventory to promote sales. For example, when a label wants to promote an artist's new CD, they approach a retailer (through their distributor) and offer to take out a media ad that features the retailer selling the release at a special price. The retailer must purchase a certain quantity of the CD (a "buy-in"). The store also agrees to give it good placement in their store(s), and puts the CD on sale for a limited time. Basically, this is a win/win situation for all the parties involved.

Returns

It's standard practice that 100% of defective and overstocked product can be returned to the distributors by the stores. They insist that every label they deal with accept this policy. If a record label deletes a specific title from their catalog, the label must notify the distributor and it can take many months for the distributor to get deleted product back from the larger chain stores. These larger chains will withhold up to 20% of their payables to distributors as a reserve against returns.

Shipping Instructions

A packing slip must be enclosed with each order the record label sends to a distributor. This must include details of what was ordered, what has been shipped, the number of cartons in the shipment, and the purchase order number from the distributor. All product must be shrink wrapped. In most cases, the jewel box is the standard package for CDs. Shipping charges are usually paid for by the label, but may be negotiated after a label has established itself as a customer of the distributor.

Invoices are sent separately, through the mail. The invoice should include an invoice number, invoice date, details of what was shipped, a ship date, unit prices of each title/format sent. The distributor's PO number and the total amount due should also appear on the invoice. Each shipment must have its own invoice.

The Big Picture

The job of the distributor's sales staff is to make the buyers at on and offline retail outlets aware of a label's product. They use promo copies and one-sheets, as well as airplay, press, and live performance reports to convince the buyers at music retail stores to stock a label's product. If a specific title sells, it's the job of the distributor, in cooperation with the record label, to provide the retailers with a continuous supply of that title.

It's essential that a record label has a consistent, professional, and mutually respectful relationship with their distributor. **Your distributor will only be as good as your ability to sell the record.** Don't expect them to do your work for you. Remember, all they do is get records into the stores. Work your product relentlessly on as many Fronts as possible—commercial and non-commercial airplay, Internet airplay and sales campaigns, on and offline publicity ideas, and touring, eternally touring!

Getting Your Music to the Customer

These charts show distribution options for getting recordings from an artist or label to brick-and-mortar retailers, and then to customers.

STAGE 1 Direct Sales Opportunities

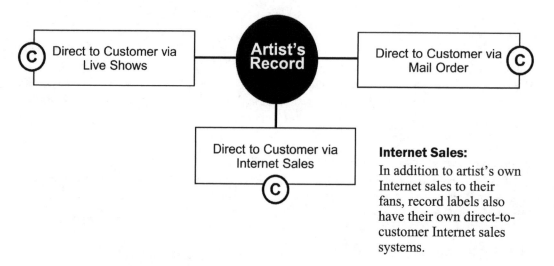

Internet Sales:

In addition to artist's own Internet sales to their fans, record labels also have their own direct-to-customer Internet sales systems.

STAGE 2 Independent Options

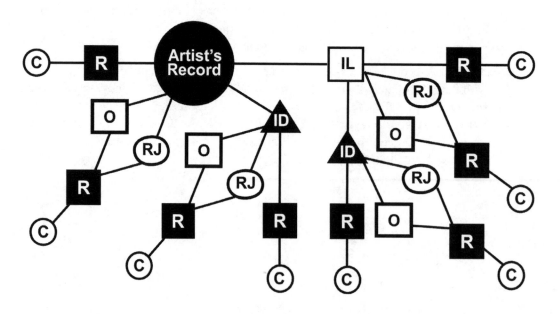

STAGE 3   Major Label Options

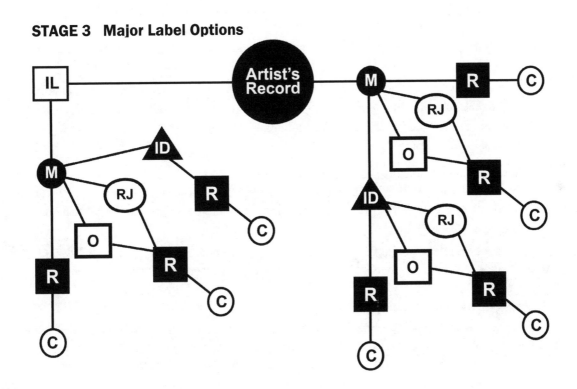

CODES

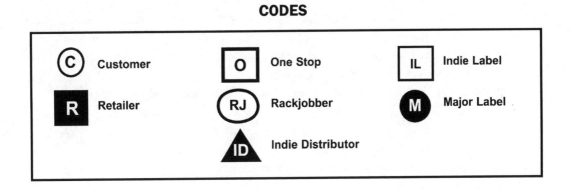

A FourFront Marketing Plan for Independent Record Releases

Writing a marketing plan benefits not only you, but everyone you'll be working with as you begin to implement your plan. The more details you can put into each section of your plan, the easier it will be for other people to understand what you're doing to promote and sell your release.

Don't hurry this important phase. A marketing plan is a necessary tool to help you organize all the different tasks that go into making and marketing a record properly. It acts as a starting point by forcing you to think about all the little things that might easily be forgotten in your rush to release your record.

Another helpful thing to realize about a marketing plan is this. It's just a plan! Once you start implementing it, the results of your plan will or will not work out the way you thought. A good marketing person reacts to those parts of the plan that are working out the best and adjusts the plan as needed.

Plan your record release as if you were releasing a CD in three months. You have 120 days from the day you complete your studio recording to get your record into stores.

You Need to Do Two Things:

- Write a marketing plan that details the tactics and strategies you'll use to promote and sell your CD. In each of the areas listed below describe clearly what you'll be doing to market the record. Remember, all your ideas must be focused on one goal—sales.
- Create a timeline that sets daily and weekly deadlines for each step of your plan.

1. What to Write about in Your Marketing Plan:

Objective: State a clear and concise objective or goal for your marketing plan. Who is your audience? How will you reach them?

Artist/Band Bio Brief: Give a short description of the type of music you make and a brief summary of the band's background.

Image: Maintain a clearly defined image in all graphics connected to your release.

Packaging: Give a detailed description of the artwork and layout to be used for the cover of the CD. List the information you'll have to obtain for the CD booklet, back cover (including bar code), the spine, and the CD disc.

Sales: Describe distribution and retail marketing plans.

- Any in-store play material (P.O.P.s)
- Purchasing any in-store listening station programs?

138

- What other specific sales opportunities: mail order, live shows?
- Create distributor one-sheet summarizing all sales and marketing ideas.

    Include bar code, catalog number, and list price of record, and street date of release.

Promotion: What radio format(s) will be targeted, what songs? Special promotions? Hiring independent radio promotion?

Publicity: Describe which broadcast media—trade and consumer publications, magazines, fan-zines, and e-zines—you'll be implementing. Internet promotions? Describe ingredients for press kits and topics for press releases. Create fact sheets.

Touring: Describe the time frame and tour schedule. Include other promotional activities to coordinate while on the road, such as radio station visits, record store appearances, and press interviews.

Advertising: What, if any, ads will be placed in the trade and consumer press and online? Describe the costs/benefits?

Internet Marketing: Outline how you'll use the Internet to market and promote your music. Mention everything you can think of; affiliated sites that you work with, blogs and podcast plans, song give-a ways...anything that is digital marketing.

Miscellaneous Ideas: Record release party? Novelty promo items?

2. Design a Twelve Week Timeline:
- Lay out what needs to be accomplished each week to get the record out.
- Consider the design and layout of your website, as well as the CD artwork, mastering, credits, sequencing, printing, pressing, and booklets. Schedule enough time to prepare and deliver these items.
- Include when to start working on the promotional tools that you'll need for your plan, (photos, press releases, novelty items, display material, ads).
- Set specific deadlines for each element of your project.

Sample Marketing Plan for a Band

This is based on a marketing plan from a major label. Some of the names have been changed to protect the innocent. If you look, you'll find the Four Fronts of music marketing here.

Prototype
Street Date October 3rd
The CD: **Some Kinda Band Are We**

RADIO
First single "We're So Optimistic"
Ship to local field staff on Wednesday, Sept. 13 – Overnight delivery
Ship to Modern Rock radio—Friday, Sept. 15 for Monday Delivery
Ralph-E to edit track
Ralph-E to produce a 30 second hook of "We're So Optimistic" for radio to tease listeners
    Weekend of Sept.15-17
Ship overnight to Modern Rock on Sept. 13
Ship full LP to Modern Rock on Friday Sept. 22 to land Monday Sept. 25
Ship full LP to College radio on Thursday, Sept. 21 (Retail Ship date)
Radio stations sponsored listening events - Weekend Sept. 30 - Oct. 2
"Are You a Real Prototype?" campaign
Possible live feed from select radio stations
    Interview with band/Playback of new CD on Monday, Sept. 18
    12 noon PST – Lamar Goodbar interview
    Manufacture discs for future playback
Website campaigns
Key programmers going to Playback party in L.A. for Sept. 23 show (List being finalized now)
Tip sheets

PRESS
Press play backs - Long lead press
LA - Spinoza Hotel (Santa Barbara) - Tuesday, July 18
NY – Super Grand Hotel - Thursday, July 20
    On-line press internet website being set up: grinandbearit.com
Preview site up beginning in August
Full website ready in early September
Journalists from around the world will be able to ask questions, download photos, etc.
Series of answered questions will always be posted.
Spin cover - 1st week of October - Lead review early Sept. street date
Vanity Fair - Fashion spread / November street date
SNL – October

NEW MEDIA
Playback occurred on Thursday, 7/20 @ MTV office 12:00pm /For programming and on-line Meeting with Redd Roundabout Mgmt. / Peter Gulag - Aug. 14 and Aug. 22
Build band 'branding' (name recognition) campaign with:

MTV live performance - Mid-Oct. in studio
5-6 songs
Can be a 30 min. (22min.) or 60 min. (44 min.)
Tie in chat after performance
Air on 120 Minutes/M2
120 Minute specials - create 50 min. programming
   Play entire album - need visuals
      Video blips / Sell advertising
MTV Worldwide playback of album
   MTV across Europe
MTVi website
   Streaming/Download - song/album
   Chat
   Premiere listening party
   Sell tickets to Spring tour
      Tied into Ticketmaster
"Are You A Real Prototype" contest
Winner gets first CD off the presses, autographed by band and delivered to their home 2 weeks prior to street date. Winning fan will host own listening party.
Spinit.com
   Band as guest D.J.s: play favorite records
Garageband.com
   Garageband promotion w/ **Prototype** graphics
   P/U at retail locations needed to stream tracks
   Possibility of internet music kit-card/disc for streaming - Mgmt. considered
Other partners awaiting management approval
Real Audio
Live365.com
Entertaindom.com - Live performance stream - Heavy advertising
Flash Video
Intel
Amazing mail (Pull photos from web)
On-line retailers - digital postcards (mid-August)
Amazon and BestBuy download 1st week of Sept.
Working with management on exclusive content for partners

SALES
Street date - October 3rd
Solicitation begins August 28
Listening parties - Week of Sept. 11
   Key markets - create listening experience
Listening stations – Timed to street date
Visibility
   Virgin - Flags/Boards
   Qtip - Boards
   Advance P.O.P (early August)
   Dump Bin - Sept. 18 in-stores
   Lite Boxes
Pre-Sell
   Added value possibilities
      Artwork give-a-ways
      Live tracks/Bonus Tracks
On-line retailers

National contest to see **Prototype** in Amsterdam Sept. 29 / Paris Oct. 7-8
    Pre-set up mid-Aug. / mid-Sept.
    In-store P.O.P
    Tie-in on-line and brick-and-mortar retailers
National label display contest
Regional Mktg. plans

ADVERTISING
Print

Spin	*tbd*		
Rolling Stone	3/4pg. 4-c	o/s	10/3
Alternative Press	1/2pg. 4-c	o/s	10/5
Entertainment Weekly	1/3pg.4-c	o/s	10/23
Snowboarding	2/3pg.4-c	o/s	10/3
Jane	1/2pg.4-c	o/s	10/16
Maxim	*tbd*		
Interview	1/2pg.4-c	o/s	10/24
Nylon	*tbd*		
CMJ Monthly	Full page	o/s	10/17
College Print	*tbd*		
College Campaign	1/2pg.	o/s	end of Sept.
Billboard Magazine	*tbd*		

TV

Kick off on MTV Awards, Sept. 7
MTV
VH-1
Comedy Central
FX
Fox
WB
NBC - Thursday night block

Radio

Key markets - Look at buying block programming to playback entire album

Outdoor

Snipes - 20 markets
Billboards
    Los Angeles
    Boston
    San Francisco

Classifieds

Rolling Stone
Regional weeklies

Consumer Print Campaign

Rolling Stone	1/2pg. 4-c	o/s	10/5
CMJ Monthly	Full pg.	o/s	10/17
Interview	1/2pg. 4-c	o/s	10/24
Wired	1/2pg.4-c	o/s	10/16
Ent. Weekly	1/3pg.4-c	o/s	10/23
Snowboarding	2/3pg.4-c	o/s	10/3
College Campaign	1/2pg.	o/s	End of Sept.

IN-STORE MERCHANDISE/P.O.P – Advance notices

Utilize band logo of **Prototype** 10-03-08
- Stickers
- Bin card (die cut)
- Banner
- Dump bin (available 9/18)
- Buttons – band logo
- T-shirts
- Car door decals
- Floor decals
- Postcards featuring cover art

PACKAGING

24 page booklet with 12 page booklet that sits under tray - initial run only
10" Double gatefold
Special CD/vinyl packaging for promo & possible sale - Management and band under discussion
Special package - metallic cover special DVD with CD 5.0 audio mix

MISCELLANEOUS MARKETING IDEAS

Possible added value to disc –free 45 of single

Place CD computer and gain access to a treasure chest of rarities - always changing (management working on)
iPod and iTunes special edition
Flash drive give-away for key radio / retail / press prior to release
Contacting Indie Retail Coalitions for select trendsetter store promotions

POSSIBLE ADDITIONAL MARKETING IDEAS

Air studios performance 7 + songs from **Some Kinda Band Are We**
September 4-5
200-300 invited guests
4 Hour Webcast - End August from studio
New tracks - live
DJ session
Create e-mail lottery competition - 200 people + will get to stream webcast.
Create playback parties
Record and use for other internet / retail partners
Prototype t-shirts - worn by selected fans around college campuses.
Possible additional contest, upon conclusion of initial contest
Lifestyle campaign with Hotels/Motels: CD in every room promotion
College television network - utilize Burly Bear Network
Modern Rock radio / Radioshack Contest
CD delivered to your home as part of a Surround Sound equipment giveaway - 2 weeks before street date.
October 20 - Los Angeles - Greek Theatre
Coffee cups around CMJ - NYC
Clear Channel Rock formatted stations: special broadcast 9/18
Sony Playstation - Added value disc 40,000 + units
Ticketmaster to be tagged for all live shows on tour

TOURING

Watch for complete tour date announcements to be announced

The Distributor One-Sheet

A distributor one-sheet is a marketing document created by a record label to summarize, in marketing terms, the credentials of an artist or band. The one-sheet also summarizes the promotion and marketing plans and sales tactics that the label has developed to sell the record. It includes interesting facts about an act's fanbase and target audience. The label uses it to help convince a distributor to carry and promote a new release.

Once a distributor has agreed to carry the release, the distributor's sales staff uses the one-sheet to convince retail buyers to "buy-in" a record and have it in stock at a music retail outlet. A one-sheet is an important sales tool that will help all the parties involved with a new release know specifically what will be done by the record label to help them sell the record.

The distributor one-sheet is designed with the buyers at distributors and retail stores in mind. In order to stand out from the one-sheets of the hundreds of other releases coming out each week, the design should be *attractive,* and *compelling.* It should declare WHY this record is being released. A well written and designed one-sheet is proof of a strong commitment by a label to its recording act.

Include the Following Information on Your Distributor One-Sheet.

* Artist or band name (logo) and album title
* Record label logo and contact information (name, phone numbers, etc.)
* Description of artist's audience
* Artist or band bio brief
* Catalog numbers, list prices, and UPC/bar codes for all configurations
* Release date and street date (if different)
* Track listings and "single" selection
* Past publicity, radio, sales, live appearance accomplishments
* Miscellaneous facts about recording: producer or studio, etc.
* At least five specific marketing ideas for the Four Fronts: retail, radio, press, live tours
* Internet marketing plans: branding relationships, contests, and music download plans
* Any distributor or retailer discounts or co-op opportunities
* Anything else of potential marketing interest

Take care to write and design an effective distributor one-sheet. Believe me, good and bad one-sheets are sent out all the time. However, it's fairly easy for anyone in the record business to tell when a new release is a "priority" for its record label, or if the label has a serious commitment to support the album.

Do not cut corners. The record you save could be your own. See page 145 for a sample of a major label distributor one-sheet.

COSMO TOPPER- Just Another Outcaste

BIO/ARTIST PROFILE:
One cannot simply classify the raw appeal of Cosmo Topper. He is a musician, an artist, and an individualist. Whether it's roots rock, British blues influences, or late '70s punk, Topper is an explosive, energetic live performer. He's a flawless studio hound who's absorbed in each song. Topper is a quintessential artist. With album sales close to two million, Topper has proven himself wildly popular among alternative rock lovers and earned critical acclaim in the process. The release of **Just Another Outcaste** aims to broaden his fanbase, by continuing to quench the thirst of devotees as well as converting those tasting Topper's brew for the first time. He is the people's artist.

BUY! HERE'S WHY!
Just Another Outcaste is Cosmo Topper's first album of new material in two years. Topper's visibility is at an all time high in the marketplace leaving his fans eagerly anticipating this new album.

COSMO TOPPER Just Another Outcaste

MARKETING:
- "Left Side of the Dial" samplers, stickers and postcards will be serviced to over 1200 board shops and extreme sports tastemakers
- Included on TEVA sampler, & handed out at outdoor events
- Annoucement stickers will be handed out at action sports events throughout Feb/March.
- Featured on the Landmark Theatres/Sundance Festival Sampler Jan/Feb
- Video of the song will be on the **Do What I Say** compilation
- Featured on the SPIN MAGAZINE sampler
- "Left Side of the Dial" will be on the Urban Outfitters sampler in spring

PUBLICITY:
- The Late Show with David Letterman CONFIRMED for 3/10
- Leno performance will be confirmed for April
- SNL, Sundance Channel appearances will be confirmed for springtime.
- Extensive press campaign in full swing. Confirmed coverage includes cover of CMJ cover, Billboard, Newsweek, Rolling Stone, Details, Elle, Entertainment Weekly, Esquire, Los Angeles Magazine, Men's Journal, New York Times Magazine, No Depression, Paste, People, Seventeen and much more.

ADVERTISING:
- Print advertising placement includes: Rolling Stone, Spin, Dirty Linen, Guitar Player, Utne Reader, The New Yorker, Bust, Resonance, Offbeat and Paste.
- Pre-release outdoor posting in major markets
- Melrose Wall in Los Angeles, month of April
- TV advertising campaign in May
- MySpace.com campaign

TOOLS:
- Poster • Flat • Bin/Tent Card
- Bio & photos • Video • Stickers

RADIO:
- First track for radio nationwide will be "Left Side of the Dial"
- This tune will be serviced and worked at key AAA, modern rock/specialty shows for an add date of January 28
- Full album will be serviced to college radio and AAA prior to release
- Second single will be "Modern Humans"

VIDEO:
- Video for "Left Side of the Dial" was shot in LA and directed by The Mollys
- Video will be serviced worldwide to all traditional (national and local stations) as well as non-traditional video outlets
- There will be a video for "Left Side of the Dial"

RETAIL:
Cosmo's previous two albums together have sold more than 1.3 million units in America to date. Cosmo Topper's top ten sales markets according to Soundscan are Los Angeles, San Francisco/ Oakland/ San Jose, New York, Seattle/Tacoma, Denver, Chicago, Boston, Portland and San Diego.
- In-store displays
- Listening stations
- In-store play copies
- Visibility will be high at all levels of retail
- 5% Discount for first 30 days

NEW MEDIA:
- The New Media campaign for Cosmo Topper will first focus on addressing his core "Outcaste Nation"/jam band audience through music previews on key genre sites and placement on community hubs.
- The second part of the campaign will develop awareness of the artist and his music among rock

TRACKLISTING	
1. **Left Side of the Dial**	8. I Left Sacramento on Purpose
2. Howie Had a Girlfriend (once)	9. The Human-be-in Boy
3. I Rocked with a Zombie	10. Shopping for Cool Records
4. **Modern Humans**	11. I'm a Heretic and I'm OK
5. Cigar Box Jam	12. Ballad of Norman & Butch
6. Who Started This Whole Thing?	13. The Donahue Connection
7. Find Me at 90.3 FM	14. Outcaste Party

and singer/songwriter fanbases, through early seeding of the music and information on core music and zine sites and select digital music partners, as well as online street team activities.
- As we get closer to release date we will build awareness and give an opportunity to participate in the project with an aggressive interactive outreach campaign to fan websites.
- A strong push for exclusives with AOL and MSN will further broaden Cosmo's audience.

INTERNATIONAL:
- This will be a worldwide release.
- Cosmo is currently on an extensive international promo tour (UK/Europe) setting up this release including TV performance on "Top Of The Pops" France and national TV in Italy. Tremendous response from Radio 2 in the UK.

TOUR:
- Cosmo will tour extensively throughout 2007-2008.

HOME: Seattle

In Stores July 11, 2007 (Order due date 5-14-07)

COSMO TOPPER Just Another Outcaste	**Topper Tune Records** 1234 5th St. Seattle, Wa 99999	**FILE UNDER: ROCK** **List Price: $16.98** **Produced by Keith B**	**CD: F415-1234**  7 2435 81922 23

Sample of a Distributor's Letter of Instructions to an Independent Label

Blankety Blank Record Distributors
4444 Knuckles Lane • Seattle, Wa. 98000
206-123-4567 phone, 123-7890 fax, beavisblanketyblank@blanketyblank.com

TO: **Newly Distributed Labels**   DATE: July 5, 2007
FROM: Beavis Blankety, Marketing Director
RE: Blankety Blank Record Distributors—Protocols & Expectations

What Blankety Blank Distribution Needs -

A letter on your label letterhead designating Blankety Blank Record Distributors as your National Exclusive U.S. distributor. (If not exclusive, a letter designating Blankety Blank Record Distributors as your distributor for Silver Platters, Valley, Virgin, HMV, etc. as applicable).

Example: "As of the date of this letter, I designate Blankety Blank Record Distributors as our National Exclusive U.S. Distributor. This is for all product on the following label imprints owned by my company (list them here, if any). All future sales AND returns of my titles should go through Blankety Blank Record Distributors." Fax this to Sales Rep Beavis Blankety **immediately** (206-123-7890), and to Reavis Blankety in the Seattle office; our reps need this to get your titles into all the mainstream retail databases.

Information about your label and your priority releases. Send our Sales Reps (8 reps, including the above mentioned individuals) 10 play copies & all pertinent info on each of your releases. TELL US whether or not you've serviced the reps directly; mark the promos you send to Seattle "FOR RETAIL ONLY – REPS ALREADY SERVICED (if they have been!)"

For "catalog" (releases that have already been out for several months or years), one promo + a Distributor One-Sheet (and/or a label overview with a list of releases w/ descriptions).

For new releases, the optimal quantities are already listed above.

New release information: We will send you a schedule with all of our **deadlines** along with a "New Release Solicitation Worksheet as soon as we receive the play copies mentioned above. As soon as you receive this:

Fax the **New release solicitation worksheet** along with a descriptive release sheet (aka "Distributor One-Sheet") to Beavis (info above) and to Reavis Blankety in Seattle: 206-123-7890.

Artwork (CD Cover or 300 dpi, 2.25" x 2.25," gray scale .tif or jpg file on disk) should be **sent to Beavis in Seattle. (No email!)**

Inserts (descriptive one-sheet). If you'd like us to insert a copy of your one-sheet in our New Release Book, please check this option on the New Release Solicitation Worksheet & send us *1,600* copies of your one-sheet; the cost is $175 or $200, payable as a charge-back. You can also place an ad in the New Release Book we put out monthly.

New Release Discount If you decide to offer a new release discount, indicate the amount on the New Release Solicitation Worksheet, initial your authorization where indicated, and fill in the "deal period". Discounts of 5%-10% are typical. *NOTE,* we offer this discount off our retail and one-stop customers' cost price, which is 20% higher than your price to us (if your price to us is

$8, for a $15.98 list price record, our price to retail is $9.85; a 10% discount means a $.98 per unit discount for the retailer, and THIS is the amount we will ultimately charge you back.) New release deals are typically in effect from the day the New Release Book mails until the Friday after Street Date. (This is the "deal period.")

Information on an existing release. If you are coming to us with a release that is already available to ship, you have two choices.

1. Hold it for the next available Street Date, and the title will get a quarter page feature with artwork & description in the New Release section of our monthly book.

2. Release it immediately—it will be listed as "Newly Available" in the back of the New Release book (& we'll fax our Sales Reps about its availability).

News about your release that affects consumers
Radio play. Fax or e-mail call letters, city, state to Reavis.
Print Reviews. Send to Reavis: publication name, issue date, city if regional.
Consumer advertising on TV, Cable or in print. Ditto
Tour dates—E-mail (as an excel.xls file) or fax to us.

I will also create a weekly "Record Stock Check" report for our Sales Reps which is printed in our New Release Book mailed monthly to Retail. I'll include your title if there are things happening in the marketplace that will drive consumers to stores. Please don't fax your weekly radio updates or tour dates, etc., to our Sales Reps. Only do this if something REALLY IMPORTANT happens (artist appearance on the MTV or NPR's All Things Considered, etc.) You should fax or e-mail all Reps. When events of regional significance occur (review in the Seattle Times, airplay on KUBE, KEXP etc), then DO inform the affected Sales Reps, and copy me too. If you are sending any materials to a particular Rep, then please 'cc' all of us at the home office as well. We will really appreciate this, and it will help us all communicate better, and stay informed on your important successes.

What you'll get from us: SERVICE SERVICE SERVICE!

Inventory reports are available monthly upon request via phone or fax to "Attention: Beavis."

Coverage questions or concerns should go to Beavis or Reavis Blankety.

Payment questions: send a monthly statement of your account to Accounts Payable Manager, Karleene Blankety. She will reconcile your account promptly.

Retail marketing options Many opportunities come up from time to time, that are presented to us with very short time frames for commitment (including Borders, Barnes & Noble, Qtip, and I use e-mail to get the word out. Note that "Co-op" programs are all ultimately paid for by you. In some cases, we will do "charge-backs" whereby we pay the retailer for the promotion and take a credit from whatever we owe you at the end of the month. In other cases, we require a check up-front from you so as not to get upside down with your account.

If you'd like to participate in any of the programs defined in the retail marketing package, fax or e-mail me your **"wish list."** Our advertising department will then work with you & the Sales Rep whose account is affected to set up the programs. Note that most programs require account (buyer) approval, and they will need to hear your release before making a decision.

Tour Support. We will be happy to set up print or radio ads as needed to support your artists on the road, but we need a minimum of **4 weeks lead time <u>IN-STORES</u>**. When you set up an in-store performance, note that we need at least 4 weeks lead time to guarantee product will be there!

We look forward to working with you. Don't hesitate to call if you have any questions.

Bevis Blankety

25 Things to Remember about Traditional Record Distributors

1. Distributors will usually only work with labels that have been in business for at least three years or have at least three previous releases that have sold several thousand copies each.

2. Distributors get records into retail stores, and record labels get customers into retail stores through promotion and marketing tactics.

3. Make sure there's a market for your style of music. Prove it to distributors by showing them how many records you have sold through live sales, internet sales, and any other alternative methods.

4. Be prepared to sign a written contract with your distributor because there are no "handshake deals" any more.

5. Distributors want "exclusive" agreements with the labels they choose to work with. They usually want to represent you exclusively.

6. You'll sell your product to a label for close to 50% of the retail list price.

7. When searching for a distributor find out what labels they represent, and talk to some of those labels to find out how well the distributor did getting records into retailers.

8. Investigate the distributor's financial status. Many labels have closed down in recent years, and you can't afford to get attached to a distributor that may not be able to pay its invoices.

9. Find out if the distributor has a sales staff and how large it is. Get to know the Sales Reps.

10. What commitment will the distributor make to help get your records into stores?

11. Is the distributor truly a national distributor? Or only a regional distributor with ambitions to be a national distributor? Many of the large chain stores will only work with national distributors.

12. Expect the distributor to request that you remove any product you have on consignment in stores so that they can be the one to service retailers.

13. Make sure that your distributor has the ability to help you set up retail promotions such as: co-op advertising (where you must be prepared to pay the costs of media ads for select retailers), in-store artist appearances, in-store listening station programs, and furnishing P.O.P.s (point of purchase posters and other graphics).

14. As a new label you'll have to offer a distributor 100% on returns of your product.

15. You must bear all the costs of any distribution and retail promotions.

16. Be able to furnish the distributor with hundreds of distributor one-sheets (attractively designed summary sheets describing your promotion and marketing commitments). Include barcodes, list price, picture of the album cover, and catalog numbers of your product.

17. Distributors may ask for hundreds of free promotional copies of your release to give to the buyers at the retail stores.

18. Make sure all promotional copies have a hole punched in the barcode, and that they are not shrink-wrapped. This will prevent any unnecessary returns of your product.

19. Don't expect a distributor to pay your invoices in full or on time. You'll always be owed something by the distributor because of the delay between orders sent, invoices received, time payment schedules (50–120 days per invoice) and whether or not your product has sold through, or returns are pending.

20. Create a relationship that's a true partnership between your label and the distributor.

21. Keep the distributor updated on any and all promotion and marketing plans and results, as they develop.

22. Be well financed. Trying to work with distributors without a realistic budget to participate in promotional opportunities would be a big mistake.

23. Your distributor will only be as good as your marketing plans to sell the record. Don't expect them to do your work for you; remember, all they do is get records into the stores.

24. Read the trades, especially *Billboard* for weekly news on the health of the industry, and/or the status of your distributor.

25. Work your product relentlessly on as many Fronts as possible...commercial and non-commercial airplay, Internet airplay and sales campaigns, on-and-offline publicity ideas, and touring...eternally touring!

What a Record Label Should Know about Music Retailers

Record sales are the "report card" for record labels. All the Four Front strategies—the work done on Artist and Product Development, Promotion, Publicity, and Performance—whether online or through brick-and-mortar retail stores must lead to record sales or those marketing efforts are in vain.

There are only two grades on a music retail report card. It's the pass/fail system; either you sold records or you didn't.

If a record doesn't sell, it's usually because the marketing plan was poorly conceived or poorly executed (unless, of course, the music sucks). Many musicians who put out their own records know something about music and a little bit about business, but they know next to nothing about selling music.

A record label traditionally sets up distribution and sales for a record before they begin to market it. They get exposure for a record by getting airplay on radio and TV, securing publicity from the print and broadcast media, and by supporting live performance tours. Online promotional tactics are now part of the retail marketing mix as well. But once the marketing campaign is underway, the focus of a record label should be to stay in touch with their distributor and work closely with the music retailers.

How Record Labels Work with Record Stores

For well over fifty years the relationship between record labels and record stores has been a rocky but consistent one. Labels need stores to sell their records as much as they need radio stations to play their records. So, labels have developed many in-store marketing programs for retailers to take advantage of. They create point-of-purchase materials such as posters, flyers, endcap displays, bin cards, and counter displays. They offer discounts on some new releases and back catalog items. They also offer advertising plans for print and broadcast co-op advertising to most music retailers. This is to guarantee that their current hit records will be available at specific record stores for a specific sale price.

On the retail side, listening station programs are available from all major record store chains, many independent record stores, and the newer independent store coalitions that formed during the '90s to compete as a group against the large music chain stores. Ambitious new record labels need to study these programs and participate in them or be able to offer them to stores.

Record Store Realities

Today, record stores sell music recordings, but they're selling a lot of other products too. Have you been to an independent or major chain record store lately? If not, and you're planning to release your own record, I suggest you get yourself down to one as soon as possible. Things have changed recently; here are three things to notice.

1. A smaller selection of CDs and vinyl from independent labels are on sale.
2. More "lifestyle" products such as clothing, DVDs, videotapes, comic books, candy, and clothing are being sold.
3. Digital delivery of music is finally beginning to appear at brick-and-mortar music stores.

The commitment of record stores to support new music hasn't changed. What has changed is the extent to which many of these stores can support the hundreds of new releases that come out each week. Since the mid '90s, many mom-and-pop stores that specialized in alternative music have been forced to close or sell out to larger record store chains because they couldn't compete with chain store prices.

Mass merchandisers, such as Circuit City and Best Buy, decided to use music CDs as loss leaders to get people into their stores. They started selling a current hit record for $9.99 and lost money on each sale in order to entice the consumer to their store, where they hoped the music fan would buy related products; CD and MP3 players, TVs, and computers. This had a dramatic effect on smaller music retailers who couldn't afford to sell music for less than they paid for it.

In the mid '90s, a record industry policy known as MAP (Minimum Advertised Price) was initiated. It required stores to stop advertising these low priced CDs or forfeit the label's offers of advertising and in-store promotional support. It took too long for the MAP policy to take effect. After almost two years of lowball pricing, over 500 independent record stores across the country went out of business or sold out to large music store chains.

By the late '90s, the MAP policy had finally proven to be an effective deterrent, but in the year 2000 the policy was found to be anti-competitive by the Federal Trade Commission and has now been repealed. The lowball pricing policies have started to return.

So, What's This Got to Do with Your Record and Your Plans to Sell It in Record Stores?

This whole sorry MAP episode contributed to an environment at brick-and-mortar independent record stores where they had to change in order to survive. Selling DVDs, MP3 players, clothing, and other entertainment and lifestyle products is their solution. Carrying your record may not be.

CDs don't leave a store much of a profit margin. Granted, if a store could sell every record in stock at the *list price* things might be different. But they can't. Even if a nearby chain store isn't selling a CD at $9.99, they're usually selling a $16.98 or $17.98 list price record for around $12 or $13. However, a store pays around $10.85 to $11.40 for those records—so do the math. Independent stores have to compete with prices of other neighboring stores, so they can't sell their records for the list price.

This situation has forced most independent stores to find other products to sell that have a higher markup. Lifestyle products, used CDs, collector CDs and vinyl, and blank CDRs provide that higher margin. Your new release does not, unless you can convince them that they'll sell *lots* of your record and the quantity of sales will make up for the low markup.

Some major chain stores are ready for the digital distribution of music. They offer kiosks that enable shoppers to request a selection of songs to be downloaded directly to a customer's iPod or MP3 player. It's about time, isn't it!

As things stand today, the labels still need the traditional music stores and will continue to work closely with them. We are, as of this edition, just on the dawn of the age of retail stores embracing downloadable options for their customers. Those who embrace it and stay ahead of the curve will most likely succeed and continue to also offer traditional CDs. At the same time, record stores are stocking their shelves with whatever music-scene "lifestyle" products they can get their hands on. This is something to watch, because new opportunities for in-store merchandising will be necessary for cutting edge record labels and musicians alike to take advantage of.

Working Retail

Music retail is the weakest link in most record label's marketing plans. But very little has been written about the realities of the brick-and-mortar record retailers, so let's take a look at this much misunderstood and neglected link—the independent record store.

When you think of an independent record store, what comes to mind? Did you see the movie (or read the book) *High Fidelity?* That's the best picture of what an independent record store can be (and maybe should be)—records, records, and more records, and a staff of goofy but passionate retail clerks who love music and want every customer to love music as much as they do. This kind of record store still exists, but it's getting harder and harder to find. Why? Because it reflects a way of doing business that's getting harder and harder to maintain.

Independent record stores are the places where the music matters more than any financial bottom line. Independent, or mom-and-pop music stores, are where passionate music lovers can find the latest and the greatest new releases. They're the places where an independent record label can go to put their CDs on consignment, where a local buzz can be created, where the impassioned, music-loving staff can play your record for shoppers. They can take pride in helping you launch your career—if you take the time to study who they are, where they're located, and what they want from you.

Major record store chains and mass merchandise entertainment stores obviously have a commitment to music, but they can't afford to be too experimental or too niched in selecting the music they stock. Seek out the hipper large record stores in your community. You'll be surprised at how much of a commitment many of these stores have to their local independent bands and artists.

It's Up to You to Convince Record Stores to Carry Your CD and Work with You

When record store buyers choose records to buy, it's a business decision, not an emotional decision. I know this from first-hand experience. I owned a record store for ten years. The first lesson I had to learn was that I couldn't carry every record I wanted to carry. I had to choose the ones I felt I could sell, out of all the new releases coming out each week. Today that decision is harder than ever to make.

It's estimated that over 1,000 plus new CD titles are released each week! Yow! Just a couple of years ago, there were about 500 new CD titles released each week. No store on the planet can carry that many new titles. So, music retailers can only select those titles that they feel they must have.

This gets us back to the marketing plans you must create to get your music on the air, reviewed in the press, and heard from concert stages. Do those things well, and the report card you'll get at the record stores will look pretty good.

If the buzz you create about your music reaches store employees, and your label can create excitement about your release, that can make it a necessity for the store to stock your record.

If you want record stores to carry your record, it's your job to convince the store buyers that they have to have it.

- Keep the stores up to date on your other marketing efforts (radio airplay, press reviews, concert attendance figures). Contact them regularly.
- Think up some value-added promotions to offer the retailer. Value-added promotions are things like giving a free live-CD to all the customers who buy your record, or discounts off your older, back catalog releases, or discount coupons for your upcoming live show.
- Give things to the retailer to make their job of selling your record easier. For example, a packaging option that can make CDs more appealing as holiday and birthday gift ideas are slip covers that come in shapes, (heart shapes, etc.). The label must create these slip covers, but they go a long way toward showing a retailer that you want to help them sell your CD. What cool item could be a future collectible?
- Work with your distributor to offer a special price on your debut record. Even though you want to price your CDs competitively, do what many labels do when they introduce a new artist: make the list price cheaper. So, instead of making your first record $16.98, make it $12.98. The store's price is cheaper and of course it's cheaper for the customer too. But only offer the lower price for a limited time.
- One of the most common tricks the labels use to create demand for a record is to release a song to radio three or four weeks ahead of the street date (the day the customer can buy the record). If you decide to do this, work with the retailer to encourage them to take advance orders, or set up a special late night purchase party if the demand for your record merits it.
- Give them point-of-purchase items to put up in the store (posters, postcards, bin cards).
- Check with your local retailers to see which independent distributors and one-stop distribu-

tors they buy their product from. Perhaps you can get in on some seasonal promotion campaign or new artist program one of these outlets are offering.

- If you use a distributor, get to know the Sales Rreps and find out which stores they call on to solicit new releases. Much of this business centers around personal relationships and a Rep who knows and respects you, your label, and your artists, can do a lot for you at the retail level.

- All the major chain stores have comprehensive listening station programs that record labels can buy in to, but be sure to research this carefully. Stores like Borders, Barnes and Noble, Virgin, etc. are very expensive to participate in.

- Try to get your CD into as many independent record stores as you can. Some of the spots on the listening posts at these stores are not for sale to any labels. The best indie stores leave room for staff favorites or CDs from local bands and solo artists. Also, since many of these independent stores belong to a coalition these days, find out which coalition your independent stores belong to.

- Give free copies of your CD to the store owner or buyer, and be sure the record store clerks who might like your music get their own copies. I can't tell you how many records I've sold simply by playing them in the store. Actually a good record store is much like a good radio station. In this case the customer is a captive audience and to this day you'll spot hip store clerks scanning the shoppers and finding the perfect record to pique their interest.

- Ask permission to post your live show posters or flyers at the store and give some free passes for your shows to the staff.

- Check for any in-store artist promotions, like store concert series or autograph parties, and be sure to bring your mailing list sign-up sheets to these events.

- Put your records on consignment (at a competitive price with other artists of your style) and call the stores regularly to check up on how they are selling.

- Consider pressing up some cheap limited edition sampler CDs that can be given away to store shoppers. Put your contact information on these.

- Many independent and chain stores have their own music publications, so be sure to submit your records for reviews. Also research the cost of buying ads in relevant store magazines.

- Ask about the store's website. Do they have any online promotional opportunities for you to take part in? How about links connecting your site to their store's homepage? If they do have downloadable kiosks in their stores, ask how you can get your CD into their system.

- Think about any combinations of online and offline experiences your fans will use while shopping for music. The future of music retailing will be one that finds creative ways for a music fan to go from a store's actual brick-and-mortar site, to the store's website, to a favorite band's homepage, to radio stations that are playing the band's music, to content at cool Internet magazines and e-zines—with links allowing the fan to hear the music all the way down the digital line. And, don't forget to include some clubs and other live venues in your linking strategies.

To sum things up, every record store is in business to do one thing; sell music. Granted, the music retailer's world isn't what it once was. Gone are the days when they could make a buck selling music and nothing else. But this change can work in your favor as well. If they sell entertainment lifestyle products like t-shirts and other stuff, give them a reason to sell *your* products.

It will be a long time—like never—before the record store disappears from our cities and towns. So, take some time to study the stores available in your area and in the regions of the country that your marketing strategies expand into. Internet or no Internet, you'll always need to work with record stores. Bank on it.

The creative record label and entrepreneurial musician will make sure to leave no stone unturned when working with a retail music store. It may not always be a music fan's final destination, but it will be an essential player.

Music is Your *Internet* Business

In this day and age you can't talk about the music business without discussing the Internet as well. Music and the Internet have become intertwined and, to a large degree, synonymous with each other. If you ask me about the Internet, I think of music, and if you ask me about music, I relate it to the Internet. That's how it is for a LOT of people, especially the up and coming "plugged-in" generation. As for independent musicians, the Internet is where it's at. It's the sales, promotion and distribution medium of choice for those who know how to use it.

Frankly, there's no way I can cover the topic of online music promotion in this book and do it any kind of justice. The subject is just too large for a single chapter or two. The most practical thing for me to do is to refer you to another resource, one that is not only complete and detailed, but necessary for anyone who wants to promote their music online. That resource is *How to Promote Your Music Successfully on the Internet* by David Nevue. It is, simply put, the best of its kind available on the topic.

What makes it so great, aside from being an inspiring, educational, and entertaining read, is that it's written by an independent artist who's actually done the work. David has done so well promoting his music business online that five years ago he was able to quit his day job. He's still reaping the rewards—*The Wall Street Journal* included him on their July 2006 list of the nation's "New Media Power Players."

I asked David if he'd let me use some of the text from his book to give you a little "getting started on the Internet" coaching. He agreed, and that excerpt starts on the next page. For more information, visit www.MusicBizAcademy.com.

And now, here's David…

Selling Your Music Online—A Reality Check

by David Nevue, Musicbizacademy.com

I'm often asked how much money a person can *really* make selling music online. I hear both extremes; from artists who think they'll use the Internet to make it rich, and others who don't believe you can make *any* money online selling music. The truth is somewhere in between.

Will You Make Millions?

Let's get real for a moment. Promoting your music successfully on the Internet is *hard work*. Don't ever forget that. I've spent *years* doing this. The Internet isn't a shortcut to success—it's simply another tool, one that can be very effective in the hands of someone who knows how to use it. Still, it's important to have realistic expectations before investing your time and money marketing your music online. You're going to face some very heated competition. There are literally *tens of thousands* of musicians out there who already have web pages on the Internet (as of this writing there are over 143,000 artists registered with CDBaby.com www.cdbaby.com/ alone). How can you compete with all those artists? They're just the tip of the iceberg. Once you embark upon your promotional journey, you are, in a very real sense, competing with every other web page out there. How can you possibly stand out in *that* crowd? Pretty daunting, isn't it?

According to the Nielsen Netratings web site, there are over 317 million people actively using the Internet (see www.nielsen-netratings.com/news.jsp?section=dat_gi for current web usage stats). A Georgia Tech survey of *actual buyers* provided some very interesting statistics: 70% of all buyers searched for the item they bought, 16% searched for a topic *related* to what they bought, and 4% searched for the name of another product which led them to the final product they purchased. Adding it up, 90% of all buyers used the Internet as a modern-day, digital Yellow Pages. So the question is, what does this tell you about selling your music on the Net?

Quite simply, it means that **creating a web page to sell your music is *not enough*.** That's something I discovered very early on. Even if you submit your site to the search engines, you're not likely to see a significant traffic increase. Think about it. If 90% of the buyers out there already know what they're looking for, and are searching the Internet for that particular item, how will they find *you*, someone whose music they've likely never heard of? If they're not looking for you, they won't find you. So, what *are* they looking for? Therein lays the key.

Here's the slap-in-the-face reality: In my experience, the average musician sells between two and five CDs a year from their web site. Sales that low do not justify the expense of putting your music online. Can you do better than that? Yes, you can do much, much better, selling not only CDs, but digital music downloads, ringtones, and even sheet music. But you'll only find success if you have a quality product people care about and market it properly. Let me be up front with you. To succeed on the Internet, you must prepare yourself for the long haul and prepare to work hard. Success on the Internet won't come overnight.

As you read on, keep the following questions in the back of your mind. They hold the key to successful online music promotion:

- What is unique about my music?
- What general style of music are my fans most interested in?
- What other artists do my fans compare my music to?

  and most importantly...

- Who is my target customer?
- What kind of information is my target customer searching for on the Internet?
- How can I use that information to bring that target customer to my web site?

To answer the question I posed earlier, no, you're not likely to make millions on the Internet doing just music. But you can bring in a good, steady income. In 2005, I was able to generate an average of about $6,000 per month in total sales just from the Internet (that doesn't include gigs and CD sales at gigs). This income comes not only from CD sales, but sheet music sales, book sales, partnerships, advertising revenue, and other sources. But every single thing I do online is related to the music business I love.

It's Not Just about the Money...

Of course, money isn't everything. There's still the question of using the Internet to advance your music career, and that's something the Internet can help you do also. I've been able to generate a lot of publicity for my music online, and as a result not only do I sell CDs, but I often receive requests to have my music used in independent film and media projects. I've negotiated three distribution deals overseas as a result of someone finding my music online. One company is using my music on an internationally distributed DVD series that raises funds for various charities. NBC contacted me to inquire about using my music in a made-for-TV film. Photographers are regularly asking permission to use my music for their web sites. Even *The Wall Street Journal* took notice of my efforts, and included me on their "New Media Power List" of people "being catapulted into positions of enormous influence," (July 29, 2006). Finally, I'm playing a lot more gigs in a lot more places as a direct result of marketing my music online and as you know, the more you play live, the more doors open up for you. You, like me, can use the Internet to create a huge amount of exposure for your music. The more exposure you generate, the more likely you are to gain new fans, sell more music, get more gigs, and of course, make those contacts you want to make within the music industry.

Getting Signed...

I get e-mail almost every day from musicians looking to be signed by a major record label. Perhaps you, too, have aspirations of making it big in the music business. But if there's one thing I've learned over the years, it's that record labels aren't looking for fly-by-night musicians to turn into stars (American Idol and a few other copycat TV shows being the exception). They're looking for musicians who are already *doing the work.* They are looking for artists who have proven they can create a huge fan base, sell thousands of CDs and sell out shows all *on their own*. What I'm saying, in a roundabout way, is this: **If you want to make it big and get signed to a major label, the best way to do that is to forget about being signed to a major label and do the work yourself.** Get out there, play your music, build your fan base, and sell your CDs and downloads. Your goal should not be to "get signed," but to bring yourself to a point to where you don't *need* the backing of a record label anymore. Once you've reached this point, and you have a marketable name and product catalog, *then* you might find some A&R people knocking on your door. Maybe.

My intent with these comments isn't to discourage you, but to *empower* you. You don't need a major label deal to have a successful music career. If you're seeking only *fame*, then yes, you may need the backing of big money to help you achieve that. But if you're just wanting to do music full-time and be the quintessential artist, that's something you can do all on your own, and the Internet can help you reach that goal. I'm living proof of that.

Selling Your Music Online: Starting from Zero

The nice thing about doing business on the Internet is that you can start with very little cash up front. If you already have a computer and Internet access, you can get going for as little as $50. Below is a short list of items you'll need to get started, along with estimated costs.

The "Right" Computer System

Any computer system you purchase today will come with built-in Internet connectibility. You can easily purchase an Internet-ready computer for less than $1,000, but expect to pay $1,200–$1,300 for a system that comes with all the most up-to-date goodies. If you're buying new and for the first time, you may want to consider purchasing your system locally. That way, if you encounter difficulties, you can take your system right to the dealer for repair. I recommend you avoid buying a computer from mega-stores like OfficeMax, or Staples. You'll get better support from a small, localized computer professional who cares about you as an individual customer.

There are basically two ways to go when looking for a computer system: you can buy one with Microsoft Windows pre-installed, or go the Macintosh route. Many musicians prefer the Macintosh operating system as the Mac is known for its friendly, easy-to-use interface and innovative design. Personally, I prefer the Windows environment, but that's just what I'm used to. Either way, once you have a system, getting onto the Internet will be a relatively simple process. Today's high-speed systems come pre-configured with all the hardware and software you should need.

If you don't mind buying via mail order, and if you, like me, prefer the Windows operating system, let me recommend Vision Computers www.visioncomputers.com/. Every desktop system comes with a three year warranty (which is virtually unheard of) and their 24/7 lifetime support is known for its excellence. However you go about it, when you're ready to buy your computer make sure you ask what kind of warranty you're getting. For a new system, your warranty should cover labor for at least one year and parts for at least three.

A Fast Internet Service Provider

Once you have the computer system, the next thing you'll need is an Internet connection. Most systems you buy today will come with two or three ISP (Internet Service Provider) choices preconfigured for you (MSN or AOL are common examples). I'd suggest, however, that you do a bit of research before going with one of these companies. Ask someone who is already hooked up and happy with their service for a referral. You can also look in your local Yellow Pages under "Internet." Your local providers will be listed there. If you still have difficulty finding one, try searching "The List" at www.thelist.com/ .

The last few years have seen the rise (and fall) of ISPs that offer FREE access to the Internet. While most of these companies have failed, one called NetZero www.netzero.net/ has survived and is still fairly popular, though these days they limit their "free" service to just ten hours a month. You'll find other free services at All Free ISP, www.all-free-isp.com/. When using a free ISP you can expect to make certain trade-offs. You'll have to deal with viewing sponsor pop-up and banner advertisements of one form or another, and some free ISPs require you fill in and return marketing surveys on a regular basis to continue your service. In other words, using a free service can be rather irritating.

For the absolute fastest and hassle-free Internet connection possible, I really recommend you look into a cable modem, DSL (Digital Subscriber Line), or wireless Internet connection. I currently use Comcast Digital Cable www.comcast.com/, and if you can afford to plunk down $50/month to get this kind of connection, by all means get hooked up. A less expensive option is a wireless company called Clearwire www.clearwire.com/, which offers high-speed wireless Internet at prices starting at $36.00 per month. Unfortunately, they're not yet available in all areas, but if they service your area, this is another viable option for a fast connection. If you're doing business on the Internet, you'll need the speed.

To research other companies providing fast connections in your area, check out Broadband Reports at www.broadbandreports.com/. And, if you don't know a thing about DSL and want to learn about the technology before jumping into it, check out the Everything DSL at www.everythingdsl.com/. It's a great place for beginners to do research.

A Personal Firewall

If you go with anything other than a dial-up connection, you MUST have a personal firewall to prevent unwanted tampering on your system. Especially when using a cable modem connection, you're *continuously* connected to the Net and thus vulnerable to hacking. Windows comes with a firewall built in, but if you just can't bring yourself to trust Microsoft, check out ZoneAlarm at www.download.com/ZoneAlarm/3000-10435_4-10039884.html. It's free.

Choose Your Browser

The next item you'll need is a web browser. I doubt I need to say much about this, since if you are reading this book, chances are about 99.5% that you already have one. If not, a web browser is the tool that allows you to view web sites on the Internet. You have three basic choices: The first is Internet Explorer, which dominates the market. Internet Explorer (and soon, Vista), come pre-installed on the Windows operating system and you can download the latest version (or any updates) from www.microsoft.com/windows/ie/default.mspx. Your second choice is Mozilla Firefox, an up-and-coming competitor to Internet Explorer. Firefox is also free, and can be downloaded from Mozilla's web site at www.mozilla.com/firefox/. Finally, there's Netscape Communicator, which has a small but loyal fan base. If you want to try out Netscape's browser, you can download a copy from http://browser.netscape.com/ns8/. There are dozens of other web browsers available (for a list, see http://browsers.evolt.org/), but Internet Explorer is all you really need.

Got a Mac? Many Mac users prefer Safari: www.apple.com/macosx/features/safari/.

Finding the Perfect Web Host—A Place to Call Home

You'll need a place to call "home" on the Internet, a place to put your web pages so others can view them. A web hosting service will allow you to put your web site on their servers for a monthly fee. You are, essentially, renting the space from them. The fee for web hosting varies, but generally lies between $8 and $30 dollars a month depending on the options you need. The more space, features, and bandwidth you want, the more it will cost you. You may also be asked to pay a one-time setup fee which can run anywhere from $20 to $50. The company I currently use for web site hosting is Aplus.net at www.aplus.net/. Hosting plans start at just $5.95 per month, and their web servers are very fast. While their setup and configuration isn't the most intuitive, you're just one click away from being able to chat with someone on Aplus' excellent support team who will gladly step you through any setup questions.

Other hosts recommended to me by readers have included Site5 www.site5.com/ and Surpass Hosting http://surpasshosting.com/. I haven't tried them out, but on the surface, everything looks very reasonable.

Finally, I can't talk about music-related web hosting without suggesting you take HostBaby www.hostbaby.com into consideration. HostBaby is run by the same great mind that started up CD Baby, and if you want a web host for no other purpose than to have your own artist page up on the Internet, HostBaby.com will provide everything you're likely to need.

Claim Your Domain

You'll need to register a domain name (such as mywebsite.com) to serve as your web site address. I use DirectNIC www.directnic.com/ to register and manage all of my domain names. The cost of their service is $15.00 per year, per domain, and while you can find cheaper registration services, you'll be hard pressed to find one that's easier to use. I highly recommend their service.

You can search DirectNIC to see if your desired domain name (you web site address) is available right from the home page. If the name you want is already taken, DirectNIC will make some suggestions based on your initial search. As you explore your options, do your best to choose a web site address that's *easy to remember*. Keep in mind, as you search, that you'll be repeating this web site address to not only your fans, but to important contacts you make. Avoid the use of hyphens (such as my-musicplace.com) or oddball naming conventions and spelling (such as 4starmuzik.com). Keep your name simple and its spelling obvious. Finally, if at all possible, use a dot.com (.com) extension. Although .net, .us, .org, .biz, and other extensions are available, the .com extension has become synonymous with the Internet and will be the easiest for your fans, contacts and visitors to remember.

Here's an article worth reading: "Are Hyphenated Domain Names a Good Buy?" You'll find it at www.netmechanic.com/news/vol6/promo_no19.htm. The article provides examples of the use of hyphenated domain names, both for and against.

Once you've selected and registered your domain name, you'll need to tell the name registration service where to direct traffic for that domain name. In other words, when someone types "yourwebsiteaddress.com" into their web browser, to what server should they be directed? To set this up, simply find out from your web host what your primary and secondary domain name server (DNS) information is. It will either be an IP address (i.e., 12.345.67.8) or a hostname (ns1.hostname.com). More than likely this information was e-mailed to you when you signed up for your hosting service. Take this information, go to your domain registration service, and add it to your nameserver (or they might call it DNS) configuration. The process sounds more complicated than it is. Once you get started, the techno-speak above will make more sense.

Tip: If you find domain name registration and configuration difficult, talk to your web host provider. Most providers will take care of the entire registration process for you at no extra cost. You just pay the cost of the actual registration.

Designing Your Web Site

One of the first things you'll need to decide is whether or not you want to design your own web site. If your goal is to simply have your music available *somewhere* online, you might want to just sign up for CD Baby's services at http://CDBaby.net/. For $35 bucks, they'll take your CD and put it on a beautiful web page for you. And that will give you somewhere to direct your fans to purchase your music online if they wish.

However, if you wish to *grow* your online presence into a long-term income generator, at some point you really *must* have your own web site. The next question then becomes whether or not you have the know-how to design a quality web site that will sell your music.

If you know nothing about web site design, your options are many. First, consider your fan base. Are any of your fans talented designers? You may find a fan will design a very nice web site for you for little or no money. My fans do a LOT of great things for me just because they want to support my music.

Plus, there are all kinds of places you can go to create an "instant" band web site. Some examples include www.TotalBand.com/, www.BandZoogle.com/ and www.Broadjam.com/.

There are many places on the Internet where you can search for and make contact with professional designers. At GetaGraphic.com for example www.getagraphic.com/, you can post your design requirements and graphic artists will bid for your job. You can evaluate each bid, and each bidder's portfolio, before committing to anything. If you see something you like, you can hire them on the spot. Similar options are available at Compare Web Designers www.CompareWebDesigners.com/, the Elance Agency http://agency.elance.com/, and Host-Baby.com www.hostbaby.com/wddb/.

If you design your web site yourself, you'll need to decide what kind of web design software to use. Macromedia's Dreamweaver www.adobe.com/products/dreamweaver/ software is a popular choice. I like a simple, WYSIWYG (what you see is what you get) page editor. I recommend Namo WedEditor www.namo.com/products/webeditor.php. I LOVE this software! You can download a free trial version from Namo's web site. If you decide to buy it, your cost is only $99, as opposed to nearly $400 for Dreamweaver.

FTP Client Software

FTP is an acronym for "File Transfer Protocol." The basic function of FTP client software is to upload and download files to and from your web host's server. Once you have your web page designed, the HTML document and graphic files that make up that page need to be transferred from your computer to your web host's server via an FTP client. FTP client file utilities are readily available on the Internet. I recommend either of these FTP client tools:
CuteFTP: www.cuteftp.com/cuteftp/
CoreFTP: www.coreftp.com/

Personally, I use CuteFTP. CoreFTP's free FTP tool is a good alternative, especially for those of you just starting out. The web hosting service you sign up with can help you set up your FTP client and upload your files. The process is very simple, and only requires you fill in two or three fields with configuration information your web host will provide you. Once it's set up, you can upload or download your files to your host service with the click of a button.

E-mail: Your New Best Friend

E-mail makes it easy for potential customers to contact you. Most services, including web hosts, ISPs and online services will provide you with a free e-mail address to go along with your web site. If you'd rather, you can use one of the many free web-based e-mail services such as Yahoo! Mail http://mail.yahoo.com/ or Google's Gmail http://gmail.google.com/. The advantage of going this route is that you can check your e-mail with ease from any computer with an Internet connection. For a quick study on all the services available to you, check out the Free E-mail Address Directory at www.e-mailaddresses.com/.

Getting Started

The tools mentioned above are all you should need to get started on the Internet. You'll use these tools just about every day as you run your online business. If you're a beginner and new to this kind of technology, some of what I described above may sound a bit complicated, but it's really not. If you take the time, you can learn all this stuff pretty quickly and soon you won't even think about it—you'll do it all automatically. If you find you need more assistance with any of the above, free tutorials are available online for every aspect of connecting to the Internet. To find help with a particular topic, just go to Google at www.google.com/ and search for the specific item you need help with, for example; "ftp tutorial." It won't take you long to find a number of useful resources.

What you just read is a brief glimpse into the opening chapter of David's book, *How to Promote Your Music Successfully on the Internet*. Take a look at the topics below. His book will give you answers to all these important Internet marketing issues:

How to build a web site designed to maximize CD sales.

How to put music online and offer it for streaming or download. The technical stuff made easy.

How to take credit card orders from your site—in just 15 minutes.

How to optimize your web site for search engines (without the hype)

How to register your web site with the search engines (without paying a dime.)

How and where to target customers most likely to buy your CDs, and drive them to your web site.

How to build a street team of fans, put them to work for you, and keep them energized.

How to write your press release and where to send it online to make an impact.

Proven strategies for selling music online. Great ideas just waiting to happen.

Little known marketing secrets that will easily double your CD sales.

How to turn casual visitors into buying customers.

How to build and maintain an e-mail list that will bring you business for years to come.

How to get your music onto podcasts as well as hundreds of Internet radio stations.

How to launch your own Internet radio station and use it to attract tens of thousands of new fans.

How to use the Internet to get gigs, book your own tour and become your own tour manager.

12 things to do right now to improve your Internet sales.

The absolute best places to promote, sell and distribute your music online. Very detailed.

How to use www.myspace.com/ to build your mailing list, fan base and tour options.

What NOT to waste your time and money on. Learn from my mistakes.

How to use advertising to pump cash into your music career. A little success can go a long way.

....and a HUGE directory of proven resources to help you take you to the next level.

Getting the Most out of Your Music Website

If you're a regular cruiser and user of the Internet, you know that the design of a website affects how, or even if, you use that site. But you may not be connecting the dots from what you like to see on *someone else's* website, to what you've created on your own band or artist site. To help you get some perspective, I've put together a few thoughts on what to do (and not to do) on your music related webpages.

Your Electronic Press Kit

In the offline world, there are press kits that contain such things as your CD, bios, fact sheets, cover letters, press clippings or quotes, and a photograph (8 x 10 inch, black-and-white glossies). In addition, your kit may need to have other useful promotional items such as lyric sheets, stage plots, equipment lists, song lists, gig listings, etc.

When you create your website, many of those traditional items should still be a part of your electronic press kit. But the uniqueness of the web, and the new challenges and opportunities that it brings, require you to re-think your online presence. One simple fact of music promotion that exists both off and online is this; the first impression an artist makes on the music industry at large is a *visual* impression. The gatekeepers in the Four Fronts will always *see* your music first—in the form of a CD cover, logo, letterhead, or a homepage on the Internet, before they *hear* it.

Here Are Some Tips for Creating the Content at Your Band/Artist Website.

Bios: Make the first paragraph stand out, with a clear description of who you are and what kind of music you make. Next, mention what you're currently doing, (a new CD, an upcoming tour, whatever). After that, summarize your career background by highlighting significant facts and achievements. Wrap it up with a reminder about your current activities. As with a traditional bio, no long-winded information should be included. Also avoid clichés and overblown statements ("the greatest, most original music ever") unless you have a quote from a significant person who actually said the cliché. Then use that quote with appropriate credit to the person who said it.

Fact Sheets: A fact sheet is nothing more than one page on your website with bulleted information about your current projects and highlights from your career. Fact sheets are useful because they're a quick and easy way for a busy industry person to get a fix on you and what you're up to.

Photographs: One of the best things about a website is that you can creatively insert cool photos of you and your fellow musicians throughout your site, or in a special section or photo gallery. Be sure that the photos are as professional looking as the design of your site. Amateur looking *anything* can really hurt you in an industry that is image addicted. You *must* have a consistent image which you control. Photos are often the most neglected and poorest parts of an artist's presentation.

Tour Dates/Performance Schedule: Most genre of music require an act to play live, so be sure to play live as often as you can and keep your performance sections on your websites updated constantly. Nothing is more of a turn off to industry reps than visiting a site where the performance schedule lists gigs are weeks or months old. It's a sure sign that you're unprofessional and perhaps have even called it quits.

Your Product: This means you have a page or pages dedicated to your CDs, vinyl, or downloadable music tracks. State clearly what past, present, and even future releases you have for sale. Then, design this section of your site to steer your fans and customers to *how* they can buy your music. It can be as simple as directing them to an address they must send a check to, or linking them to online retailers like www.Amazon.com or www.CDBaby.com. *(Restricting your fans to only one purchasing choice isn't an effective e-commerce marketing decision.)*

You should also include fun and interesting descriptions of your songs, any stories about the making of the record, quotes from your producer or engineers, or other musicians. Have some fun with this too. This *is* the entertainment business, you know!

The issue of how you'll use sound samples, (via Windows Media Player, iTunes samples, or MP3s) is up to you, but you must have some samples, if not a rotating selection of some of your complete songs. Unless you've been living under a rock, you know that the compressed audio technology of the unsecured kind—MP3—has taken the music world by storm. My view on which to choose for downloading whole songs is *all of the above!* Why miss out on a customer?

Blog/News and Views Section: This is where you post any and all information about yourself and your music that doesn't fit in any other section. Mention your hobbies, political and social concerns, gossip, or anything else that might be of interest to your fans. *You must create reasons for your fans to re-visit your site!* This section of your site could help provide those reasons.

Contact Information: You would be shocked at how many sites forget to have an e-mail link for visitors to contact you. Just like in the offline world, the number of musicians who forget to put their phone numbers, addresses, etc., on their promotional materials is astounding. So, don't forget this basic, essential tool on your site. And put that contact link on *every* page. You have no real control over what pages your fans may visit.

Some Other Issues for a Music Related Website

- Make sure your page is easy to read. No light green type on a yellow background, for example. Use type effects like drop shadows sparingly.
- The font size you choose should be at least 12. And don't use hard to read fonts, like Old English in all capital letters. Make it something you could *easily* read yourself.

- Watch out for tricky moving images. Java applets and animations may be very slow to load. You may have sophisticated broadband connections because you're really into technology, but many users still do not and you'll make your site unavailable to them.

- Obey the eight second rule! If your web pages do not load up within eight seconds, most web cruisers get frustrated and move on to other pages or sites.

- No more web-counters! Stop putting those silly little mileage-readout type thingies on your sites. They were cool in 1994, but they're stupid now.

- Think about creating a chat room for your fans to gather and spread vicious rumors about you…just kidding. When your fanbase gets big enough for this, then be sure you schedule regular visits to make yourself available. At least once a month, you or a member of your group should commit to being available in your chatroom.

- Be sure you have a guestbook for your fans and visitors to sign. This is really your mailing list, but you don't have to call it that. Whatever you call it, you must have a way for visitors to sign up for a newsletter or a mailing list of some kind. If you're not hip to the value of a growing mailing list, please leave now and do some research on this essential topic.

- Research the Internet for the best e-commerce technologies to sell your music. Credit card processing services such as Paypal.com and Propay.com are a good starting point.

- Choose an easy to remember URL. Your web address should not be something like *www.meanderingfreewebsite.com/members/bands/* or whatever. You should invest in an easy to remember domain name like www.knab.com, or www.fourfrontmusic.com. Think about it, the most visited websites are the ones that are easy to remember!

- Don't forget to promote your website by linking to as many other genre-related sites you can find, and offer to exchange links with like minded artists and bands. Include your URL on all your promotional materials, flyers, posters, business cards, CDs, and yell it out from the stage at all your live shows too.

- Consider adding a search service to your site to make it easier for fans to find information from your site. Also consider archiving your older data in a special "Collector's Corner."

- Sign up for the free daily newsletters www.musicdish.com, and www.mi2n.com. They report on the evolving e-commerce music scene. Also there are many other e-commerce and music newsletters on the Internet. Get out there and learn new ways to promote your music online.

- Be sure to link to a page you've created at www.myspace.com, or www.youtube.com. These sites have changed the way music fans and music industry gatekeepers find new music. You *must* create some presence on both these sites.

Before the Internet arrived, musicians and record labels were already busy working their releases in the old analog way. But a great looking, easy to navigate website is now a necessity for any musician who is serious about making money with their music. It's an added responsibility for every artist and band.

You need to ask yourself how much time and money you have to market your music. Which of the two worlds is most important for your style of music? Is it the everyday (analog) world of FourFront marketing with the brick-and-mortar stores, radio stations, print media and live performance venues; or the digital FourFront way with dynamite web sites, e-mail lists, blogs, and podcasts that may be used in all marketing sections?

This is an important question to consider. There are only so many hours in a day, and so many dollars in your bank account. Some kind of compromise is necessary. You must market your music in tried and true traditional ways *and* you must market your music over the Internet. Only you can decide how much of a commitment must be made to both kinds of marketing.

Online E-Music Promotions

For bands and artists who are releasing their own records, the Internet offers many new and exciting opportunities. But—getting online retailers to pick up your CDs (and other music related product) is as much a business as getting offline distributors or brick-and-mortar stores to carry your records. **Be sure you distinguish between websites that may offer your CD for sale on their site from websites that sell your downloadable music, or arrange for your music to be available through other music sites.**

How it Works

Like a good brick-and-mortar record store, online music stores like www.cdbaby.com www.amazon.com, www.barnesandnoble.com, www.borders.com, and others check out the new releases that come out each week. Each store then uses different methods to decide what to carry, but basically they'll decide to buy your record if they feel it's a potential seller. When they're deciding whether to re-order your record, they check their stock and decide how many units they should buy. Their goals are to monitor what their online customers are buying and to get them the music they demand.

For these sites that sell actual CDs, each CD is called a "unit." The better a title sells, the more units an online store may keep in its inventory. The more a record label "works" a record, (the more they actively promote and market a release by trying to secure airplay, putting the act out on tour, and securing publicity opportunities for them), the more likely e-music retailers (like their brick-and-mortar cousins) will find it necessary to carry the record.

Online Promotions

Brick-and-mortar stores use P.O.P.s (point of purchase items) like posters, cardboard stand-ups, and counter display materials. Online music retailers have their own version of P.O.P.s. When significant "action" occurs, (increased sales of a record, usually the result of a label or independent artist's marketing activities), the label will have to supply album cover art files and track listings to the online music retailers who are carrying the CD. Contact Muze Inc. to learn about their services to labels. You'll need your UPC or bar code to work with them.

Muze Inc., Label Liaison, 304 Hudson St., 8th Floor, New York, NY 10013, phone: (212) 824-0321, www.muze.com.

My Online Fave Sites for Marketing Your Music

My personal recommendations for the most effective online music marketer are www.cdbaby.com and www.tunecore.com. They're always making changes and sometimes they reduce or change the marketing options they have for you, but their traffic is so strong you should make it a real priority to work with them.

I still love www.Amazon.com/advantage and what they have to offer, too. Go to their site and read how to get your CDs sold through their system. They have a powerful way for an independent label or artist to sell their music over the Internet. You'll get your own "page," which you create. Detail everything you want a customer to know about your release; include a thumbnail of your CD cover and the song listings, as well as audio samples of selected songs. Over the last year I've spoken to dozens of acts who used Amazon and I have yet to hear a negative word about them. Remember though, Amazon isn't a record label—you have to steer people toward them with your on and offline marketing ideas. They'll help you get started, but you're on your own, like any other label, to get the word out about your release.

Sales from Your Own Website

I feel that all serious cyber music marketers should consider selling their product on their own websites. Let's face it, direct sales have the best royalty rate going, don't they? For the novice cyber-seller, simply posting a PO Box where fans can send their money is a primitive but valid alternative. When you get too busy to handle all the orders, there are many secure-server e-commerce companies around, eager to have you as a client. Two such companies are www.propay.com and www.paypal.com. They both provide a simple online way for entrepreneurs to take credit card orders from their websites. Personally, I like Propay better than Paypal.

A Final Note

Streaming your songs, or having them available for downloading, is a big part of today's music industry for both major and independent labels. But remember, the business of marketing your music over the Internet is in a transition mode. Just as it takes time to get a record from the manufacturer to a brick-and-mortar distributor, for the distributor to get those records into a store, and for the store to sell them, (possibly returning product to you later)—it takes time for the online version of that process. You'll need patience as you wait to collect money from online retailers. Many online e-music retailers at this time in history may still sell good ol' plastic storage devices wrapped in paper and plastic, and if so, they may face many of the same challenges as brick-and-mortar stores; dealing with payments on records sold, return policies, and lots of rules and regulations.

To not mention iTunes.com when talking about selling your music digitally would be like not mentioning Burger King when talking about hamburgers. iTunes *is* the king of downloadable music. You must have a presence on this site. For other digital download websites I will refer you again to *How to Successfully Promote Your Music On The Internet,* David Nevue's book. One other good resource is at www.mosesavalon.com. Moses has a constantly updated comparison chart of all the websites or digital aggregators (digital music distributors). This chart shows who is doing the best job of helping you sell your music digitally. While you're at this site, you should really check out all other the great information available there.

What is SoundExchange and Why Should You Know about Them?

SoundExchange is the first organization formed in the United States to collect performance royalties for sound recording copyright owners (SRCOs), featured and nonfeatured artists. SoundExchange is an independent nonprofit performance rights organization that currently represents over 1,000 record companies, their 3000+ labels and thousands of artists united in receiving a fair price for the licensing of their music in a new digital world. Their members include small, medium and large independent record companies, as well as the major label groups and artist-owned labels.

SoundExchange was created to collect the revenue stream created by 1995's Digital Performance Right in Sound Recordings Act (DPRA). Before 1995, U.S. copyright law did not provide a performance right in sound recordings. So, unlike SoundExchange's counterparts in other countries (United Kingdom, France, Germany, the Netherlands, Japan, etc.), record companies and recording artists were not entitled to license and collect royalties for the public performance of their sound recordings. SoundExchange administers the compulsory licenses once they're taken by those who wish to engage in the public performance by digital transmission of music, collects the license fees and distributes royalties to those whose music was performed.

Before its spin-off in September of 2003 as an independent organization, SoundExchange was originally created in 2000 as an unincorporated division of the RIAA. The Digital Performance Right in Sound Recordings Act of 1995 (DPRA) and the Digital Millennium Copyright Act of 1998 (DMCA) granted a performance right in sound recordings for certain digital and satellite transmissions. In exchange for this new right, SRCOs are subject to a compulsory license for the use of their music, provided the user complies with those conditions set forth in the copyright law. SoundExchange was established to administer the collection and distribution of royalties from such compulsory licenses taken by noninteractive streaming services that use satellite, cable or Internet methods of distribution.

SoundExchange collects and distributes royalties from statutory licenses, including:
- Digital cable and satellite television services (Music Choice and Muzak)
- Noninteractive "webcasters" (including original programmers and retransmissions of FCC-licensed radio stations by aggregators)
- Satellite radio services (XM and SIRIUS)

For more information go to www.soundexchange.com.

Product Development Questions
for Music Sellers

- Does the record store specialize in a certain type of music?
- What is the demographic makeup of the customers?
- Where is the store located?
- Which commercial radio stations in the area affect sales?
- Do college and/or public radio stations affect sales?
- What, if any, in-store promotions help increase sales?
- What factors determine which records will be promoted?
- What other types of music product are sold?
- Do they sell any non-music related product?
- What kind of display area is there?
- Is the display area free or is it for sale?
- Are "listening posts" available? How much do they cost?
- What is the buying policy for new product and catalog product?
- What new music trends do they detect?
- What kind of support do stores want from labels?
- Is the store aware of any new local or regional talent that is selling well?
- What would the stores like the labels to do more of?
- What would the stores like the labels to do less of?
- What kind of customer services are available?
- What is the store's sales breakdown by format (CD, tape, vinyl)?
- What percentage of store's sales are major label product?
- What percentage of sales are independent label product?
- Does the store purchase direct from any labels?
- Is product purchased from independent distributors?
- Is product purchased from one-stop distributors?
- Does the store have a website?
- What are your own plans to sell your music over the Internet?
- What kind of sales come from the websites you work with?
- What type of on and off-line media sales advertising is planned? (Newspapers? Magazines? Fanzines, E-zines?)

3

The Second Front

Promotion

Promotion: The Second Front

Getting Airplay for Your Music

Promotion means only one thing to a record label—airplay. While most Promotion Front efforts are focused on getting songs played on radio (primarily FM radio), today those efforts can also mean trying to get your songs played on Internet radio stations, satellite broadcasters like Serius and XM, and the new kids on the block—the High Definition FM radio broadcasters. Promotion can also include the work of getting videos aired on public access TV, commercial broadcast TV channels, and networks such as MTV, VH1, and BET. But those efforts are all secondary to securing radio airplay.

Promotional Representatives (Promo Reps) are the employees at record labels whose job it is to secure airplay for the label's releases. Promoting songs to radio stations is a skill that challenges record labels at every turn. Commercial radio airplay is the most effective way to expose new music to people, but it's also the most difficult kind of exposure to get. Securing commercial radio airplay is a serious game played by crafty and well funded record labels who have developed business contracts and personal relationships within the broadcast industry. The result is an environment that excludes, rather than includes, most independent record labels from getting their songs played on commercial radio.

But there are opportunities for radio exposure on many non-commercial stations—college radio in particular—for those who know where to look and what to do to promote their music to these stations.

The first step in preparing a promotion campaign is to learn about the different music formats on radio and how record labels work with radio stations. The next step would be to learn something about the business of broadcasting. Much of the business of promoting music involves establishing and maintaining relationships. That is true when dealing with any music-formatted radio station. There are also rules of conduct and weekly promotional routines that must be honored, all with the intention of doing everything that can be done to convince stations that the songs being promoted will attract and keep radio's listeners tuned-in.

Radio Station Music Formats

The first decision a record label must make—after recording an artist's record—is to determine what radio format or formats would most likely play the music of their act. A "format" is the industry term used to describe the type or style of music a station plays. According to the music industry trade publication *Radio and Records (R&R)*, (recently bought by the publishing company that owns Billboard…hmmm), there are twelve popular formats that dominate current commercial radio stations programming.

CHR: (Contemporary Hit Radio) Otherwise known as Top 40, it's been split into **CHR POP** and **CHR RHYTHMIC** to accommodate the growing category of dance-oriented pop music.

URBAN: Once called R&B, it has divided into the more rap and hip-hop oriented **URBAN,** and the softer adult contemporary or R&B sounding **URBAN AC** format.

ROCK and **ACTIVE ROCK**: Formerly called Album Oriented Rock (AOR), this format has split into two types of traditional heavy rock. Even though both formats play songs performed primarily by white, male, rock bands, they're slightly different in their programming mission. With many musical styles, music formats must adapt to the times and adjust their music to appeal to aging listeners. So, the old AOR stations of the past have morphed into these two commercial rock formats.

ROCK formatted stations usually only play new releases of surviving heritage rock bands, mixed in with the tried and true classic rock songs of the recent and not so recent past. For example, if Motley Crue or Aerosmith have a new record coming out, rock oriented stations would probably play songs from their new albums as well as their past releases.

ACTIVE ROCK stations add one significant difference to their mix of heavy rock songs. While they embrace the heritage rockers from past, they would also play some songs from the more contemporary mainstream/alternative rockers of the grunge era (Pearl Jam, Soundgarden) with today's rockers like the Arctic Monkeys and Franz Ferdinand.

ALTERNATIVE/MODERN ROCK: This format is in rapid transition, evolving more into Active Rock in the new millennium because what was once considered very alternative music has now become the norm. In the mid 1990s, Alternative was the most popular rock format going (thanks to the tireless efforts of the non-commercial college radio stations, who, over the last twenty years had been the breeding ground for all significant rock artists who moved on to the commercial airwaves). Commercial radio discovered alternative music in the mid 1990s and gave the Gen X'ers a format of their own.

By 1996, alternative rock had peaked, and the labels began to search for the next big thing. This turned out to be a new form of bubblegum Top 40-CHR Pop Music with such multi-platinum selling artists as Backstreet Boys, 'N Sync, Britney Spears, et al. By the late 1990s and into this new millennium however, Alternative found room on their playlists for the then-new hybrid sound of rap/rock bands. This format will always be somewhat on the edge, but nowhere near as adventurous as the true Alternative sounds found on non-commercial/college radio stations. (Stay tuned for more on this.)

ADULT CONTEMPORARY: (AC) This female targeted format still plays the mid-tempo pop music of the 1980s and 1990s, but also plays current, more mainstream songsters. It's divided into HOT AC, for more dance oriented but less Urban sounding artists, and **NAC (NEW ADULT CONTEMPORARY)** stations who play the easygoing, relaxed "soft jazz" artists.

COUNTRY: This format fragmented in the 1990s. New, younger country artists have taken over the airwaves and forced the more mainstream-sounding country to incorporate a new generation of country music in much the same way that Rock stations had to make room for the Alternative rockers. (The relatively new **Americana** Format is a more country roots-sounding format that has made small inroads into several markets, but isn't recognized by *R&R* as significant enough to have a chart of their own.)

ADULT ALTERNATIVE: This format supports the older singer/songwriter or mellow rock that began in the 1970s with artists like James Taylor and Joni Mitchell, but incorporates into that a fairly broad spectrum of contemporary singer/songwriters. It's surprisingly liberal in its pro-gramming mission. A good Adult Alternative station can span quite a spectrum of sounds. For example, they might play a Beck tune, followed by an old Roxy Music song from the early '80s, and then segue into some new Neko Case cut. They support many song-oriented artists, and can also include in their programming mix everything from roots-oriented rock to some of the more approachable alternative artists of today.

Crossover Hits

If a record label could make a wish and have it come true, it would be for every record to be what is called a crossover hit. This is a term used to describe those songs that can be played on more than one music-formatted station. In other words, if you have a song that can reach a CHR POP audience, like much of Mariah Carey's records do, then it's quite possible that the same song could also be played on CHR Rhythmic, and cross over from there to AC oriented stations too. Crossing over to as many formats as possible is the real goal of every popular music release. In fact, without a crossover hit, the multi-platinum artist would not exist.

To appeal to other music formats, record labels often do several radio "re-mixes" of the same song. By hiring producers known to make hit records for each desired format, record labels can ensure (as much as anything can be ensured in this crazy business) that a special remix of a popular song will reach as many different kinds of music fans as possible.

Once a record label has selected the song and the music formats they wish to target with their promotion campaign, they begin to make contact with the decision makers at each radio sta-tion who select the music a station actually plays.

Promotion: How Record Labels and Radio Stations Work Together

If you understand the business relationship between record labels and radio stations, you understand the very essence of the music business. **To put it simply, they need each other**. A record label needs radio airplay to deliver the music of its artists to an audience of radio listeners. A radio station needs music programming to broadcast to that audience. But of course there's a little more to it than that.

Anyone who is interested in getting their music on the radio must realize that the relationship between these two businesses is complex. Understanding some of the basic issues of record promotion and radio broadcasting will better prepare you for the challenges that await, should you ever attempt to solicit your music to a commercial or non-commercial radio station.

The Record Label Side

Radio airplay is the chief way for a record label to get their recorded music heard by the public. The more a song is played on the radio and heard by listeners, the more chance the song has to become a part of the public's consciousness. If people hear a song often enough to get familiar with it, they may like it and want to buy it—that's the only reason a record label invests so much time and money to get airplay. It's a proven marketing tactic that, when successful, leads to billions of dollars in record sales annually.

Although MTV, VH1, and other cable and broadcast television exposure can significantly increase the popularity of a recording artist, it's radio airplay that initially creates excitement about a new song. So, music formatted radio stations work closely with the record labels to coordinate promotional events surrounding music releases. Today, Internet promotions, publicity efforts, retail store promotions, and live tours by recording artists each play an important role in supporting the radio airplay a song gets, all with the hopes of creating sales of that record.

Radio airplay is the primary tool used by the major labels for selling recorded music product. The money from the sales of CDs is a label's only real source of income. So, until some newer technology comes along to replace radio airplay, the number one priority for most record labels will be to promote their new releases to commercial and non-commercial stations. However, for independent recording artists putting out their own records, or those signed to small independent labels, getting significant commercial radio airplay can be very difficult and very expensive.

Getting songs played consistently on national commercial radio stations and getting songs aired on non-commercial radio are two different things. Commercial airplay is the most effective type of radio airplay, but the costs of promoting songs to commercial radio may be prohibitive to many independent artists and labels. Opportunities for some radio airplay do exist for independent artists on many commercial stations through local music programs, but such airplay is usually spotty at best. However, many non-commercial radio stations (especially college radio), as well as Internet stations, air independent music on a regular basis.

The Radio Side

Realizing how record labels need radio airplay is only half the picture. Because record labels and radio stations need each other, let's take a quick look at the radio side of things before we talk about promotion in greater detail. Record label combatants in the music promotion wars arm themselves with an arsenal of information to convince stations to play their songs. They prepare for a promotional campaign by studying some facts about the business of radio. Basically this is how the broadcasting business works.

Music-formatted radio stations get their music for free from record labels. The radio industry uses that music to attract listeners to their stations. If they get enough listeners, consistently, they can attract advertisers who are eager to reach a select demographic group of consumers. So, in a sense, a radio station uses music like bait to attract people of a certain age group, gender, and ethnicity so they can deliver listeners of that demographic group to their advertisers. If they do their programming right, radio stations can charge advertisers handsomely for the radio ads they air, and the income from advertisers is radio's primary source of revenue.

To help you better understand this relationship, I'll start with a definition of what a Promo Rep at a record label does and describe how the Promotion Departments at many labels are organized. I'll describe radio's decision makers (the Music and Program Directors). Then discuss some facts about the business of radio broadcasting and the relevance of the music-industry trade publications to all record industry players. I'll finish with the importance of consistent communications between radio promotion personnel, label departments, and radio station decision makers when a promotion campaign is underway.

What Is Record Promotion?

Promotion is the word used to describe the work done by record labels to get radio airplay for their releases. Promotional Representatives, or "Promo Reps" are record label employees who present the label's new releases to radio stations and try to persuade the station's music and/or program director to play the song the label has selected for promotion. Record labels decide very carefully what specific songs from an artist or band's new record would most likely get the airplay they need to attract consumer's attention, and at the same time fit into the radio station's format.

The Promotion Department is a key department for any record label—major or independent. If a Promo Rep is successful in securing airplay for a record, the overall marketing plan conceived by the label will be given a significant boost. If a Promo Rep can't secure airplay for a release, it's very difficult for that record to become a hit.

Promo Reps are like sales people. If you've ever had any experience selling anything, then you know how important enthusiasm and a positive attitude are in convincing potential customers to buy your product. Staying positive and upbeat is essential in the music business. Every label Rep knows that they're not the only label releasing new music every week, and that radio stations can only play a few of those new songs.

Record labels, big and small, release several hundred CDs every week. Radio stations have an over-abundance of records to choose from when they pick which, if any, songs to add to their playlists. A "playlist" is a list of songs a station is airing and it's created every week by the station's Music Director. So, a recording that gets a passionate and honest sales pitch (filled with information about the act and what support the label is giving the record) will have a better chance of being listened to by the radio station's Music and Program Directors.

In order to fully appreciate what's involved in promoting songs to radio, it's essential that some basic understanding of the business of radio broadcasting be known. So, let's take a brief look at who decides what music gets on the air at a station, why they choose the songs they choose, and other issues that affect music broadcasters.

Radio Station Decision Makers: Music Directors and Program Directors

Every music-formatted radio station, both commercial and non-commercial, has a Music Director and Program Director. The Music Director (MD) is the main contact for a record label's Promo Rep. The Music Director's immediate boss is usually the station's Program Director. The PD is responsible for everything that goes out over the air and reports directly to the station's General Manager. These General Managers (GMs) are then, in turn, responsible for the entire operation of a station and report directly to the owners of the station.

At most commercial radio stations, Program Directors approve all songs that their MDs recommend. There are variations on this, of course. Some PDs leave all music selection to the MD, while others are deeply involved in choosing the music with the MD, or act as the MD in addition to their other duties. Those duties can involve hiring and firing DJs, working with the station's Sales and Promotions departments, meeting with the station's Chief Engineer, Production Director and General Manager. A Program Director has to coordinate any and all issues that may affect the station's sound. Radio stations, like record labels, are run by people in separate departments who act as a team.

Over the last decade, technology has radically changed the way radio conducts its business. In the early '90s, at the same time as the **SoundScan** company was revolutionizing the way record sales were monitored, a company called **Broadcast Data Systems** (note: now called **Nielson BDS**) unveiled a new software to help radio stations and record labels keep better track of the number of times a record got played on a station. Today's music-industry trade magazines now track the exact number of spins a song gets every week on all stations that report playing it. These spins are called Plays Per Week (PPW) in the charts. Knowing exactly how many times a song is played can be very beneficial to both radio stations and record labels. Think of it…every time a song is played on a commercial station, the song's unique ID number tracks it. Reports of the number of plays each song gets are sent via e-mail to the BDS offices in New Jersey, where they can compile very accurate national PPW reports on the cumulative number of spins each song gets every week on the various music-formatted commercial radio stations.

To help a Music Director and Program Director put together their playlists and devise effective rotations of their programmed songs. The dominant company today is **Mediabase**. It has contributed to streamlining the job of creating and maintaining accurate programming logs. And as technology creeps even more into the business of radio, most commercial radio stations today no longer play actual CDs, which are cumbersome to organize and subject to too many technical glitches. Instead, radio stations invest in computer programs that store the selected songs on massive hard drives with hundreds of terabytes of storage which are then simply accessed by the DJ on duty, and played or recalled from memory at the time they are scheduled for airplay. (Did you think DJs actually play vinyl records, or even CDs? Times have changed, my friends.)

Music Directors have one main job to do. They deal with the glut of new releases coming into the station every day. That means they have to listen to every record and decide on its merits for airplay, keeping in mind the format of their station, the target demographic they are appealing to, and whether or not that song will work in their programming mix.

In addition to that awesome task, they must talk with the many Promo Reps who call them every week seeking airplay for their new releases or increased airplay of the songs they *are* playing. Then, in regular weekly meetings with the Program Director, they usually recommend specific songs to be added to the playlist. In most cases, the PD makes the final decision on what particular songs will be added.

By the way, for every new record added to a station's playlist, another record is usually taken out of the playlist. Commercial radio stations play a very short list of songs in varying degrees of rotation. Around the clock, seven days a week, 365 days a year, music-formatted radio stations play a mix of new songs, fairly recent popular songs (called "recurrents"), and some older songs from the history of their format. No radio station on the planet plays only new songs, one after the other, around the clock. If they did, they would have very few listeners.

Music Directors and Program Directors are professional broadcasters who have studied the listening habits of radio listeners for years. They know how listeners use radio in their daily lives, and the fact is that most radio listeners listen to radio as background accompaniment to various tasks they're involved in throughout the day.

Radio stations' most listened-to times of day occur in the early morning and the late afternoon. These times are called "drive time." Morning drive time is roughly from 5 am to 9 or 10 am. Afternoon drive time is approximately from 3 pm to 7 pm. More people listen to a radio station early in the morning than at any other time of day.

Americans use radio as a companion to whatever else they may be doing. Getting ready for work in the morning, driving to work or school, doing errands throughout the day, performing chores around the house, working on our computers, or playing around with our hobbies— whenever we want it, radio is there for us.

When Music Directors and Program Directors check out the new releases sent to them from the labels each week, they listen with an ear tuned to how most listeners use the radio and how each particular song can fit into a listener's day. They know instinctively if a particular song would work for them in the morning, afternoon, or perhaps in the late evening or over- night off-time hours. Music and Program Directors are acutely aware of their audience's lis- tening habits. The time of day and even the day of the week play a role in their decision to play a record a lot, a little bit, or not at all. MDs and PDs may choose a song because they personally happen to like it, but as professionals, they've learned how to listen to songs for their audience. They are paid handsomely, in most cases, for having the ability to choose songs that keep listeners listening. They can tell if they're making good programming choices when they read the Arbitron reports.

The Role of Arbitron

Arbitron, for many decades now, has used a system of measuring which stations people listen to, when they listen, and even how long they listen. Arbitron reports also show the ages, gen- der, and ethnic backgrounds of the audience that a station has attracted. These audience re- ports are used by the radio broadcast industry to gauge their success or failure at attracting a *specific* audience, out of all the men, women, boys, and girls who live various lifestyles and come from different ethnic, financial, and religious backgrounds.

How does Arbitron get this information? They send station diary forms to randomly chosen people in all the different geographic regions of the country, requesting them to keep track of their radio listening habits for one-week periods. When these diaries are returned to Arbitron, the information is collated and published in regular reports sent out to their subscribers. Radio station PDs, MDs, General Managers, and the station's ownership scrutinize the results of the listener surveys to find out how well they've been able to attract as many listeners as possible to their stations.

Remember, a radio station plays music to entertain their chosen demographic audience. If they get Arbitron reports that report large numbers of listeners tuned in to their stations, they can approach companies that advertise on the radio with products targeted to the same demo- graphic that the station has selected. To put it simply, when a radio station has a lot of listen- ers, especially in those crucial morning and afternoon drive times, they can charge advertisers a lot of money to air their commercials on their stations. If they can consistently keep listeners listening to their station, year-in and year-out, they will have long and successful careers in the broadcast industry. If they can't, well, the weekly music trades are full of job listings and reports on stations that have changed formats—stations looking for the magic formula that will make them money, the right mix of songs targeted to the right audience for those songs.

Music Directors and Program Directors have one goal and one goal only—to choose music that they feel will attract a large and loyal audience.

Think of it like this. If you're a songwriter, the song you wrote and recorded becomes the programming content of radio stations who are trying to lure advertisers to their stations. Your music becomes something else when it enters the marketplace. Other businesses make money from your song. In the case of commercial radio, if the station executives feel their station will benefit from airing your songs, there's a good chance they will air them. If not, there's no chance they will air them out of any sense of duty to support the arts.

MDs and PDs are the gatekeepers for the radio station's owners. They must protect the owners' huge investments in buying those stations and the even larger investments made by those owners in operating the stations; buying the equipment, paying the DJs and the other station employees. They protect the station as best they can by doing their job; selecting, and then programming songs, (maybe your songs) to their targeted demographic of listeners.

About Nielsen BDS

Nielsen Broadcast Data Systems is the world's leading provider of airplay tracking for the entertainment industry. Employing their own patented digital pattern recognition technology, Nielsen BDS captures in excess of 100 million song detections annually on more than 1,400 radio stations in over 130 markets in the U.S. (including Puerto Rico) and in thirty Canadian markets.

Radio formats monitored include Adult Alternative, Adult Contemporary, Album Rock, Classic Rock, Contemporary Christian, Country, Alternative Rock, Oldies, R&B (including Rap and Hip Hop), Spanish (including Latin Contemporary, Regional Mexican and Tropical Salsa), and Top 40. Additionally, Nielsen BDS monitors twelve U.S. Music Video Channels and nine Canadian Video Channels.

Executives from all facets of record companies, radio stations, publishing firms, performance rights organizations, music retailers, independent promoters, film and TV, and artist management are among those who have access to more than **10,000 reports daily** from Nielsen BDS products; ENcore, BDSRadio.com, BDSexpress.com, and BDS RealTime.

Nielsen BDS information is utilized exclusively by _Billboard_, _Billboard Radio Monitor_ and the _Canadian Music Network_ in determining their radio airplay music charts.

This company's services are critical for getting accurate and up-to-date data. That data can be used to make the critical marketing decisions that must be made for every recorded project that is released.

The Business of Radio and the Role of Consultants in Choosing Music

There are now only a handful of huge corporations that own most of the commercial radio stations we listen to. In today's complex world, powerful media companies have taken control of over 80% of what we read, see, and hear on the radio, the print media, and television. In recent years, billions of dollars have changed hands to consolidate the radio broadcast industry. Most major markets have only four or five companies who own all the commercial stations in any given city. To protect their investments in these radio properties, many ownership groups hire radio-programming consultants who take over much of what I described as the jobs of the Music and Program Directors. It's very possible that the stations you listen to, and want to approach to play your record, can't do so because they hired a consultant who determines what songs are programmed.

These programming consultants may be the only decision makers for whole groups of stations. Because of this, record label Promo Reps may have to deal with the consultants directly if there's any hope of getting their songs aired in the markets these ownership groups have stations in. Consultants will go so far as to tell a station what they can or cannot play. They can have a great deal of influence over the playlists of their client stations, so they will share information on a song's success or failure with other client stations. Unfortunately, more and more of the stations owned by these large media corporations are using consultants to program dozens of their stations nationally.

To be clear, radio is a business first, and a news and entertainment source second. Everything I just described to you is basic information for anyone wishing to play the promotion game. Once you've made peace with the facts about the broadcast industry, unpleasant though they may be, the better prepared you are to promote your records to this industry.

The Record Label Promotion Department: Who Does What?

The Vice President of Promotion is the head of the department. This person makes the final decisions regarding national radio promotion tactics and strategies. There may be more than one VP. There are twelve major commercial music formats and several of them require specific experience dealing with the different lifestyle marketing strategies used in today's competitive music marketplace. So, one VP of Promotion may oversee all the Rock formats, another may oversee the CHR/Pop format, while another works the CHR/Rhythmic/Urban formats, Country, etc.

The VPs of Promotion may also supervise various National or Regional Promotion Directors. For example, these VPs may be in charge of radio promotion for the West Coast, Midwest, or East Coast. These directors usually oversee yet another group of label promotion staff—the many Local Promo Reps across the country, who cover specific metropolitan areas. These local Reps spend their time calling and visiting local program and music directors at radio stations to solicit them for airplay. When it comes down to it, the local Promo Reps are like the infantry for the record label's armed forces. They're the ones who maintain day-to-day contact with radio stations and must develop a good rapport with the music and program directors—good relationships are vital to any promotion success.

The National or Regional Directors as well as the VPs of Promotion may intervene in a promotion campaign when an especially important priority record has been released, and/or when promotion problems of some kind develop that the local Reps can't handle. There are many cases of egotistical program and music directors butting heads with young Promo Reps, for example. Other promotional challenges come up regularly.

The local Promo Reps keep in constant touch with their National or Regional Directors, and if necessary, the VP of Promotion. Clear and constant communications are a necessity in the promotion business. Every addition of a song to a playlist (an "add") is a small victory for the label, and every movement up the national radio charts is another victory. It works like this: the more stations that add a record, the more airplay that song gets. The more airplay the song gets, the higher the likelihood that record sales will increase. Any missed communication could endanger the whole promotion campaign.

Promotion Reps are in the trenches, day in and day out, communicating any successes, challenges, or failures to each other. But it will be the National or Regional Directors and VPs of Promotion (described earlier), who confer with other label departments like Sales and/or Marketing to make final decisions about continuing or ending a particular promotion campaign. All parties will study the results of every record's acceptance or rejection at radio and at music retail, and then decide at their weekly department meetings to continue working a particular record or stop, if the results show the battle for airplay has been lost.

The Promo Rep and Getting College Radio Airplay

Most major labels also use college interns who deal primarily with college and other noncommercial stations. These College Reps are essential when a label has an act that's on the cutting edge musically. College radio airplay can be a make it or break it opportunity for artists or bands whose songs are perceived to be too risky for commercial airplay. But, if the College Reps can get enough of a buzz created, even regionally, and the college music trade magazine *CMJ* reports a growing number of stations playing the act, it's possible that the other Promo Reps who work the commercial stations will be able to influence the more progressive minded MDs and PDs to check out the act.

The more adventurous or controversial an act's sound may be, the more likely college radio will be the label's primary target. Since the late '70s, college radio has been the proving ground for new trends in mostly rock and urban music. Once college radio airplay has been secured, the battle to cross over to commercial stations can begin. Many big name artists and bands from the last two decades got their first airplay on college radio. As their record sales increased and their popularity grew, the record labels could more easily convince the commercial music stations to add the song to their playlists.

The College Rep position can be a good entry-level job for anyone wanting a career working for a record label. The major labels and many independent labels offer internships for hip, young, men and women who know what teenagers and alternative lifestyle people are listening to. College Reps who do well in these internship positions—by securing college station airplay for their label's releases—often move up in the label's ranks.

When approaching a college station, or any non-commercial station, the Promo Rep's pitch is substantially different than the pitch to commercial stations. The people who staff most non-commercial and college stations care a great deal about non-mainstream music. These stations rarely play the commercial hits, but air a wide range of music. A good college station today will program separate blocks of airtime for specific genre, or program a variety mix of music; alternative rock, world music, rap and hip-hop, and roots music like blues, jazz and folk. Electronic music, dance music, punk and metal will not be ignored, either. The more eclectic and non-mainstream sounding the music the more likely these stations will be interested in airing it. There are non-commercial stations that may air hit records, but they're mainly found at colleges and universities that use their stations as a school for students who want to train for commercial radio DJ jobs.

The most important thing to remember when approaching a good non-commercial radio station is this: talk to the MD or PD about the *music* first, and bring up the promotional business information later, if at all. When the time is right—if they're spinning the record—the most useful business request to a good non-commercial station is to ask the station to do a live broadcast of the label's act. THAT can be music to a non-commercial station's ears. Non-coms are into music, and are usually fans first and business people second. The label sees a live broadcast as an invaluable exposure opportunity that will probably increase sales of the release, and help create a good turnout at the band's show in the city where the station is located.

Remember, since non-coms are more music oriented, they can actually be put off by a Promo Rep that starts spouting off a bunch of PPW (plays per week) information or sales statistics. The best relationship to have with these MDs and PDs is an honest one, based on why the music is so good and how it can fit into their eclectic programming. Also, they like to get little gifts from the label Reps. So send them a t-shirt or a coffee mug with your act's logo on it, or give them tickets to an upcoming show.

Independent Record Promoters: Who Are They and What Do They Do?

For many decades, record labels have hired additional help to convince radio stations to play a particular song. They hired Independent Record Promoters, experienced radio promotion people who may have once worked for a label but went out on their own to start their own radio promotion companies. These Indies, as they're sometimes called, are hired by the major and independent labels when a priority is given a song to secure airplay.

In the history of popular music from the '50s to today, the influence of Indies is marked with controversy and payola scandals. Payola was made illegal decades ago. Payola occurs when a radio station accepts money in exchange for playing a particular record, but does not disclose those payments to the public. To get around this law, record labels and radio stations have had to be creative. (For a sordid history of payola in the 1980s I recommend the book *Hitmen* by Frederic Danon.)

The truth is, money influences airplay. Money is spent, in combination with the other "favors" a label will offer a station; that's the nature of the business. Contests, exclusive radio station artist and band promotions, promotional trinkets—all play an important role in the game of getting songs on the radio. Record label Promo Reps and Indie Reps use all the tricks they can think of to get the attention of radio programmers. It's part of the promotional dance between record labels and radio stations.

Former New York Attorney General (and current Governor) Eliot Spitzer's investigation of the payola arrangements between commercial radio stations and labels has led recently to the exposure of many violations of the payola practices. He caught Sony/BMG Music Entertainment and other major labels red-handed, and his investigation resulted in an agreement prohibiting Sony/BMG and other major labels from making payments in exchange for radio airplay. Record labels usually hire independent Promo Reps, to remove themselves from direct contact with the stations and any illegal offers or "arrangements" for airplay. However the record labels themselves have not had clean hands when it comes to payola deals.

Don't let me give you the impression that every Indie Rep is involved in criminal behavior. That's not the case. There are many legitimate and powerful Indies who continue to work records to radio. Today those legitimate Indies are being challenged by a new generation of Indie Promoters who have aligned themselves with an army of lawyers and powerful radio ownership groups, and secured contracts that state that certain stations will only take promotional phone calls from one particular Indie. This new breed of Indie promoter has made the job of getting songs added on commercial radio stations very expensive. Among the many things the Spitzer investigations uncovered; a record label would have to pay $1,000 or more per song, per station to the Indie just to get a song added to a station's playlist. When a record label needs dozens of stations to play their songs nationally in order to create hit records, it's not uncommon to see hundreds of thousands of dollars being spent by the labels on these Indies, just to get some initial airplay.

The typical honest deal between a label and a more traditional independent radio promoter is a fee ranging from $500 to $1,000 a week for the Indie to work a record. Also, it's important to remember that any label wishing to hire the services of a legitimate Indie will have to hire their services at those prices for at least six to eight weeks.

I hope I'm making it clear that the cost of securing national, commercial radio airplay is expensive. Any label starting up today should be well financed if they plan to promote their records to commercial radio stations on a national level.

There are, by the way, many independent promotion companies that work the non-commercial, college radio circuit. But, the cost of hiring those Indies isn't much cheaper than hiring the independent promoters who work for commercial radio stations.

More on the Job of the Record Label's Promo Rep

The Promo Rep's major responsibility is securing airplay at as many stations as possible and then finding ways to increase that airplay. But they also have other duties. They must stay in touch with the label's A&R department, which is always looking for new talent. When a label wants to sign a new act, it's a good idea for the A&R department to introduce the new act to the Promo Reps and get their feedback on how the act's sound fits the needs of today's tightly formatted radio stations. Likewise, once an act has signed and made a recording, Promo Reps can suggest which particular songs have the best chance of getting radio airplay, and on which specific commercial or non-commercial stations.

The Promotion department also consults with the label's Publicity department, and based on radio's acceptance of the song, may suggest specific television shows, radio programs, magazines, Internet sites, or newspapers that might be best suited to secure reviews, articles, or interviews with the act.

Promo Reps talk regularly with the label's Sales department. They check with the music retailers in their area to see how sales of their record reflect the public's reaction to radio airplay. Their feedback to the Sales department can be very valuable. Often, reluctant music retailers won't stock a record until they hear that some local radio stations are playing it. (Or, conversely, a reluctant radio station may wait to see if the record is selling locally, creating a catch-22 situation.) So, the relationship between the Promotion department and the Sales department should be very close. After all, they're really a team working toward the same goal—to create excitement and sales for their label's releases.

Also, the Marketing department needs to hear from the Promo Reps. Their reports on any airplay successes, or the lack thereof, can affect marketing plans such as special contests, advertising, video promotions, retail merchandising programs, Internet and media publicity campaigns. The Marketing department must help coordinate the overall promotion activities for every release the label undertakes. Since airplay is so important to the overall success of a record, the Promo Reps must make sure to keep this department up to date on any relevant happenings at radio.

Promo Reps will also find it necessary to keep in contact with an act's management, especially when one of their bands or artists are out on tour, and playing a show in a city covered by the Rep. They may help arrange visits by a touring band to those radio stations that have been supporting the act's music.

Good Promo Reps have their eyes and ears open for every opportunity to take advantage of the radio airplay they have received. So, almost every department at the label might have to be contacted if there's something those departments can do to help keep the Promotion campaign running smoothly.

The Promo Rep: Fine Tuning the Pitch for Airplay

The Promo Rep has to know everything I described earlier about the business of radio. Before Reps call on a station seeking airplay, they must have a song that meets the needs of a station, but Reps must give the radio station other assurances too, based on the answers to such questions as:

- Are any other similarly formatted stations playing the record locally or nationally?
- Has any "call-out research" been done by the label to suggest that music fans might like the song? (Many stations do their own testing in addition to the label's own tests, to determine the likelihood that the listening public will enjoy the song.)
- Have there been favorable reviews in the music press?
- Is there a buzz on the band or artist as a result of their live performances?
- Are the early sales favorable to the record?
- What are the downloadable song sales currently, and the results of streaming the songs?
- Has the label by-passed radio to go straight to MTV, VHI, or BET with a video? The results?
- Has there been any dance club response to the record? What were the results?

In many cases, Reps will approach certain radio stations across the country known as risk-takers or leaders in their particular format. If a Rep can secure airplay for a song on these influential stations, it's quite common for the more conservative stations to add the song to their playlist. This copy-cat syndrome has resulted in many a hit record. So, any label wishing to break a new record nationally should research the leader stations most likely to play their genre of music and concentrate their promotional efforts on those stations. This is where the services of the Indie Promoter can come in quite handy—if the label is well funded and has established a relationship with an influential Indie Promoter.

When Promo Reps have gotten a song added to enough stations, they switch their efforts to getting the song played *more often*. This is important. Because if other, more resistant stations see substantial increased airplay, they may get interested in adding the song to *their* playlists. This obviously gives the Reps more ammunition to work with when they call back stations who have yet to add the record.

Once a station has added a song, they expect a reaction from listeners. Reps are well aware of this and check with their stations to see if listener requests have been coming in for the song. If a station gets consistent requests for a song, both the stations' MD and PD, as well as the label Rep will take a deep breath knowing that their decision was right on target.

If a station asks for a favor of any kind—an exclusive interview with the artist, a few free tickets to a show, a record from the label's past catalog of releases—the Rep better not let the station down. Whenever possible, any favors offered by the Rep or requested by the station must be fulfilled. The MD or PD you disappoint can hurt you more than you know.

The music business is built on relationships. People make things happen in this business. Building and then maintaining relationships within the industry should be the primary goal of anyone who wants to have a long career in the music industry.

Because so many new records arrive at radio stations every day, MDs and PDs spend hours each week auditioning the CDs and music files they feel are most appropriate for their music format. With so many records looking for airplay, the reality is that only a handful can be played at any station. The Promo Rep must prepare his pitch to the station with this in mind.

Good Promo Reps go over a lot of information when they prepare their pitches for the MDs. Before making any phone calls they must know all the facts about the artist or band they are soliciting. They also have to know the personality of the MDs and PDs and keep in mind the personalities the stations have developed. Every station has a unique image and that image has to be maintained when the MDs and PDs choose what songs, if any, to add to their playlists. Reps who do their homework can better represent a song to a station because they'll know when a particular song is right for that station.

It also helps to know what records the stations added recently. The Reps can find this reported in the weekly trades and tip sheets. For example, if a station added two alternative rock ballads a week ago, chances are slim they're looking for that sound now. The Rep's record should be compatible with the station's format and fit into the sound that station is trying to project. In short, Promo Reps must know the stations they work with and have a feel for the type of listener their format attracts.

Reps must also know their competition. It can easily be forgotten that your label isn't the only label releasing records every week. When Reps are focused on their own records too much, they may find that a similar sounding record, released around the same time as theirs, beat them to the punch.

Music Directors and Program Directors hear dozens of pitches every week, even every day. Many novice Reps make the mistake of not being prepared for their promotional pitches. Here's a list of things that should be covered in a good initial promotional pitch:

- Updated information on the artist or band's current release and any relevant past achievements; previous album sales, radio and media support, etc.
- Updated information on the station's format, playlist, and ratings.
- Several specific reasons why the song being pitched is right for that station.
- Mention of any special label promotions to involve the stations in. Such as:
  Exclusive station-sponsored live shows
  Special contests or in-station appearances by the act online or in-person
  Co-sponsored events with retailers, music publications, or Internet promotions
  Free promotional items: t-shirts and other clothing with the act's logo, special edition CDs, trinkets, or artist/band novelty items

Methods of Promoting

There are a lot of radio stations across the country and individual Promo Reps may cover dozens of them, depending on the size of their region. The ideal situation would be to meet in-person with every station MD or PD, because an in-person promotional appeal can be far more effective than a phone call. Because that's impossible, phone calls are the main focus of record label radio promotion.

People in the business of promotion live on the phone. I'll spare you the bad jokes about telephones and Promo Reps and pass right on to some tips about the art of using the phone. There's an etiquette involved in this work, rules governing what to do and what not to do when you're calling stations.

The cardinal rule is to call the MD during the designated hours of the specific days these people set aside for label calls. All MDs post the times they take label promotional calls, either on their voice messaging services, or by informing their receptionists of those hours. *CMJ,* the college radio trade magazine, posts the "call hours" of most of their reporting stations in their annual directory, available to subscribers. It's very unprofessional to call a station outside of their call hours. Listening to music is only one of many tasks that MDs and PDs must do every day, and they would get no other work done if they spent their whole time listening to sales pitches from eager Promo Reps.

When it comes to calling during the specified hours, the problem for any label is that dozens of calls from other label Promo Reps are also pouring into the station. Be prepared to hear a lot of busy signals when you begin calling radio stations. When you finally do get through, that well prepared presentation I mentioned earlier will serve you well. Be polite and try to sense if they are very busy and want you to get down to business, or if they're in a more relaxed mood and feel like talking shop.

A newer tactic for getting songs to stations is to e-mail stations advance copies of priority songs as digital downloads. This is a faster and less expensive way for the labels to deliver and then promote a song to a specific music-formatted station.

Tracking

Tracking is the method of keeping a written record of which songs are getting airplay at a station, and how often a station is playing a particular song. Each week, the Promo Rep creates and maintains a list of the new adds they get, as well as a record of any increased airplay or reduced play. Tracking data is essential for the Rep when he discusses prospective airplay with a station's program or music director. Tracking is the only way Promo Reps can keep a log of what each station is doing with the Rep's songs. It's like a weekly report card from every station they've contacted on every record they're working. It lets them know which songs are doing well and which songs are having trouble.

Music Industry Trades and Tip Sheets—Why They're Important

The music industry trade magazines and tip sheets are valuable for both Promo Reps and radio personnel. A key trade such as *Radio and Records* or *Billboard's* tipsheet *Monitor* can give a good picture of a record's national activity. Promo Reps can also see how their record stacks up against the competition. Trades and tipsheets have information on current label promotions, industry news, gossip, reviews, charts, commentary, and advertising.

Radio and Records

Radio and Records is the most respected periodical for radio airplay data. It offers a chart for each of the major radio formats and its listings carry unquestioned credibility. It will be interesting to see over the next few years how much, if any, the purchase of *R&R* by *Billboard's* parent company will affect their decades-old reputation as a reliable and honest trade that reports accurately what radio stations are playing.

Radio stations that report to *Radio and Records* (or *R&R* for short) are the most desirable targets for commercial airplay and are classified according to their ratings strength and market size. Most records begin their progress through the *Radio and Records* chart in the "Significant Action" section. Every song is listed by artist, title, record label, and followed by a series of numbers. The first number lists the total number of stations reporting the song that week, followed by a break-down of total moves—upward moves, downward moves, frozen moves—as well as chart debut information. The final number shows the total number of adds, (stations that have added the song to their play lists) that particular week. Once the record obtains a minimum of reporting stations, it moves into the "New and Active" section. Every week in *R&R* the number of reporting stations is listed, with criteria for movement tied in with the number of stations reporting in a particular format.

When a specific number of *R&R* reporting stations have added the song, it becomes known as a "breaker." Usually at this point the remaining stations *not* playing a song have to consider it seriously. When the song becomes a breaker, it usually debuts on the "Back Page" chart of *R&R* and, depending on the strength of its reports, begins its upward progress on the chart.

Billboard Magazine

Billboard already has a radio tip sheet of its own, *The Billboard Radio Monitor,* which is recognized as a very reliable source of weekly airplay information.

As a music business trade magazine, *Billboard* is the oldest of the trades, over one hundred years old. *Billboard's* retail sales charts are the "gospel" so to speak, and they're determined mainly on the basis of sales action compiled by Neilsen/SoundScan. A record that climbs the *Billboard* charts is more likely to attract the attention of an MD or PD, and that's good for the record label's Sales Reps. *Billboard* has dozens of charts reporting airplay and sales in various categories. The Promo Rep should check all the charts.

CMJ (College Music Journal)

College and alternative radio has its own weekly music trade, the *College Music Journal.* It has a comprehensive listing of new CDs, reviews, and charts, most of which fall outside the musical mainstream. For over twenty years *CMJ* has also been an essential tool for *commercial* radio—they use it to find out which new bands and artists are getting their first airplay on non-commercial college radio. Remember, most new trends in music are avoided by commercial radio at first, but get a chance to find an audience at college radio. *CMJ* is a leader in tracking the new sounds that are coming from the underground, sounds that may find their way to a broader pop audience eventually. I'm especially impressed that CMJ was the *first* music business trade of any kind to make their weekly editions available online by subscription, thereby setting a new standard for fast and accurate feedback on up and coming acts from rock to hip-hop and everything in between.

Tip Sheets

A tip sheet is a weekly publication that covers the music business as it relates to radio airplay. CHR and Rock formats each have their own tip sheets. *Hits,* like *Billboard's Radio Monitor* is a tip sheet that covers several formats and is actually a glossy magazine with slick graphics. *Hits* has changed a lot in the last few years, but it still has a fun and irreverent style. Its information, however, is quite serious. It's loaded with full-page color ads on the priority record releases of the week, all targeted at the MDs and PDs. Those ads have information about how many stations in a certain format are playing the song, how sales are going, and any other updated information that could sway a station that *isn't* playing the record, to do so.

Trades and tip sheets provide valuable information about new music and industry news. Promo reps use these valuable resources as they prepare their weekly strategies.

Communication: The Most Important Link in Record Promotion

I've mentioned the importance of communication several times. Promo Reps who stay in touch with all the players in the promotion game are usually the most successful. Communication is everything in the promotion business. Good Reps always stays in touch with their National or Regional Directors and the VPs of Promotion whenever necessary. They constantly have to relay information about adds, sales, or any problems that have come up.

Thankfully, technology has helped them out a great deal. They may live on the phone, but they're armed with the latest in bluetooth and wifi cell phones and laptop computers, as well as the good ol' fax machine. It used to be easier to hide from your boss when there were only land phones to keep track of you. Not today. If all that isn't enough, company intranets and/or voice mail systems allow a Promo Rep to call a central phone number, punch up an individual code number, and hear a recorded message as well as personalized instructions. Or, more likely, be inundated with instant messages coming at them faster than the speed of light.

Once or twice a week, the VPs of Promotion will organize a conference call, or require Reps to travel to different cities where an airplay crisis is happening, or ask the Promo Reps to fly to the home office on short notice to attend an in-person departmental meeting. With a conference call, the national and regional personnel can speak to the entire staff and receive feedback from everyone at once. Promo Reps can find out what's happening in other parts of the country. Conference calls can be tedious, but they do reinforce the feeling that the Rep is part of a team. That should never be forgotten.

The Promo Rep is a soldier on the front lines of the continuing effort to attain radio airplay. Reps are a record label's direct link to radio; they *are* the record label in the eyes of the broadcast industry.

The way record labels and radio stations conduct their daily business is always changing. The term "broadcasting" has now taken on a new definition with the advent of Digital Satellite Radio (XM and Serius to be exact) along with the thousands of Internet radio stations that bring a wider variety of music to people's ears. But no matter what new kind of radio broadcasting technology is developed, there will always be record labels sending their releases to those stations, and there will always be Promo Reps trying to influence the broadcasters to get that essential airplay exposure for their label's releases.

Getting College, Non-Commercial Radio Airplay

by John Richards, "The Morning Show" Host, 90.3 FM in Seattle, and www.kexp.org

There are so many thoughts on how an artist gets airplay both here at KEXP radio, and radio in general. I can't speak for those other radio stations, but from my experience here at KEXP, at my indie label Loveless, and other music related activities, I can give you some advice that might help cut down on the confusion and help you get your music heard and hopefully played on radio.

The Package:

First you must prepare a package to submit to radio stations. Here's a list of what should be inside (I assume you know to put a return address on the outside).

The CD or Record. The finished product with full artwork is always best. However, if this isn't possible, clearly display the song list, album title, and record label info. Please put it in a jewel case, otherwise it might get lost in the shuffle.

MP3/Sending Music in Digital Form. This has made it *so* much easier for bands to send music. It's also made it *so* much easier for someone who gets hundreds of e-mailed songs to delete them without listening to them. Think about the amount of music that's probably being sent to a DJ, and whether it's realistic for you to think they'll take time to open your e-mail and listen. You also have to consider that they might not be able to play the MP3 directly in most cases, so they have to physically burn the song onto CD to play it. You don't want them doing anything physical, trust me. I think it's great to send music this way, but don't expect direct airplay to come from it.

MySpace. When you send a link to your MySpace page to a DJ so they can listen to your song, it seems like a great and easy way for them to hear your music, and for you to get the word out. I agree; it is! But right now, in my MySpace Inbox, I have at least 400 bands asking me to do that. It's much easier to ignore those messages, even if I don't want to. It's just a question of time, really. So again, use MySpace for that purpose, but don't have unrealistic ideas of the success of this practice. Oh, and don't post bulletin after bulletin on a DJ's or station's site. It really pisses them off. Going in with the attitude, "How can I not piss off a station?" is half the battle.

Radio One-Sheet. The "one-sheet" is designed to outline what you're sending and why it should be listened to. Limit it to one page; multiple pages create desk clutter and most likely won't be read. Avoid cramming the "one-sheet" with too much but do include this essential information:

- A song list
- A list of any songs the FCC wouldn't like, such as those with obscene language.
- "Go To" tracks (three to five of your strongest)
- A few press quotes if you have them. Don't try to be funny; assume that music directors

don't have a sense of humor, because they don't.

- A comparison to other bands but make sure they apply. (Not everyone sounds like Radio-head.) You could also include the "genre" of your music.
- Avoid too much clutter; get to the point and let the music speak to that point.
- Unwrap the CD and fold the one-sheet inside the CD case. Don't ask music directors (MDs) to contact you, assume that you must contact them. Most MDs don't have time to return calls. Call them during their office hours and continue to do so until you reach them. E-mail is great as well. Send one e-mail a week until you've heard from them, and thank them for their time. If they are playing your CD, offer up CDs for giveaway, tickets to your show, or whatever you can offer. They may not have a use for it, but can't hurt to try.

Other Promotional Items. Send other promotional items that will help your chances...but use good judgment. Don't toss in things that spoil or appear unprofessional. I once received a package with a hotdog in it. I happened to be on vacation at the time and when I returned the package smelled so bad I threw it out...CD and all. Plus, what does a hotdog have to do with getting airplay? Don't spend time, or money, or energy on a sweet picture of yourself. Why on earth would you do that? Stations like this one are interested in the music, not your looks. I've seen more bands get caught up on this.

Who Do I Send My Package To?

Research, research, research. Use the Internet to identify appropriate stations. If they play twang, then sending your new rap release is a big waste of time. You can usually find a "play list" or "rotation" section on station websites. Does your music fit? Send your package to the station's music director. If the station has multiple MDs, then send the CD to the main MD and to any other MDs who might play it. If there's just one MD, then send him or her at least one copy of your CD. If you send your package to a station in your hometown, send it to the local show. This is your best chance at airplay as they are usually in need of new music.

Okay I've Sent It, Now What Do I Do?

Follow Up. *Do not* assume that just because you've sent your package, your CD is being played. Wait at least two weeks after you've sent it before you follow up with a phone call. Most music directors have call hours a couple of days each week. You can usually find these hours listed on a station's website, or you can call the station to ask when they are.

Patience and Politeness. Keep trying and once you get through to them, remain polite and to the point. Ask the following questions. If any of the answers are "No," stop asking, and politely tell them to have a nice day.

- Did you receive *so-and-so* CD on *so-and-so* records?
- Were you able to review *so-and-so*?
- Are you going to add *so-and-so* to your rotation?
- Where are you going to add *so-and-so* to your rotation?
- Is there anything else you need?

Most stations have a "Heavy, Medium, and Light" rotation system. If you're put into any of these, it's good news: you're getting airplay. At this point, thank the music director, and let them know you'll be calling back later to see how the record is being received and where it's charting. Continue to follow-up for six to eight weeks, the life of a new release in rotation. Or, if you like, keep an eye on the station website's play list.

Requests. Inform your supporters what station is playing your CD; however, make sure that they don't overload the station with requests or turn bitter towards the station because your music isn't being aired enough. DJs can tell when a band's supporters are overloading them with requests, and this will not win you friends or more airplay. Most stations will play music based on merit and not on requests.

National Promotion

There are several top-notch radio promotion companies that specialize in helping musicians get radio airplay around the country. They generally service 300 to 750 stations for a fee of $500 to thousands of dollars. Promotional mailings to radio stations will cost you money, both for postage and lost CDs. Usually you handle the mailings while they track your release by calling the MD each week to find out where in rotation it is and how many plays it's getting a week. Most of these companies service your CD for six to eight weeks, and can assist with setting up in-studio visits and giveaways. Most will recommend the type of stations to target.

Here are a few of these companies:
> Planetary Group, www.planetarygroup.com
> Spectre, www.spectreradio.com
> Mcgathy, www.mcgathypromotions.com
> Revolver, www.midheaven.com
> AAM, www.aampromo.com
> Fanatic, www.fanaticpromotion.com
> Team Clermont, www.teamclermont.com
> Nice Promotions, www.nicepromo.com
> Pirate! Promotion and Management, www.piratepirate.com

It's not easy to do it yourself: write the music, book gigs, manage the tour, release the CD, and get radio airplay. But once you connect with the right listeners for your music, there are definitely rewards. I hope you now have a better idea of how to approach a radio station and get airplay for your new CD. Good luck!

The Promotion Game: A Day by Day Summary

The players in the Promotion game have a lot of different tasks to juggle throughout the week. Record label Promo Reps are talking to the Music Directors and Program Directors at radio stations, communicating with their label's other departments, preparing reports, and tracking song movements up or down on the charts as they work to get adds to radio station playlists. The MDs at radio stations are busy taking calls and responding to e-mails and instant messages from the label Reps, meeting with their PDs, and preparing their playlists to submit to the music industry trades and tip sheets. The trades and tip sheets have to compile all the information they receive from the thousands of radio stations each week.

With all this in mind, here's a daily summary of how the game of radio promotion is played. Some of these routines and daily tasks have been made easier thanks to computers, fast Internet connections, e-mail, and faxes. But, anyone wanting to play this game themselves should pay attention to the way things are set up. I suggest you learn the rules before you attempt to promote your music with ideas of your own.

For starters, a week in the life of a Promo Rep doesn't start with a clean slate on Monday morning. In many ways, Wednesdays have more in common with our notion of the start of a new work week.

Monday

Promo Reps will spend hours on the phone calling or e-mailing radio stations they had previous contact with, to remind them that when the MDs put together their playlists on Tuesday, they hope they'll decide to add their new song. If the song has already been added and the station is playing it, perhaps the MDs could increase the airplay and move it from a lighter number of spins to a heavier number of plays.

Good Promo Reps are armed with tons of information when they make these Monday appeals for airplay. They'll refer to favorable updated radio and sales chart data to when they talk to the MD. The purpose of all this work is to make the stations feel like the song is going to be a hit, or already is, but just needs continued airplay to become an even bigger hit.

By the way, when a new record is being promoted, and a station has not decided to add the song yet, the Rep can use the contacts they have at the stations to at least get some kind of commitment from the MD. If they haven't even listened to the song yet, this could be a good time to ask for that favor. These days the Reps will also mention any increase in legal downloads or reports from increased Internet streaming sites.

Music Directors may or may not let a Rep know their decisions on adding a song or increasing the rotation of the song. It depends on that station's policy, and even on the individual MDs personality. At any rate, throughout Monday, if any significant news should come down about a station's acceptance of a new song or increased airplay of it, the Rep will also stay in contact with his superiors at the label to inform them of any important station feedback. Mondays are really the last chance a Rep has to make a pitch to the stations before they report to the music industry trades the next day. When they've done all they can do for that day, they just have to wait a little while to see if their efforts paid off.

Tuesday

This is the day most radio stations either fax or e-mail their playlists to the music trade magazines and tip sheets. The reports include each station's new song adds, plus any increase in the number of spins of the song. The trades and tip sheets collect all the station reports that come in. It takes a couple of days to prepare a new edition of their publications, and they're on a tight schedule to meet print deadlines. The magazines must be published and in the mail to arrive on the desk of industry subscribers by Monday of the next week. However, several trades, *CMJ* being the first in the late '90s, and all others today, use electronic editions posted on the Internet by Thursday. Reps have a chance to get the results of their promotional efforts a few days earlier than their competition this way.

There isn't much for a Promo Rep to do with the stations on Tuesday, so they prepare for their new and next attack on radio. By the way, they may be in label department meetings on Monday to discuss with other departments what's on the plate promotionally that week and these Monday meetings may lap over into Tuesday.

Tuesdays are the best day for planning new strategies in general, or to arrange for any personal visits to priority radio stations, so making travel arrangements might also be on their Tuesday agenda.

Wednesday

From an organizational point of view, Wednesday is the Rep's Monday. By that I mean the Rep can use this day to plan out new sales pitches for upcoming calls and e-mails to MDs. Any playlist information in the print edition of the trades and tipsheets should now be in their hands.

Promo Reps have to scrutinize all the relevant playlists and take note (track) the addition of their new songs or movement of their songs on the individual station playlists, as well as on the national radio charts. In *Radio and Records,* for example, you'll see pages of playlists printed in very tiny type in the back of the magazine. Promo Reps compile all the information on the dozens of stations under their responsibility. It's time consuming, but it's an essential job that can't be overlooked. If a station actually adds a song or increases its rotation and the Promo Rep misses that action, the repercussions could be devastating to the whole promotion campaign.

Wednesday is also the day to send out any new records, or re-service any station that claims they didn't receive a record the first time the Rep sent it to them. Any special record promotions discussed in department meetings could also be pursued today.

Occasionally a Promo Rep may have to talk with an artist's manager about the success or failure of a client's song at radio. This may happen any day, but Wednesdays might have more time for such work.

All jobs have paperwork, and radio promotion is no different. Time on Wednesday could be used for filling out any required written promotion reports or other required paperwork that needs to be e-mailed or sent to their superiors at the label.

Thursday

On Thursday, phone calls or more e-mails may be used to thank the stations for their recent adds or increased airplay may the priority of the day. Many stations also set aside Thursday for Promo Rep visits. It's a good opportunity to play new records for programmers or take a key PD or MD out to lunch, or even bring a pizza by on their station visit.

The initial pitch for the week's new releases will probably be made today. Armed with the marketing plans from the label, the Reps spend their day communicating with dozens of MDs and even PDs trying to convince them yet again, that a new song they just released is just perfect for their format.

A reminder: most commercial radio stations, as well as college stations, have only certain hours on certain days of the week when they will take calls from Promo Reps. So, getting through at those times and on those days can be frustrating, as dozens of other Promo Reps are calling at the same time. It's essential for a Promo Rep to honor the posted hours for label phone calls. Calling outside those hours would hurt a promotion campaign more than help it.

Remembering my comments about the changing face of Independent Radio Promoters, many commercial stations today cannot talk to any Reps if their station ownership has signed a contract with a particular Independent Promotion company.

Thursdays are traditionally a day for Reps to contact stations, but how many stations may actually be able to talk to you is another issue. In the radio promotion business, you do what you can, then move on.

Friday

This day can be called clean-up day. Whatever didn't get finished earlier in the week can be dealt with on Fridays. This can mean more phone calls, station visits, meetings with label superiors, or just catching up on paperwork. Many Reps find that Friday is a good day to visit music retail accounts. Record stores post the playlists of popular radio stations as a service to customers. An important part of the Promo Reps' job is to browse the aisles, looking for any displays or special in-store merchandising of their artists and bands. Remember, the sole purpose of securing airplay is to expose record buyers to new music, so if the Rep gets airplay in a particular market, but retail sales are poor, something is wrong. The Rep needs to be on top of this and help find a remedy for the low sales. Low retail sales would be a topic for the weekly label department meeting.

The Weekend

When a record label's act comes to a city for a live show, weekend or no weekend, a Rep will probably have to meet the act and help with pre-arranged publicity or marketing events. This could entail driving them to radio stations for interviews, or taking them to meet a local newspaper reviewer, or helping set up a record store autograph party. Reps from the label's Sales department may be more involved with such promotions, but for the sake of goodwill with the act, if nothing else, the Promo Rep's presence at those events is quite important. The actual concert could also be on their weekend agenda.

Bands and solo artists are on tour constantly, and weekends are not the only day of the week when the normal routines of the Rep could be affected. But, major acts and the priority artists usually play their concerts on the weekend.

So, you want to be a Promo Rep? If so, you'll be a very busy individual.

Promotion Front Questions
for Radio Stations

- What is the specific format of the station?
- What is the signal coverage area of the station?
- Who is the regular contact at the station—the Music Director or Program Director?
- Who makes the final decisions about adding songs into the station's rotation?
- What are the specific days and times of day that MDs or PDs take record label calls?
- Is the station "consulted" or are all programming decisions made by the station?
- How does the station decide on what to put into rotation?
- Does the station have the reputation for breaking new artists or bands?
- Does the station notice any new music trends developing?
- How many copies of the CD does the station need?
- What specific trade publications and charts do they report to?
- Which retail stores do they track sales of?
- Is the station aware of any new local or regional artists or bands?
- Is the station involved in any on-going music focus groups?
- Has the station been involved in any co-promotions with stores?
- What specific kinds of station/store co-promotions have been most effective?
- Does the station subscribe to BDS (Broadcast Data Systems), and/or SoundScan data?
- How well is the station doing in the Arbitron ratings for their area?
- How well is the station doing in the ratings against competing stations?
- What kinds of label or station promotions have been most successful for the station?
- Does the station give airtime to artist or band interviews?
- Does the station air live concerts?
- Will the station consider hosting a live performance by an artist or band?
- Does the station have a presence on the Internet with its own website?
- Does the station stream its programming on the Internet, and will it stream any live broadcasts it has recorded of your band?

The Third Front

Publicity

Publicity: The Third Front

Creating a Buzz in the Media

Let's be clear about the Publicity Front. Publicity is the job of getting the print and broadcast media to talk about your music by printing or broadcasting a story, an interview, or a review of your music.

There's good news and bad news about getting publicity. The good news is that there are literally thousands of print publications that cover music exclusively or as part of their service to their readers and listeners. The bad news is that everybody and their sister and their sister's dog are trying to get their CDs reviewed, their band interviewed, and their concerts listed.

It's a lot of work to put together an effective campaign to convince the print and broadcast press to review your release, and interview you about your music. If you're prepared with professionally designed, image-focused press kit materials (bios, fact sheets, cover letters, photos, press clippings and/or press quote sheets), you'll be ready to get the attention of the many magazines, newspapers, fanzines, and e-zines that cover music entertainment. In addition, with these same materials and your databases of media connections updated and ready to be used, you can take a shot at getting some broadcast media exposure for yourself and your music. You'll need to learn how to write effective press and promotional materials that will stand out from the mountain of press materials these people receive every day. And you'll have to learn the best way to work with these media people.

Your publicity ideas must concentrate on proving to the media gatekeepers that your music is worthy of mention in their media. There lies the rub. No media outlet can give you their support unless you can prove, (as you had to prove to the buyers at distributors, the buyers at retail stores, and the music directors at radio stations) *why* they should do a review, story, or interview about your music.

Publicity by itself doesn't sell many records. But, as any professional publicist will tell you, a consistent presence in the media helps support the overall marketing campaign for a recording, and indirectly affects the overall support generated by all your other Front activities.

The Internet has helped tremendously to help create a buzz for an act. With such sites as www.myspace.com it's easier than ever for a buzz to be created. If you've spent any time on that site, you already know how powerful it can be and how much fun it is to tell friends about a new artist or band you've discovered. No matter what stage you're in as a musician, MySpace is a must for free publicity!

Kits, Kits, and More Kits

Demo kits, promo kits, and press kits. You've probably heard of each of these, and maybe thought they're all the same thing. They're not. Let's set the record straight on each of them.

Demo Kits: Short for "demonstration," a demo kit usually contains three to five songs on a manufactured CD or home-made CDR, plus a cover letter, a bio, and maybe a fact sheet that summarizes key information about who you are and what you've done to promote your music. Demo kits are often sent out indiscriminately by musicians in a misguided attempt to "get signed" by record labels or music publishers. **Demo kits should only be sent out after researching which publishing companies and record labels are appropriate to the genre of music, and actually accept unsolicited (un-asked-for) demo recordings.** Never send them out randomly to a list of companies you found on the Internet.

Promo Kits: Promotion means "radio airplay" in music business lingo. So, a promo kit would be a kit sent to a non-commercial or commercial radio station with the intent to secure some kind of airplay of your music. Some stations have local music programs during the week and offer limited airplay to independent artists and bands. Your promo kit could contain a CDR of three to five songs that are suitable for the station's music format, or your complete CD (with two or three songs highlighted for airplay consideration), a bio, a fact sheet, and a cover letter introducing yourself and saying what type of airplay you're seeking.

Press Kits: A press kit is an informational package about you and your music for the media. Broadcast, Internet, and print media can be targeted with your press kits. Of all the kits, the press kit is probably the most comprehensive. You would NOT want to send a CDR or any demo material to the media. They should only get CDs that are professionally promoted and marketed. Include a bio, a fact sheet, an 8x10 black and white publicity photo, a cover letter, and perhaps a lyric sheet. Also, send them a quote sheet and/or examples of press clippings you've received.

Note: If you're sending a kit to a booking agent or a club, either a demo kit or a press kit will suffice for them. You may want to include a "stage plot" that describes the equipment setup you use for live shows, and/or a list of past live performance venues you've played.

As you can see, demo/promo/press kits have some similar ingredients to them, and in the following pages you'll see a list of things that might be included. But, think of this list as you would think of a toolkit you have in your basement or garage. You don't use every tool each time; only the appropriate ones. Look at the ingredients of a demo/promo/press kit the same way. You want to have many different "tools" in your kits but choose the ones that are appropriate. For example, radio stations get a lot of kits with photos in them. Why? What the heck is a radio station going to do with your photo...put it up to the microphone? Prepare your kits with only those things that will help the person on the receiving end to do their job effectively. If you're not sure what they need, just ask them before sending it.

Ingredients of a Demo/Promo/Press Kit

1. **Attractive, creatively designed folder**

2. **Cover Letter:** A letter of introduction to the person you are sending the kit to.

3. **Bio :** One or two pages long.

    Include:

    Introductory statement

    Summary of current project

    Additional information

    Background of artist/band

    Elaboration of any other key information

    Ending paragraph

4. **Fact Sheet:** One page long! Point out key information on the artist/band from the bio.

5. **Photograph:** 8x10 inch black and white glossy ONLY!

6. **Press Clippings:** Two or three sheets of photocopied reviews.

7. **Quote Sheet:** Six or seven positive quotes from music professionals about your music.

8. **CD/CDR:** Three or four of your best songs.

9. **CD/CDR cover:** Well-designed cover with song titles, artist/band name, copyright and contact information, production credits.

10. **CD/CDR Label:** Well-designed label with song titles and copyright information. Contact information.

11. **Options:** Business card, lyric sheet, itinerary information, equipment list, and brief information about your website and/or myspace.com sites.

Note: Put contact information on every part of the kit!

How to Write a Bio and a Fact Sheet

What is a bio? A bio is a one or two page document describing the musical genre, current activities, and background of a solo artist or band. It's a short story of your professional life as a musician.

What's the Purpose of a Bio?

A bio should get music business "gatekeepers" interested in your music. It should motivate the reader to want to get involved with your music.

Who are the "Gatekeepers" and How Do They Use Bios?

Gatekeepers are influential people in the music business who either directly or indirectly affect or control access to key music business exposure areas.

A&R Reps at record labels and publishing companies use bios to learn about your musical style and background. The bio describes your past and present activities and accomplishments. Reps will use a good bio to help them understand where you are professionally, and see what talents or skills you may need to develop in order for them to consider you for a record or publishing contract.

Program Directors and Music Directors at radio stations use bios to help them decide if your music is appropriate for airplay at their stations. Radio station programmers use your bio to get interesting background information about you for their listeners. Programmers also find background information useful if they need to interview you.

Editors and writers at consumer and trade magazines, newspapers, fanzines and Internet e-zines need to use your bio for information about your music, influences, and experience. They might include this information in the reviews or articles they write about your CDs or live shows. The bio also helps them come up with interesting or provocative questions to ask you during an interview.

Booking agents or club bookers use your bio to get an idea of what other experience you've had playing live. The bio also tells them what your music sounds like, and what kind of success you've had up to that point in your career—in selling your music, getting airplay, or getting print media reviews.

Buyers at record distributors and at retail stores receive distributor one-sheets from record labels that include a short artist's bio summary. These bio summaries help the buyers decide whether or not there are valid business reasons why they should carry the artist or band's CD.

Industry showcase coordinators from national and regional annual music conferences like SXSW and CMJ Marathon will invite solo artists and bands to submit a demo along with a bio. The information you provide in your bio will help them decide if you, as an unsigned artist, are ready for the showcasing opportunity. (Each of these events has its own rules and regulations for submitting demos. These rules should be followed to the letter.)

To review, a bio is simply a document that introduces you to the reader. It's a tool the gatekeepers of the Four Fronts use to evaluate you and your music.

How Do You Decide What Information to Put in the Bio?

A bio can be written in two ways. Either you are interviewed by a publicist, (a person who's job is to conduct the press and public relations aspects of an artist's career), or you take a careful inventory of your professional life and accomplishments and choose facts that might be appealing to a music industry gatekeeper.

One of the most important things to remember about writing a bio is to write it as if *you* were in the professions listed above. In other words, if you write it with the intended reader in mind, with an understanding of what that person's job is like, then your bio will have information that is useful to that gatekeeper. Many artists and bands just throw together a bunch of stuff about how "good" their music is and infer that the music will speak for itself. No doubt about it, the music is the centerpiece. However, that music may not reach the gatekeepers' ears if the artist doesn't write a good bio. The bio will often be the first introduction a gatekeeper receives from an artist. It should speak clearly and directly to their needs.

It can be quite useful to take an inventory of your talents, skills, lyric content, stage presence, and attitudes toward life and the business of music. (See Artist Development: Questions to Ask Youself, page 66.) Band members should take time to sit down and talk about the music they make, what they feel their image is, and how they can best preserve an honest image throughout their career. Being clear about who you are—even recognizing who your influences have been and what you want to say with your music—can make writing the bio an enlightening and useful experience.

Fact Sheet: A Way to Outline the Key Parts of a Bio

Is there a way to outline the topics to cover in a bio? Yes, it's called a "fact sheet," and it can become an easy guideline for writing the bio. It's another promotional tool that can be included in a complete demo or press kit. The fact sheet is simply an 8½ x11 inch sheet of paper that lists essential facts about the artist or band. The following topics should be included in the fact sheet, with the following "fields" filled in with the proper information.

Band or Artist Name:

Musical Style:

Hometown:

Names of Band Members and Instruments Played:

Background Information:

Current Activities and Plans:

The last two sections should include interesting data about any previous successful bands, accomplishments, website hits, awards, education, or recognition that you have received, as well as what is currently going on, and the promotional/marketing plans that are being used.

It's best if these facts are listed in order of importance. Make sure that you list four or five items under each of the last two fields, and make them short bulleted statements such as:

- Released two previous CDs that sold over 1,000 copies each
- Planning tour of the Northwest in the fall of_____.

After you put together the fact sheet, it's easier to begin writing your actual bio. You can take the information from the fact sheet and elaborate on it in the bio. It's important to use words economically. A well-written bio doesn't waste words, and avoids superlatives and cliché language. Use quotes from music industry professionals or zealous fans to describe your music. That is far more effective than saying something about oneself.

Are There Any Simple Instructions for Putting the Bio Together?

Following the instructions listed below is the safest way to go. But let's review some simple but important facts about writing the bio first.

Before you begin, be sure you've taken an inventory of your background, accomplishments, goals, and objectives as a musician. Remember who you're writing for. A&R Reps at record labels, media contacts, booking agents, and management contacts are busy people. They may read dozens of bios every week, so make your bio informative and upbeat. Put in useful comments, descriptions, and quotes that can make them want to listen to your music and help you on your way. Writing your bio with this outline will keep you focused and organized.

- **First Paragraph:** Start with an introductory sentence that clearly states your band/artist name, and defines your specific genre of music. Say where you are from. Perhaps put in a positive quote about your music from a contact you've made in the music business.

- **Second Paragraph:** A reason why the bio has been written should be clearly stated early on. What are you doing at this time? Mention a current activity you're involved with. If you have a new CD coming out, that should be the main topic of the first sentence of the second paragraph. Hints about promotional activities that will be occurring to support the CD are also useful in this paragraph.

- **Third and Fourth Paragraphs:** Introduce the band members. You can include background information about how the group was formed, your past experience, accomplishments, and recognition. If you've developed a plan for your career path, you can write additional paragraphs elaborating on this to demonstrate how your current project is part of a larger career development plan.

- **Ending:** As stated earlier, the bio should not waste words. For a new artist, one page is sufficient. For more experienced artists, a page-and-a-half to two pages should be the maximum. End the bio efficiently; use another quote from a gatekeeper who supports you, or summarize the second paragraph information, reminding the reader of current activities.

Sample Band Bio

This is an example of a Bio for a band. Use the layout and content for inspiration only. Be sure to include similar information on your Fact Sheet.

Prototype Bio

Prototype is a four-piece rockabilly band from Seattle, Washington. The Rockabilly Times called their sound "stripped down to the bone rock 'n' roll." In the summer of 2007, they went on a tour of the West Coast, playing fairs, festivals, and even old hot rod car conventions. They spent that fall and winter recording their first CD *Proto-Mojo* and will release their debut album on September 15th.

The members of **Prototype** will be promoting *Proto-Mojo* with a three-month tour of college campuses shortly after they recover from their first of many record release parties beginning in September. Their debut release is filled with roots-rockin' tunes. "Carry Your Own Backpack, Baby" and "Huffa-Huffa," two live-show crowd pleasers, will be featured on their new CD, along with 9 other songs ripping up as many licks from their rockabilly heroes as possible.

From Jerry Lee Lewis to Eddie Cochran to a new millennium version of the slippin' and slidin' of Carl Perkins, **Prototype** has their own slick way of screechin' and moanin', guaranteeing that you'll be singing their original tunes like you grew up with them.

Each member of the group is a star in his own right. Singer/guitarist Toddboy shakes the kinda guitar rhythms that make even the toughest tavern girl blush, while Kettle pounds his standup snare drum silly, and bass player Rock Whittim holds down the bottom like he was sitting on his granddaddy's '49 Chevy truck to keep it from getting towed. Add to this mixture lead guitarist Wilhelm Maranda's manic adventures in feedback slide guitar, and you get the smokin' sounds of a truly fiendish band.

Prototype's debut album *Proto-Mojo* will fulfill the promise of their live shows, capturing the frenzy of a rockabilly comet headed straight for your living room.

Be sure to visit their website **Prototype.com** to find out about free downloads of some of their songs, and to sign up on their e-mail list for advance notice on band activities. Also, check your favorite record store this fall to pick up your copy of *Proto-Mojo*. And if you aren't in college now, register somewhere on the West Coast this fall so you won't miss the *Proto-Mojo* tour.

For more information contact Prototype at: (206) 123-4567. Write them at: 33 1/3 Revolution Lane, Seattle, WA, 98188 or catch them at www.Prototype.com. And e-mail them too, at Protomojo@Prototype.com.

Sample Fact Sheet

This is an example of a Fact Sheet for a band. Use the layout and content for inspiration only. Be sure to include similar information on your Fact Sheet.

Prototype Fact Sheet

Band/Artist Name: **Prototype**

Musical Style: Alternative Rock. A mix of contemporary rock sounds mixed in with strong Hip Hop and Funk rhythms

Home Base: Seattle, Washington

Band Member Names and Instruments:

Kip Stanford: Lead Vocals
John Tremmer: Lead and Rhythm Guitar
Ron Malcolm: Bass
Judy Winter: Drums

Interesting Facts:

- Currently recording new CD for spring 2007 release
- Previously released CDs, 2002 and 2005
- Sold 10,000 copies of previous releases
- Playing live since 2002 with original members
- Songs are concerned with political and social issues
- Showcased at 2006 CMJ Conference

More Information:

- Appeared on KEXP's "Live Room" in fall of 2006
- Northwest tour of alternative clubs and college campuses planned for summer of 2007
- Alternative press (The Stranger, Seattle Weekly) have reviewed all previous releases favorably
- Interviews and reviews of new release will be solicited to alternative press and radio
- Prototype website, www.Prototype.com, to feature downloadable MP3 files and contests to be announced
- Also check them out at www.myspace.com/prototype

Contact Information:

For more information on the band call or write:
Mez Mezrow
PO Box 3825, Seattle, WA 98199
Email: prototype@someotherband.com
Phone: (206) 889-8888   Fax: (206) 889-8889

Sample Cover Letter

Date

Your Name

Your Address

Name of Contact (Mr. or Ms.)

Name of Publication

Address

Dear Mr./Ms.,

Enclosed you'll find the press kit for *(your name or band name here)*. The *(your city or state)* based *(your genre: rock, jazz, etc.)* band will be releasing their debut CD *"(title of CD)"* on the *(name of your record label)* label on *(date of release)*.

I would appreciate it if you would consider the CD *"(title of CD)"* for review in *(name of the publication)*.

(Your name or band name) will be hosting a record release party for their CD in *(date)*. I will be sending you an invitation for the party shortly. I hope you'll be able to join us in celebrating the debut release of *(your name or band name)'s* CD.

Sample quote, such as: (So and So) of *(some publication)* in *(some city),* reviewed a recent show by saying "*(favorable quote)*." When you get a chance to hear the CD, which I have included in the press kit, I think you'll agree with that comment.

Our website (*www.yourbandnamehere.com*) has samples of their latest songs and a list of upcoming shows.

If you have any questions about the band, please feel free to call me any time. I can be reached at *(your phone number with area code)*. I will be contacting you next week to follow up on this letter.

Thank you for your time.

Sincerely,

(Be sure to sign the letter between "Sincerely" and your printed name.)

Your Name

The Quote Sheet

A quote sheet can be a useful addition to a demo/promo/press kit. It's one sheet of paper, preferably on your letterhead stationary. On it, you simply list positive comments about you or your music from various professionals in the Four Fronts. These quotes give the gatekeepers at stores, distributors, radio, the print media, and live venues an easy-to-read glimpse of what other industry people said about you.

How do you get these quotes? You should ask for comments from some of the following professions:

- Producers or Engineers who recorded your music
- Club and other live-performance bookers
- Writers from various music or entertainment publications
- Music Directors, Program Directors and DJs from radio stations
- Record store managers or clerks
- Other respected musicians

Note: You can ask loyal fans to make a comment, but only use one or two of the best quotes from these people.

After you've compiled the best quotes you could get, choose the best six or seven quotes, type them up and title it something like "What People Are Saying" or "A Few Comments About My Music."

Press Clippings

As your career develops and the reviews of your records and concerts increase, be sure to save as many of them as you can. When you have a dozen or so collected, it's time to organize them for your kit.

Here are a couple of ways to arrange your press clippings.

- If the reviews are small (capsule reviews) of your live shows, or you've received record reviews, cut out and arrange several of them on a sheet of paper in an attractive way, then photocopy them on your letterhead stationary.
- If you've gotten longer reviews, feature stories, or cover stories, then the whole article should be copied. Two or three of these can then be put into your kits. Don't go overboard on these clips. There's nothing more annoying than getting a demo/promo, or press kit filled with a dozen or more long clippings.

Folders and Envelopes

Whenever you have an opportunity to present your promotional materials to a professional in the music business, you should remember two things.

• What type of information does the industry contact need from you to do their job?

• Does the folder or envelope that contains your promotional materials reflect your image in a professional way?

The first impression your music makes is a visual impression. In other words, if the package your music arrives in looks unprofessional, your music may never be listened to.

The gatekeepers in the Four Fronts see hundreds of promotional packages a month, and after years of dealing with these packages, it's very easy to tell what artist or band has their act together professionally—and who doesn't.

You don't need to go overboard in your eagerness to please. The folder (or envelope) can be a thirty-five cent one, with the band or artist's logo used as a sticker on the front of it. The promotional materials inside should be neatly written and laid out.

Different styles of music demand different images. Sometimes package that looks too "slick" can work against you as much as a poorly designed package. You should become familiar with what kind of image is appropriate for your music. For example, what might be an appropriate image for an alternative rock band, or a rap group, might be completely inappropriate for a country act, or a pop artist. Basically, the more mainstream your music is the more professional the packaging of promotional materials should be.

If there's any doubt which promotional materials should be put into your kits, remember to think of it this way. You have a bio, a fact sheet, a photo, press clippings or quote sheets, and a cover letter. In addition to all those items, you may have created a list of song lyrics, a stage plot for your live show presentations, or an equipment list. So, do you use them all?

My tip on what to put into a promotional kit is this: ask the recipient of your kit what they want you to send them. It's as simple as that.

Press Kit Photos

Your official publicity photo is an important and basic item of the promo kit because it's probably the most striking and effective part of it. Your publicity photo has a significant psychological impact on how your music is perceived. Just like the cover of your CD conveys an image of your music, so does the photo you put in your kit.

Initially, photos will be sent to publicity contacts in the print and online media. These people will judge you by your visual image, as will fans and prospective fans when they see the photo in magazines and newspapers. In a business that hinges on image, photography represents image in its most immediate form. Be careful when you select a professional photographer and choose the right photo from the shoot. Remember to choose a photo that will look good reduced down to the size of photos you see in the print media.

Finding a Photographer

The best way to find a photographer is the local grapevine or word-of-mouth. Ask around and contact other bands or their management, entertainment editors, radio station promotion directors, people at record labels or PR firms, and club managers. Make sure the photographer you pick has experience in the music business. Most professional photographers tend to specialize, so hold out for a person accustomed to working with musicians.

Once you've found possible photographers, ask to look at their portfolios. Most portfolios will include widely differing subjects, compositions, and styles, so concentrate on the entertainment work—concert shots, album covers, studio portraits, and shots of parties and other functions. Also, talk to the photographers about their experience. Do they seem to have a feel for your music and appear enthusiastic about the project? Don't be timid about asking for references and a list of previous clients. Contact a few of them and ask how the sessions went.

Location vs. Studio Shots

Location Shots

For outdoor or location shots, the possibilities are virtually endless. Regardless of your musical style make sure you have at least a rough idea of an effective shot before going in. Often, you can use locations to help portray your (the band's) identity (i.e. an abandoned prison, a funky old billboard or storefront, bizarre architecture, a sunny beach, etc.). Always remember however that the photograph you are taking is about YOU, and not the abandoned prison or funky billboard, etc. A great location may distract you from your main purpose, which is to get a great photograph for your press kit.

Don't go for something so arty or weird that you as individuals aren't recognizable; this will just defeat your purpose. Also, think about getting written permission from property owners for location shots (normally this is quite easy, but if you run into trouble, go elsewhere). With abandoned buildings, this may not even be necessary.

When you shoot your photo at a venue/show, think about the following; make certain there's no alcohol or tobacco evident in your publicity photos. Many newspapers and magazines won't touch them otherwise. If banners, placards, and other promotional items show in the photo that's okay, but have the photographer watch out for empty beer cans, overflowing ash-trays, and the like.

Studio Shots

I'm often asked what is the best photo for a press kit, and I always say get a studio shot with a white background. Keep it simple. The advantage of a studio shoot is that the photographer has total control over the environment; virtually unlimited lighting resources along with control over backdrops, props, and special effects. Shooting time in a studio can be expensive, so calculate your budget carefully.

Here are some basic rules for a studio shoot:
- Make sure that everyone arrives a little early or *at least* on time.
- If you have to cancel a session, call the studio as soon as possible; if you simply blow off the appointment you'll be billed for all the time that was booked.
- Bring different outfits to the session. This will save you time and money.
- See that all cans, bottles, and other garbage are put in trash cans. If you leave the studio in a mess, you can bet you'll be billed for cleanup.

Proof-Sheets

If the photographer still uses film, you'll choose your black and white photos from proof sheets. Proof sheets are 8x10 inch photo sheets of all the shots that were taken at the photo shoot in their actual film size, either 35mm, 2 ¼ inch, or 4x5 inch. You choose from these numbered smaller images to order the final enlargements. Generally you'll pick three to five photos and have them blown up to 8 x 10 inch size. Your official photo should always be a black and white, 8x10 inch, glossy photograph.

Digital photographers will show you the digital photos of the shoot for you to choose from.

Publicity Shots

A publicity shot isn't the same as an official publicity photograph. Publicity shots are photos taken at parties, or backstage with luminaries of some kind. Publicity photos should capture your (the band's) personality and image and should say something about you. You don't have much, if any, choice in photographers for publicity shots, but you should at least ask for approval of the photos that are suggested for use by the print media. Let me point out, once more, that you are often judged by your photos—so consider the image you want to convey. Finally, any photos chosen for your press kit should be printed so that they are not be too dark or too light. A professional photographer can usually be trusted to print your photos correctly so that they will reproduce well.

Ownership of Photographs

The Film Roll or Digital File

The question of who owns and keeps the film or the original digital file has caused problems. Here's the rule: Under normal circumstances the photographer keeps the black and white original, unless otherwise negotiated. The photographer will deliver one master print per ordered frame unless more prints are specified per frame.

The Photos

A photographer's work is covered by the same copyright law that protects musical works. In practice, this means that the photographer retains all rights to the photographs except for the rights that you specifically purchase.

When you pay normal photo rates, you're actually leasing the photographic work for specific uses; you're not free to use the photo any way that you wish. Publicity shots are a good example. If you pay a publicity-photo rate, then that's all the photos can be used for. If you later decide to use the same image for a billboard, album cover, your website, or as part of an advertising campaign, you will owe additional fees to the photographer.

It's possible to purchase all rights to an image, but the applied rates are going to be much more expensive (because the photographer is giving up all rights to his artistic work). In the world of music PR, it's usually inadvisable to buy all rights to a black and white shot; it's too expensive and the odds are slim that you'll re-use any of the prints.

Duplication

For black and white photos, send the master file to a mass-duplication house. A mass-photo house can also print your band logo, the contact info, and the credits on the prints. The number of prints you order will vary widely depending on your goals.

How to Write a Music-Related Press Release

When to Write Press Releases
- Concert/show and or tour information.
- Record, publishing, merchandising deal announcements.
- Band personnel changes or additions.
- CD and video release information.
- Promotional events, marketing plans, misc. announcements.
- News about your website.

What the Print, Internet, and Broadcast Media Need
- News or announcements related to their target audience.
- Deadlines met for calendars and event listings.
- Event or information in proximity to their coverage area.

Press Release Layout and Essential Information
- Double space (or 1½ space) all content.
- Center the phrase "For Immediate Release" near top third of page.
- Date the press release is sent out.
- Contact information: the phone, e-mail, and fax numbers of the media contact.
- Print it on your artist/band stationary with full address info.
- 1 to 1½ pages long (unless for major event or project).
- End with the marks ### centered at end of the body.

The Press Release Structure
The Slug Line (Headline)
- Short, but attention getting headline phrase.
- A hint of the purpose or topic to be presented.

The Lead Paragraph
- Include the five W's and the H if needed. Who, What, Where, When, Why, and How.
- Begin with the most important part of the information.
- Who is in the beginning sentence, followed by Where and When.
- Summary of the basic topic and information.

The Body
- Elaborate on the theme or purpose of the press release.
- One thought, one paragraph. Cohesive, single ideas in each paragraph.
- Write information in descending order of importance.
- Keep information factual. Use opinions only in quotes with proper credit.
- Use simple sentences (subject, object, verb) and avoid too much hype.
- Ending option: recap essential information from first paragraph.

Tips for Working with the Press

The job of a music publicist is to create a database of contacts within the entertainment industry, and determine which magazines, newspapers, fanzines, and Internet sites and e-zines are most likely to review a client's record, interview them, or write a feature story.

Publicity, by itself, doesn't sell a lot of records. It's most effective when your name is consistently in front of music fans. That will not happen overnight. You'll probably be your own music publicist in the beginning, and it will take you some time to learn how to work with the press. But, learning some basic facts about music journalists and how they operate is as important as the tips I gave you for working with distributors and radio stations.

Music journalists are a strange breed. In large part, they're a group with a wide, and often fickle, range of inconsistent musical tastes, egos, and attitudes. If you want a local music magazine to write a story about you, or review your record, there are some things to learn about those important gatekeepers. If you want a newspaper entertainment editor to pay attention to your latest release or write a feature story on you, it can be a big help to understand the work habits of these professional journalists.

Here are some important facts about the people who may write a review of your new record.

- There's a hierarchy of influential music writers, and every one of them—from the tiniest local music fanzine editor, to the writers who work for *Rolling Stone* or *Uncut*—all have egos. Even the guy who writes reviews for some start-up dot.com site dedicated to rap and hip-hop cops an attitude. That attitude can either help or hurt you, depending on their likes and dislikes. This goes for music reviewers for any genre of music; rock, blues, folk, jazz, world music, you name it. So research the tastes of your local music writers carefully before you mail out your press kits looking for reviews.

- Never address your press material envelopes generically to any publication, *"Music Critic, Music Sandwich Monthly,"* or whatever. If you do that, most likely your record will be put into a large pile of similarly addressed envelopes, and the lowest ranking writer on the staff of the publication will be assigned to check out your music. If that happens, your music might be listened to and reviewed by someone who hates your kind of music, and uses their review to rant and stomp all over your precious release.

- Always research the music magazines, blogs, newspapers, fanzines and Internet e-zines carefully. Take time to read some of the reviews, articles and feature stories, and take note of who wrote them. When you find a positive review for a record that is close to your genre or style, remember the writer's name and when you do your mailing, address it to that person. When you find a negative review of a record that is close to what your music is like, take note of that writer, and do not send them your record for review.

- Follow-up on every press mailing you send out. Give it a week to ten days, then phone or e-mail the publication asking if they received your record. If you actually make contact, find out if the record has been listened to yet, and if they plan to do something with it. Be polite and professional. Most writers are quite conscientious about responding to publicist's calls or e-mails, but I can assure you that you'll meet your share of characters in the world of music journalists.

- When you leave a phone message or write an e-mail, be very specific in your message. Introduce yourself and state clearly why you are calling or writing them. Leave your contact information too. You'd be surprised how many people don't.

- If you've had trouble getting a response from a publication, watch your attitude. I have seen and heard many messages that start to argue with a reluctant reviewer. That's a sure way to *not* make a new contact, or to lose an established one.

- If you score with a publication and they agree to do a story on you, or interview you, keep any promises you made to get them more information or send another copy of your CD. If you flake out on an appointment or show up late for an interview, you may lose a valuable ally. Writers are busy people, like everyone else in the entertainment industry, and too many artists and bands have an unprofessional attitude when it comes to dealing with writers and editors.

- When a review or article on you comes out and you find things about it that are objectionable to you, watch your temper. No artist gets only glowing reviews. Bad or mediocre reviews are part of the game. Avoid the temptation to write or call back when you are emotionally heated about the story. Publicity is about making and keeping relationships with the press. You never want to get a reputation for being a jerk or a troublemaker. If you do lose your temper, I can assure you your tirade will show up in the next issue of their publication—and no, I'm not one of those people who believes all publicity is good publicity.

Working with the press, finding contacts, making the initial connections, and nurturing the relationships along the way from local and regional to national recognition is a time consuming commitment. But, publicity done well and consistently over time can be a career rewarding experience.

Publicity Front Questions for Magazines, Newspapers, and Internet Publications

- What genre of music does the publication cover?
- Is it a music trade publication or a consumer publication?
- Does the publication come out monthly, weekly, or daily?
- What is the distribution area and the readership of the publication?
- What specific publicity opportunities are available (features, interviews, reviews)?
- What advertising opportunities are available?
- What is the cost of advertising?
- Who is the publisher or editor, and what is his or her background?
- How are decisions made regarding cover stories?
- How far in advance are cover stories and features decided?
- Who are the columnists, reviewers, and writers for the publication?
- What is the reputation of each writer?
- What specific kinds of music does each writer like or dislike?
- Does the publication feature calendar listings for concerts?
- Will they accept press releases by fax or e-mail?
- What are the copy deadlines for each issue?
- Are there any seasonal "special issues" offered during the year?
- Does the publication get involved in any co-promotions? With whom?
- What specific kinds of promotions have worked the best for the publication?
- Does the publication notice any new music trends developing?
- Does the radio station do interviews of artists or bands?
- What other kinds of publicity opportunities are available at the station?
- Does the publication or radio station have a website?
- What Internet publicity opportunities are available?

5

The Fourth Front

Performance

Performance: The Fourth Front

Finding Your Audience

The Performance Front focuses on two important issues: using live shows and touring as a way to build a strong and loyal fanbase, and finding ways to market and sell your music before and after each show.

Many developing acts concentrate too much on trying to get club dates when they first start performing live, instead of doing more non-traditional live shows, such as house parties, school gigs, fairs, and festivals to build a strong and dedicated fanbase. Many developing acts can use non-traditional performance venues as the springboard to the clubs and concert halls of the world.

The performance industry has its own cast of characters: booking agents, concert promoters, and venue operators who all play a role in supporting an artist once they've been convinced that they'll make money when they get involved with the act. I'll introduce you to these characters and give you some tips on how to deal with them.

Record labels have long seen the value of supporting their recording acts by advancing them money to fund a tour. They keep their acts busy in between shows, by scheduling radio and press appearances, and arranging for visits to various music retailers. New artists and bands can set up their own promotional events based on these time-tested industry strategies.

This book is primarily about music marketing, so **I will discuss issues related to the live performance industry, and provide tips to you about working with key contacts, but I'll focus on ways to promote and sell music through live shows.**

Read on for more information about the live performance industry, the gatekeepers who work within it, and using the Performance Front as a marketing tool.

The Business of Live Performance

Live performances of hundreds of acts are being streamed over the Internet these days, or are available at websites in large archives of previously posted live performances.

Offline, playing a live show of any kind is glamorous and exciting. But performers don't realize that when they perform in good, old fashioned clubs and other live venues, they'll be dealing with the owners of these businesses; and these people have a different perspective on music. For traditional live venues, it's a business, a very serious business, fraught with risk and considerable competition.

Most musicians think a club date is the ultimate live gig. Granted, playing the club circuit can be lucrative. But clubs are different from other kinds of live performance venues. In order to attract the attention of the club's booker, ask yourself; what's the criteria to get a gig at this venue? The bottom line for club owners is this; they need to be able to make a living at their profession, and the only way they can do that is to book acts that fill their club. A club makes most of its money from people who buy drinks from the bar, or order food from the kitchen. A club can't book an act that draws flies; it needs an act that draws people in droves.

Artists who want to get booked should be ready to show the club's booker their promotional kit. The promo kit contains a cover letter, a bio, a photo, a selection of press clips, possibly a fact sheet, and of course, a CD (CDR) of your music.

When you send a demo, always put your contact information on the cover of the CDR (as well as every other part of the promo kit). Only three or four of your best songs should be on the demo. The demo you send to a club can be a live recording, unlike studio-produced recordings you send to radio stations. If you send a CD, mark three or four songs that are most appropriate for the venue.

There are many kinds of live venues. Besides clubs, there are:

Bars and Taverns	Conventions	Book Stores
Coffee Houses	Music Conferences Showcases	Record Stores
Festivals	Industry Showcases	House Concerts
Fairs	Non-Profit Charity Organization Shows	Frat and Sorority Gigs
Concert Halls	Association Functions	Shopping Malls
Schools	Street Corners	Restaurants
Churches	Raves	…more?

So, how many more live music venues can you think of? The above is just a partial list, the point is for you to think about all the alternatives you have for playing in front of an audience. If you do well at non-traditional venues, the nightclubs may be more inclined to book you—especially when they know that your shows have been selling out wherever you play.

When dealing with different types of venues other than clubs, keep in mind that many have a business agenda that can determine whether or not your music is appropriate for them. Each venue is out to achieve its mission or goal: to get people to have a good time and spend lots of money, to get them to donate money to some worthy cause, or to get them to take part in some larger event that's being sponsored. Your job is to convince the venue's booker that your music will help them achieve their goal.

Artists who are just beginning to perform live have a tough time getting their first shows. You can't get a gig unless you've gotten other gigs, and you can't get other gigs until you get that first gig. So be it. Everyone has to start somewhere, and many artists who are frustrated by this situation have simply rented a space, gotten a permit, rented a sound system, and put on their own show. At least then they can say they *have* performed live.

It's the job of the bookers to be aware of what new acts are causing a stir in their own backyard. It's also their job to listen to the demos that come in the mail by the dozens every week. This brings up the issue of protocol. Yes, there's an etiquette for all areas of music marketing, and the protocol for dealing with bookers is; mail the promo kit, wait a week to ten days, then call the booker to ask for their response to your kit. Believe it or not, politeness and respect are fairly uncommon virtues in the music business. Be sure not to interrupt meetings. Ask the person if it's a good time for them to talk. *If they request a call back, do so at the time requested.*

Artists and bands who think they're ready for prime time may not be. It's a good idea to have at least two or three hours of prepared material that can be performed live. If you have only half-an-hour or an hour of songs, not many venues will be interested in booking you. Remember, different venues have different needs. Some offer special open-mike nights or showcases for unproven acts. Be sure your set of music meets the needs of the venue.

It's a good policy to not be too picky about what venues to play. The more resistant venues may become friendlier if your act is out in the local scene, and your name is listed on radio station concert and print media calendars. The venue bookers check out their competition. If you're out there playing gigs, the bookers will eventually take notice. That's part of their job.

Once a venue books you, they add you to their schedule and include you in their press releases, calendars, posters, and flyers. This doesn't mean you should leave all the promotion to the venues. On the contrary, you should notify your fans with a mailing notice, print up your own posters and flyers, and promote your shows in any creative way you can think of.

A good habit for a young act is to have a member of the band's team count the ticket stubs collected at the door. This is a fairly common task that assures you of getting a correct count of the number of patrons who came to the show. More established artists who are dealing with booking agents can demand as much as 50% of their performance fee up front, before they perform. Even more established can demand their whole fee before they perform.

Performance Contracts

The music business is very fond of contracts. The record, publishing, merchandising, and management sides of the industry are contract crazy. In the performance arena, there are indeed contracts but in the beginning they're more of the "handshake" or verbal variety. When your act gets more established you can rest assured that the written contract will be around. This doesn't mean that a beginning act shouldn't *try* to get something in writing.

The verbal contract between a club, for example, and an artist may simply be an agreement that the artist will perform on a certain date, at a certain time, for an agreed upon length of time, with another specific act, and how much will be paid. Many venues require some kind of written confirmation of a verbal agreement made over the phone. This is to the advantage of the artist anyway.

Without a doubt, the single most contested area is how the artist will be paid. The act may receive a flat fee or a straight percentage of the door or ticket sales. A flat fee plus a percentage is where the artist receives a guaranteed fee plus a percentage of the door *after* the venue (or concert promoter) reaches a break-even point. Remember, the venue is concerned with making and not losing money, so the break-even point for a show is based on the costs of putting on the performance, which include promotion costs and any "guarantees" that may have been made to the artist for their performance.

Here's the information you'll need to complete a live performance contract:

- Name of Purchaser or Buyer (Name of the club promoter):
- Name of Artist:
- Terms of the Deal: The deal you accepted and the amount of money you'll get paid. Here are the four most common deals you'll encounter:

  Flat or Guarantee - Example: $300 for the performance

  Versus --------------- Example: $300 versus 30% of money collected at the door (Whichever is higher.)

  Plus ------------------ Example: $300 plus 30% door

  Points/Split --------- Example: 50/30/20 of Net
- Date of Event:
- Set Length:
- Deposit (if any):
- Who will pay to whom, how much, and when:
- Admission Fee (Ticket Price):
- Capacity of the Venue:
- Act of Nature (Force Majeure):

  The force majeure (literally "superior force") clause is applied when there's an unexpected event that causes performance of the contract to become impossible; it releases one or both parties from their rights and obligations.
- Cancellation Fees:
- Recording by Permission Only:
- Promotional Commitment: For example: this specifies the minimum amount of money you, the band, expect the club to invest in advertising the show.
- Merchandise: How much the club takes from the gross of merchandise sold.

Booking Agents

You won't need a booking agent to book your local or regional shows. Booking agents (for the most part) are people who make their living by working for established artists and bands who have a steady income from touring regularly. You may be attractive to an agent when your live performance career has grown to where the offers to do shows are coming in rapidly, and the time you need to work on your music is being taken up with booking issues. Once you've accumulated a solid list of accomplishments, it's possible that an agent may even seek you out. When you can prove to an agent that you're a money making act, *then* the agent may be interested in working with you. An agent will (help you) decide which markets to hit on, which tour route to select, which club clubs offers are best. Here are some important points to remember when you consider signing a contract with a booking agent.

Term. The agent often asks for a contract of three or more years; you'll want to keep it to one year. Shorter is better for you, because you can leave if things don't work out, or squeeze the commission down if things do. If you give more than a year, make sure you have the right to get out after each year if you don't earn minimum levels. Note that there's a very good chance you'll never sign any papers at all. This varies with the policy of the agent.

Territory. When you are a new act, it may be difficult to give an agent less than worldwide rights. As you move up the ladder, you can sometimes exclude territories outside the United States. This is often beneficial, because you can use agents in Europe or elsewhere who are skilled in those markets. In fact, many U.S. agents often employ a local subagent for foreign territories and you can thus eliminate the middleman. On the other hand, the U.S. agent doesn't just sit idly by while a subagent does the work. The agent oversees the foreign agent and makes sure the shows are properly promoted, that you get paid on time, etc. (Please note that—at any time and level—you might want to reserve the right to book local shows yourselves.)

Fee. The agent's services are primarily to book concerts and they're only paid for the area where they render services. So never give your agent a piece of your income from records, songwriting, or publishing. Usually agents don't even ask for this, but be careful of union forms. Agents are regulated by unions, such as the American Federation of Musicians and the American Federation of Television and Radio Artists. The maximum these unions allow an agent to charge is 10%. The AFM and AFTRA printed forms have a place for you to initial if the agency commissions your earnings from records. Watch out for this and never agree to it.

Termination. Most performance contracts have a clause saying you can terminate if the agent doesn't get you work for ninety days.

Roster. You want to make sure that the bands on the agent's roster play the same type of music you do. This will help ensure that the agent will book you into clubs that are appropriate for your music and you'll be saved the embarrassment of performing in a venue that's wrong for you.

Also, make sure that the agent doesn't have too many bands on his roster. If there are more than six to eight bands on your agent's roster, your band probably won't get enough attention.

Personality. An agent should be genuinely enthusiastic about you and your music. An agent should be a persistent person who fights for his clients. Remember, you don't necessarily have to like your agent's personality! Check out www.pollstar.com or the *Recording Industry Source Book* to research more agents.

Some Do's and Don'ts for Dealing with Booking Issues

Do's:
- Research the venues you think are appropriate for your music. Read the local music papers and magazines and check out the venues in person.
- Talk and network with other artists who have a similar style and ask where they've played.
- Put together eye-catching and creatively designed press kits. Always make sure that your contact number is on your CDs and CDRs.
- It can be tedious to do the mailings and make the follow-up phone calls. If you've got more than one person in your group willing to help with booking, split up the work.
- Write a general cover letter to include with your press kit that answers some additional questions a booking agent will want to know: your *style* of music, what your draw is and whether you're looking for an opening spot or a headlining spot, what kind of guarantee or terms you're willing to accept, and most importantly what *you* will do to help promote your show. Will you send out mailers to your mailing list, put up posters, handbills, buy any media print ads, update your website?
- Send press kits out well in advance. Most venues want two to three weeks to review your music before they'll even talk about booking you.
- Always plan your bookings well in advance. Booking agents usually have their calendars full by the fifteenth for the upcoming month. Also, touring acts will put "holds" on club calendars for two to three months in advance.
- When doing follow-up calls always have your calendar in front of you. Most of the time, you'll be leaving messages on answering machines. Make notes of your phone calls and messages. When leaving messages be friendly and brief. These guys get hundreds of calls per week. State specifically what you're looking for.
- Know that the bookers will be calling you only if you bring in crowds and the venue makes lots of money selling booze and other refreshments.
- Calling a venue back *once every two weeks* is plenty to show them your interest and professionalism.
- After you get a verbal offer for a gig, write a letter to the venue (or fill out a contract) summarizing the details.
- Start planning your own promotions early. Get flyers and posters in the venue and distributed around town a couple of weeks before the show.
- Use your database the week before your show and call to remind your fans. Be sure to use

the Internet to promote your shows and send e-mail reminders to people on your e-mail list.
- Network. Find bands who are compatible with your music and trade shows with them.
- Be patient about getting the hot gigs. It takes time to get those headline gigs on Saturday night. You'll usually start out with a weeknight gig and work your way up to the headliner position *if* you draw large crowds.
- Spread out slowly to other areas around your hometown. Then define your region and work that circuit.
- Remember the venue's priorities—to get a lot of people into their venue so they'll make lots of money selling alcohol and food.
- Send a thank you to the bookers after your first show and all significant shows thereafter.

Don'ts:
- Don't overbook yourself in the same area and spread your audience too thin. Move around. Three or four shows a month in one city are plenty when you're getting started.
- Don't burn any bridges. You may encounter some conniving people in this business, but watch out what you say about anyone. It could come back to haunt you.
- Don't give up. If your music is as good as you claim it is, and your audience continues to grow, that's the best news you can give any booker.

Selling Your Music at Live Shows

A record label's sole purpose in supporting an artist's tour is the strong possibility that sales of the artist's records will increase as a result of the tour. For the independent musician then, the rule for live shows is this; never perform live without setting up a way to sell your CDs.

Selling your CDs is the ultimate goal of music marketing. All the activities that have been discussed—all the planning and coordination that a label puts into marketing a record—have the sale of CDs as their ultimate goal. Live performance sales can provide you with the largest percentage of profit, per unit sold, than any other method of distribution or sales. Make the most of this opportunity, and never even think about doing a live show without mentioning to the crowd that your music is for sale at the venue.

The income you receive from your live show sales can help pay for expenses you have on the road. In many cases the amount of money you receive from sales of your CDs at live shows will be much higher than the performance fees you receive.

Most live venues allow performers to sell their music releases. Some may ask for a percentage of sales (from 10–30%), but smaller size venues just let musicians sell their merchandise without taking any percentage. So, sell your CDs and any other paraphernalia you have, like t-shirts, caps, and other clothing with your logo on them.

Be sure to have a mailing list available for your fans to sign. This is really Marketing 101 when it comes to taking advantage of a fan's enthusiasm. There's no better time to catch the emotional high of a music fan than at a live performance. It's also a good idea for every member of a group to spend some time hanging out at the sales table. Fans like to have autographs and what better opportunity to offer this gift than when you have them waiting around to buy your music.

Keep accurate records of each transaction. If you have a laptop computer, create a spreadsheet to keep track of your music product. If not, get a receipt book and write up each sale separately. Remember, you're making money from each sale and, like every other tax-paying citizen, you need to report your income from sales to the relevant local, state, or federal agencies.

I've had many discussions with musicians about live-sales opportunities but one incident stands out. A client arrived in a city where a major chain-store had put up a beautiful display of the artist's latest CD and went all out to welcome the artist to the in-store autograph party. Later that evening my client called to update me on the event and said something like this: "The record store was so nice to me that I've decided not to sell my CDs at tonight's concert. I'm just asking everyone to go to their store after the show." I was speechless and said, after a long pause, "Why did you hire me? Didn't I tell you that the cardinal rule for live performances is to sell your CDs at every show? What I want you to do tonight is this. At some point in the show, stop and thank the record store for their support and then tell everyone that at the intermission your CDs are for sale in the lobby."

The next morning I was waiting for my client in a hotel lobby when I saw her approach. She said "Chris, put out your arms." I did. She gave me a big hug and said, "I sold a ton of CDs last night, and actually made more money from those sales than I did from the fee they paid me." I rest my case.

The business of live music is a world unto itself. This is a basic introduction. For an independent artist or label, marketing means taking advantage of any and all opportunities to reach potential fans. Live performance is a very special chance for recording artists to interact directly with their customers.

Have you heard about one of the newest and most attractive live performance sources of income? The technology is now available for you to arrange to record your live show: as people arrive for your concert, they are asked if they'd like to buy a CD of *that night's show* at the end of the concert.

That's right, do this…go to www.discmakers.com and check out how affordable CD duplicating equipment has become. It's more affordable than ever to record, and then rapidly duplicate your live show so you can sell it on the spot to your fans. Do it!

Have You Ever Played a House Concert?

What? You answered "No," or "What's a house concert?" Well, I'm going to give you some information that will change your life as a musician. I've already said how hard it is to get booked in a traditional live music venue, so the idea of doing house concerts is twofold; first of all it gets you out and about in your community (and beyond) so people can hear and see you perform, and secondly it gives you a huge marketing opportunity to sell your CDs and other merchandise.

So, here's some vital information about the wonderful world of doing house concerts. All you need to get started is a place to play, and people to attend.

Where Do You Find a Place to Play Your House Concert?

Ask your friends, your family, and of course, your growing list of fans. That's one of the reasons you got their e-mail addresses, you know, so you could get them involved in helping you grow your career. What better place to start playing gigs than a fan's home, garage, or basement? Just ask them if you could hold a concert at their place.

Obviously they'll need to have a space for you to setup a most stage area, and they will need to think about how your audience will be seated. This isn't rocket science, I'm sure you can find a simple solution for seating.

In most cases a living room big enough for fifteen to twenty-five people will suffice. Also you'll need some basic live sound equipment and lighting, which can all be done with you and your host's imagination.

As with any show be sure to have the lights focused on *you,* but make the ambience around your audience mellow, or exciting, depending on your genre of music.

Do make sure the acoustics are adequate. You can easily check this out on a test run, by going to your host's space and doing a sound check. As a musician you should know if the space has good acoustics and the sound isn't bouncing all around.

Another tip from attending many house concerts; make sure by showtime that domestic pets are put in another space, and that babies or loud kids are entertained elsewhere. This is a professional show, and you want the right feel for your performance without disturbances.

Since this gig is more than just for the fun of it, you have to prepare for the business side of the concert and have a table or space set aside where you can sell your CDs and other merchandise.

You can ask a friend or the host if they could watch the table before, during, and after your show. This table must have room for people to sign up on your e-mail list. That's a must. You don't want to miss a chance to get that precious information.

If you're worried that no one will come to see your house concert, remember this fact; when you get a friend or fan to host a show at their home or yard or wherever, they're the ones who are going to get their friends to come to the show. Half the battle of filling up the venue is going to be done by the host. That's right. When you ask a fan or friend to host a show of yours in their home, they'll be so honored to have been asked that they'll spread the word like a professional publicist would for a club gig. They'll call or e-mail all their friends who they think would enjoy your music, and you only need twenty to twenty-five people to start.

What You Should Charge

This will vary. Some artists and bands charge nothing at first, seeing the show as a promotional opportunity. Others charge very little, like $5, while others charge $15 or even $20 or more. It really depends on how popular you are now, and how popular you become as your career advances. Since you're really putting on a private performance, you probably don't want to mention the cost as a "ticket price." Make it more casual. Ask your host to say that the cost is voluntary, but a musician donation of such-and-such would be appreciated. Also don't settle up with any money owed during an intermission. Wait until the show is over and people have gone home before counting money from donations and sales of CDs or merchandise.

Where to Play Next?

When you're starting out I always recommend that you look at expanding your geographic marketing and touring areas like this. Imagine a pool of water, and you drop a small stone into the pool. What happens? The stone creates ripples in the pool of water. See your expanding marketing and touring area like the ripples in the pool.

You'll only expand your marketing and touring when it's wise to do so.

One of the great things about doing house concerts is this; the guests who come to see you perform will be your base to expand into other neighborhoods and regions. Here's what happens; after your show people will come up to you and talk about how much they liked your music. Then, they'll either ask if they can host a house concert in their place, or you can ask an enthusiastic fan to host a show in their home. And on and on it goes!

Should You Have a Contract?

I suggest that in the beginning you just do a handshake deal. As you get more popular and start getting more offers for house concerts, you might write up a simple agreement based on what issues have been discussed here. One thing though, always try to convince your host to get reservations. That way the invitation is a real RSVP and you can base how many CDs to bring and how much merchandise to plan on selling.

Note: You want to make sure you post any upcoming house concerts on your website, just as you would any other kind of gig. But be sure to give your host's contact info and state that if anyone wants to go to your house concert they must check with your host first.

Here are some tips on preparing your house concert. Please remember that the tasks involved are your responsibility in cooperation with the host of your concert.

Six weeks or more before your show
You show is booked. Host agreement has been made.
Update your media database, including any Internet sites, i.e. www.craigslist.com

Four weeks before
Mail postcards and/or e-mail announcements to your fans.

Three weeks before
If show is open to the public, notify local newspapers. Be sure to check the calendar listing deadlines. Put up posters/flyers.

Two weeks before
Notify local and Internet radio of your show's date and time, if show is open to public.

One week before
Send out directions to house concert location.

Two to three days before
Verify everything's OK with host.
Purchase refreshments for your show, per agreement with your host.
Send a last reminder to local radio, friends and family, post to your website, if show is open to the public.
Check equipment needs (lights, monitors, etc.)

Day before
Make sure host is updated on all preparation needs.

Day of show!
Rearrange furniture and set up concert seating.
Put out refreshments. (Bring a friend to help with day of show tasks.)
Set up your merchandise table and have a mailing list signup sheet.
Make sure parking arrangements are set up with host's cooperation.
Set up the stage the way you want it for your performance.
Set up your merchandise table with a clipboard for people to sign your mailing list.
Select appropriate background music, compatible to your style. Keep the volume low and remember to turn it off before the show starts.

One-half hour before show—Guests should begin arriving. Refreshments should be ready. If possible, delegate a helper for this task.
Make sure your host understands the **set times** you'll be doing.

Five minutes before show—Tell your host and helper you'll be starting in five minutes. People often start a few minutes late just because that's acceptable; try not to go more than **15 minutes** late or people get restless.

Make sure everyone has a seat. Turn down the background music.

Show begins—Make sure everyone has a seat. Turn down the background music. Walk on-stage, introduce yourself, and welcome people. Thank them for coming; say whatever else seems appropriate. Keep it short. Say you're got a great show tonight and thank them for coming. Then introduce your first song. Just keep everything simple.

Late arrivals; have your helper stationed where they can be welcomed and shown to a seat. Have a few empty chairs open in back for them.

Have your helper count the number of guests after everyone's arrived.

Note the time your show started; mentally calculate when it should end, and keep your eye on the clock. Wear a watch if you need to. Estimate five minutes per song, on average. If you're running long, leave out one song and go to your last tune.

If you have an intermission; say something like, "We're going to take a 10 (or 15) minute break." (Make sure everyone knows where the bathrooms are.)

Be sure to mention that during the intermission your helper has your CDs and other merchandise for sale.

After intermission is a good time to announce your upcoming schedule and encourage your guests to spread the word.

Then just intro your next set and start playing. Note your start time and keep track of the time, leaving time for possible encores.

At the end of the show—Thank everyone for coming. Remind them once more about the mailing lists and CDs and your next show; ask them to help pick up around their chairs so cleanup is easier. Tell them house concerts are fun to give and you're available if they want to know more about hosting one. **Don't forget to thank your helpers *and* your host.**

After the show—There will be schmooze time. Bring up your background music (at low volume) after a few minutes.

You're done, for now. A house concert is a lot of work, but the payoff is in meeting new fans and getting *more* house concerts from the people who saw you there. This can be the beginning of a great alternative way to play live and make money with your music.

Sample Band Tour and Work Schedule

Most aspiring recording artists have a somewhat romantic idea about going out on tour. After watching tightly edited versions of band tours on MTV, few developing artists understand the everyday life of a band on the road. When a tour is financed by a record label, there's more to it than just showing up for sound-checks in every city. The labels put their bands to work.

The following fake tour schedule is based on a three-week tour schedule by a nationally known, major label, alternative rock act. When you get to the daily work schedule, remember that going out on tour is hard work. Press interviews at every tour stop. In-store visits, "meet and greet" schmooze events, then the soundchecks. The endless routine of checking in and out of hotels, and driving, lots of driving. Think about what kind of food you'll be eating, what kind of industry people you must deal with. You'll have to set aside time to meet with fans, sell your merchandise, sign autographs, get your mailing lists ready for people to sign. Then, it's show-time. And you'd better be *on*, because in every city your fans have been waiting to see you. They've spent a lot of money to come to your show, and they expect you to be at your best, every night, week in and week out.

Remember, this is only *one,* three-week tour. If you look closely, you'll notice that early on many details show what the band will be doing hour-by-hour. As the schedule continues, fewer details of the band's activities are listed. This is common, because depending on the success of the marketing plan, there may not be that much interest in a fairly new band in every city of the tour. Labels leave the schedule open and plug in new promotional opportunities as they develop. If the record is a hit, the band will go out for many more weeks and months and repeat the daily work routines. The band's management company will stay in close contact with the label, and alert the band for any new tour dates or other new marketing arrangements. Now you know why that classic Mott The Hoople song said, "It's a mighty long way down rock 'n' roll."

Prototype Band Tour Overview/Highlights

Dates	City	Promotional Activities	Venue
june 1	detroit, mi	CXOX / 92X radio show	@ phoenix plaza amphitheatre
june 2	cleveland, oh	WTXM / xstream radio show	@ qtip city amphitheatre
june 3	state college, pa		crowbar
june 4	lancaster, pa		chameleon
june 5	off		
june 6	old bridge, nj		birch hill
june 7	philadelphia, pa	WYPL / new 100 radio show	@ tweeter center-watefront
june 8	norfolk, va	WWWR / (wantcom-wireless amphitheatre) – the boat - new venue	
june 9	boston, ma	WBCOO / wboo radio show	@ cmgi field
june 10	new york, ny	press	
june 11	clifton park, ny		northern lights
june 12	new york, ny	press	
june 13	new york, ny	press	

june 14	new york, ny	tape mtv2 "rock show"	
june 15	off		
june 16	off		
june 17	off		
june 18	detroit, mi	in store performance at qtip birmingham	
june 19	chicago, il	in store performance at qtip schaumberg	
june 20	cleveland, oh	in store performace at fye in mentor	
june 21	off / travel		
june 22	seattle, wa	KDDN / alternative rock	@ gorge amphitheatre

Daily work schedule: The details
sat, 6.01

detroit, mi	92X radio show	@ phoenix plaza amphitheatre
promoter:	clear channel	cap / ticket: 6500 / all ages
1 pm:	station will do live interview at the venue and a meet and greet for radio winners	
press:	the news herald is a detroit paper - wants interview with steve at the venue	
	feature to run in the real detroit (weekly newspaper)	
	feature to run in the oakland press (detroit suburban daily newspaper)	
	feature to run in the real detroit paper to promote the in-store and new release	
sheets:	liberty hotel, 1245 w. levin st., detroit, mi.	
wheels:	aftershow travel to cleveland	
other acts:	the dives, slimm, pasttie, simpletomes	
guest list:	check local press contacts, and retail contacts	
1:00pm	load in	
3:00pm	doors	
6:30pm	in person interview with the news-herald- at the venue	
7:00pm	in person interview with 92x at the venue	
9:15pm	prototype on stage	
after show	meet and greet with station winners	

sun, 6. 02

cleveland, oh	WTXM xtreme radio show	@ qtip city amphitheatre
promoter:	clear channel	cap / ticket: 6000
radio:	this is the 89.3 xfest- xtreme wants a live on air interview from the venue	
press:	none	
sheets:	holiday inn, 68597 n. columbia, cleveland, oh.	
wheels:	station to provide shuttles to and from hotel to venue	
other acts:	fanta, zoup kitchen, town hall, almost ready, elbowroom	
guest list:	check local press and retailers	
11:00am	load in	
1:00pm	doors	
5:15pm	take photos with the xtreme staffers	
5:25pm	autograph posters backstage for 15 mins	
6:20pm	prototype on stage	

mon, 6.03

state college, pa		crowbar
promoter:	concerts east	cap / ticket: 650 / $15 / all ages
radio:	none	
press:	cd review to run in the centre daily times (state college daily newspaper) on june 3	
sheets:	overnight in state college guest dorm	
1:00pm	load in	

4:30pm	soundcheck
8:00pm	doors
10:15pm	prototype on stage

tue, 6.04

lancaster, pa — chameleon

cap / ticket: 750 / $13 / all ages

promoter:	stan livingston
radio:	WQQT presents - pre-show "meet and grub"
	with the band at the venue's downstairs bar
press:	the "selfless owl" is a student newspaper of tinytown college - wants interview
wheels:	overnight drive to new york
guest list:	check local press and retailers
1:00pm	load in
4:30pm	soundcheck
tba	in person interview with the e-townian at the venue
6:00pm	meet and greet with contest winners and staffers for WQQT at the venue
7:00pm	doors
9:00pm	prototype on stage

sat, 6.15

	day off
sheets:	paramount hotel, 235 w. 46th street, new york, ny
wheels:	overnight in new york

thu, 6.06

old bridge, nj — birch hill concert hall

cap / ticket: 1350 / $15 /all ages

promoter:	steve livingstone
radio:	tba
press:	"palpable" is a new jersey based tri-yearly music fanzine wants inteview at the venue
sheets:	paramount hotel, 235 w. 46th street, new york, ny
wheels:	none-overnight in new york –paramount hotel again
guest list:	check local press and retailers
1:00pm	load in
4:30pm	soundcheck
5:30pm	in person interview with "palpable" (fan magazine) at the venue
7:00pm	doors
9:30pm	prototype on stage

fri, 6.07

philadelphia, pa — tweeter center on the waterfront
@ the waterfront in camden
cap / ticket: 25,000

venue:	
promoter:	clear channel 215.569-9400
radio:	WYUU on-air interview not yet confirmed -this is the Y-100 show. station would like an in person interview at venue, station ids, photo with staffers, band to sign posters
press:	none
sheets:	hilton, cherry hill 8567 30th ave. philadelphia, pa.
wheels:	overnight in philly
other acts:	yanniyawn, bold face lie, transit x
9:00am	load in
10:00am	soundcheck (must take place before doors)
12:00pm	doors open
4:00pm	go to the backstage "green room" to interview, record liners, etc (label rep to organize)
5:00pm	prototype on stage (main stage)

sat, 6.08

virginia beach, va		WRU / the boat
promoter:	clear channel	cap / ticket: 2460
station contact:	pd	
radio	this is the wru radio show	
press:	tba	
sheets:	founders inn, 5641 indian river road, virginia beach, va	
wheels:	after show travel to boston	
other acts	elephant fainting, watchoutnow, cymbol crazzy	
12:30pm	load in	
9:50pm	prototype on stage	

sun, 6.09

boston, ma		
venue:		cmgi field
promoter:	clear channel	cap / ticket: tickets on sale april
27		
station contact:	pd-wboo	
radio:	this is the WBOO "cave-in 2002"	
press:	none	
sheets:	swissotel, 1 avenue de lafayette, boston, ma	
wheels:	overnight in boston	
other acts:	dwan of destruction, roach motel invaders, the sticks, h.o.d., barefoot, I-know	
11:00am	doors	
3:15pm	prototpe on stage	

mon, 6.10

new york, ny	off day
sheets:	paramount hotel, 235 w. 46th street, new york, ny
wheels:	overnight in new york

tue, 6.11

clifton park, ny		northern lights
promoter:	stan levinstone / concerts east	cap / ticket: 1200 / 16+
radio:	tba	
press:	tba	
sheets:	paramount, 235 w. 46th street, new york, ny	
wheels:	overnight in new york	
1:00pm	load in	
4:30pm	soundcheck	
7:30pm	doors	
8:30pm	opening act on stage	
9:45pm	prototype on stage	

wed, 6.12

new york, ny	press day being set up	
sheets:	paramount, 235 w. 46th street, new york, ny	
wheels:	overnight in new york	
retail:	in-store Qtip Records, midtown store	(pending)

thu, 6.13

new york, ny	press day being set up
sheets:	paramount hotel, 235 w. 46th street, new york, ny

wheels:	overnight in new york
radio:	college radio day (pending)

fri, 6.14

new york, ny	press day being set up
sheets:	paramount hotel, 235 w. 46th street, new york, ny
wheels:	overnight in new york
retail:	long island indie store (pending)

sat, 6.15	day off
sun, 6.16	day off
mon, 6.17	day off

tue, 6.18

detroit, mi	instore performance @ qtip birmingham, new single in store!
radio:	101x is presenting the show and doing a live weekend 6/8 and 6/9 to build up show.
	will be broadcasting live from the event from 4pm-9pm
sheets:	holiday inn, 34952 woodward avenue, birmingham
wheels:	overnight in birmingham
tba:	in person interview with 101x at the store
6:30pm	in store performance at qtip records, birmingham
	aftershow meet and greet with 20 station winners at the store

wed, 6.19

chicago, il	instore performance @ qtip schaumberg
sheets:	springhill suites, 1550 mcconnor parkway, chaumberg, il
wheels:	overnight in chicago
6:30pm	in store performance at qtip records, e. golf road /schaumburg

thu, 6.20

cleveland, oh	day off
sheets:	best western, 8434 mentor avenue, mentor, oh
wheels:	overnight in cleveland
6:00pm	in store performance at fye store, 7850 mentor avenue, mentor, oh

fri, 6.21

vancouver	day off
sheets:	holiday inn, 711 w. broadway avenue, vancouver, bc
wheels:	overnight in Vancouver

sat, 6.22

seattle, wa	KDDN /alternative rock-radio	
venue:		the gorge
promoter:	house of blues	cap / ticket: 20,000
station contact:	pd	
radio:	tba	
press:	tba	
sheets:	west coast wenatchee, 201 n. wenatchee avenue, wenatchee, wa	
wheels:	overnight in wenatchee	
other acts:	tba	
11:00am:	doors	
1pm:	prototype on stage	

tour over- (pending additional dates secured by booking agent)

Performance Front Questions
for Working Your Live Shows

- Does the venue have strong contacts with booking agents and concert promoters?
- What is the venue's seating capacity?
- How many people does the venue need to attract to shows on a regular basis?
- What is the demographic breakdown of the venue's audience?
- Who does the booking at the venue?
- Will the venue promote their own shows? How?
- What kind of special promotions has the venue done with retail to promote shows?
- Has the venue ever done a show with or for a radio station?
- What kind of relationship does the venue have with the print media?
- Does the venue have its own website?
- What kind of Internet promotions do they do for their live shows?
- Can you sell your own CDs at the venue's shows?
- How much do acts average in merchandise sales at the venue?
- Does the club or venue have contacts in other cities or regions where you could find bookings?
- Does the venue place any restrictions on where or how often you can perform in their area?
- Do you have a written contract with the venue? If not, did you write them a letter acknowledging the booking arrangements and conditions for performing?
- Do you have any special performance requirements, i.e. equipment, stage setups, lighting or sound?
- Can you arrange for some marketing activities before or after your soundcheck—visiting radio stations, record stores, or press interviews?
- Do you have a mailing list ready for fans to sign?
- Before and/or after the show, can you find time to meet and greet your fans and sign autographs?
- If you're doing house concerts, are you sure about all the details that need your attention?

Chapter

The Future Is Now

Changes in the Way Music Is Sold
Over the Last 35 Years

In the late '60s, the rules we have today were still being written about how to market and sell music. Most record labels then believed in supporting new artists over several albums and developing their careers slowly. Artists and bands in the late 1960's, like Bob Dylan and Pink Floyd, established their careers in a very different business climate than acts like Fugazi, Ani DeFranco or Jurassic 5 would do in the late '80s, '90s, and into the new millennium.

Times have changed. In the last thirty years, labels, distributors, and music retailers have adapted to demographic changes in the youth population, and advances in recording techniques that allow less expensive ways to record records. Digital technology has had a profound impact on old analog business practices. These changes have prompted the people behind the scenes—at labels, distributors, and stores—to constantly re-evaluate their investments in music, their strategies and tactics for marketing, and their business operation policies.

Significant changes have affected how records were sold in the recent past, and how they're being sold today.

Thirty Years Ago	Now
Thirty years ago, between 7,000 and 8,000 new releases a year. Introduction of CD in '82 causes catalog sales to rise.	By 1991, 17,000 new releases released. In '93 there were 26,000. In 1997 37,000 and by 2005 there were an unprecedented 60,031 new releases.
Records were perceived to be a bargain at a good price. Albums had many good songs to enjoy.	Confusion reigns. CDs are thought to be too expensive for what you get, one or two worthwhile songs. Prices vary too much from record club prices to store prices.
LPs and singles ruled, cassette tapes became more popular than the short-lived 8-track.	In addition to CDs, there are DVDs, vinyl LPs, cassette tapes, video tapes, video games, MP3 and other compressed audio file formats and dozens of digital storage devices. Cassettes and vinyl are less than 5% of the market, combined!
For non-music entertainment, we had movies, board games, sporting events, and recreational activities, am/fm radio, limited TV (few cable channels yet), nightclubs, and books.	We now have access to personal computers, satellite TV and radio, the Internet with essential sites like www.myspace.com, www.tunecore.com and www.youtube.com available for aspiring artists to promote and sell their music: plus we can enjoy home theaters with surround sound, Blackberrys and other mobile communication toys.

Thirty Years Ago	Now
Music was starting to become more portable. The Sony Walkman arrived in the early '80s.	MP3 players/iPods are the size of cell phones or smaller. Storage of music files is measured in dozens of hours. Streaming music is available.
Five main categories for popular music exist: Country, Pop, R&B, Jazz/Blues, & Rock.	Mixing of musical genres create new musical styles. There is more choice for music fans. Music styles have broken into hundreds of subcategories and niches.
Music recognized more as art, less as "product."	Emphasis is on "product." Art has taken a back seat to marketing.
Artist Development at major labels creates a generation of "classic" artists and bands.	Major labels are more selective when signing new acts, use Internet to find budding new talent. Development of an artist's career, (except young Pop acts), is left to the individual artist. Labels seek fast sales from new acts, or they're dumped.
Record sales and radio airplay charts were created by "oral reports" from retailers and radio stations.	SoundScan (for retail sales) and Broadcast Data Systems-BDS, (for radio airplay data) created in early '90s for industry to evaluate sales and airplay results quickly and easily, but expensive.
Records sold primarily at department stores and independent record stores. The record chain store phenomenon grows. (i.e. Tower Records started in 1968.)	Music retailing has consolidated, only Top 10 retailers and rackjobbers and larger chains matter. Tower Records is gone. However, niche marketing has kept Indie stores relevant.
Many regional record distributors. (Over two hundred, 30 years ago.)	National distributors dominate today. Only a handful of one-stop distributors exist. Major labels sell direct to them and through independent distributors and rackjobbers. It's very hard to get a distributor today.
Major labels had branch offices across the country. Independent distributors sold their records regionally. Major labels affiliate with more independent labels.	Only a few big cities have major label branch offices. Independent labels proliferate throughout the U.S. Many involved in coalitions to consolidate buying power and awareness in the marketplace.
Independent distributors worked on "handshake" deals, no written contracts.	Distributors now require written contracts, up to 5 pages, (single-spaced) on how labels must work with them.
More services, financial help available for independent labels with a hit record and who need money to press more records.	Independent labels expected to be self-financed and able to fund store promotions set up by the distributor, (listening station promotions, co-op advertising programs, price and positioning deals.)

Thirty Years Ago	Now
The costs of getting commercial media (radio, press) difficult for Independents. Plus, commercial radio was controlled by illegal payola tactics.	Radio ownership has consolidated. High costs of radio promotion, scandals with various payola policies still occur. Commercial radio exposure is usually only available to the well-funded labels. However, record sales/ profits have not kept up with rising costs of media exposure. Best chance for developing alternative music genres to get radio airplay is on non-commercial terrestrial FM radio, plus a plethora of Internet radio stations that have appeared over the last few years such as www.live365.com and www.pandora.com.
Costs for making (pressing) records were relatively high, and were only affordable to legitimate labels.	Cheaper to manufacture CDs today, but high costs of marketing offset any advantage. Also, the cheaper pressing and recording costs have created a deluge of independent releases. Saturation point has been reached. People can absorb only so much new product.
Fewer releases allowed retailers to stock and sell more records.	Over 1,000 releases a week come out, only a handful of releases account for most sales. High costs of running music retail means stores are more reluctant to stock product that may not sell.
Record sales are from brick-and-mortar record stores, mail order, and artist's selling records at live shows.	Internet sales a multi-billion dollar business, and online sales expected to increase with each year. Artist's sale of their own records is now more important. Consignment to local record stores very important now. CDs today are sold by many non-traditional retailers such as coffee cafes and clothing stores.
Major labels sold their product directly to all record stores. This policy stopped in late '70s. Major labels sold records at same fair price to all brick-and-mortar music retailers.	After 20 years of not selling to smaller record stores, most labels have re-opened accounts with key mom-and-pop and independent stores.
Store inventory systems not computer generated. Stores relied on hand counts and guessing on potential sales.	Point of Sale (POS) scanning systems allow more accurate tracking of store's inventory. Easier to see what music is selling, harder to convince retailers to carry your record unless you can prove it is selling. Controversial pricing policies by major mass merchandisers caused many store closures in the mid '90s. MAP (Minimum Advertised Price) enforced by mass merchandisers, enabled them to sell CDs for less than they paid for them. Independent stores can't compete with prices.

Thirty Years Ago	Now
No such thing as downloadable music files.	Threats from P2P illegal downloadable music sites continue to challenge the many legal downloadable sites, such as iTunes and the new Napster, etc.
Access to film, TV, and advertising licensing deals hard to find for the independent artist.	More opportunities for independent songwriters and artists to get their music used in films, TV, Internet deals, and video games, as well as streamed to mobile devices.
Recording contracts for "album" deals were the standard type of contract offered a new act.	Because of iTunes, MP3 file downloads, and file sharing; as well as the emergence of online community websites like www.myspace.com, www.facebook.com, and other similar sites, record labels may now offer only "song" deals for new acts. If the songs are successful, the label may offer the act a full recording contract.

New Challenges for Music Marketing

Musicians who are trying to get their music to the public are confronted with a harsh reality; changes in every aspect of the music business are an every day occurrence. Here's an overview of some of the more profound changes.

The Large are Swallowing Up the Small

For the last twenty years, many multinational corporations who had investments in entertainment products have been on a feeding frenzy. They've been buying up the smaller entertainment industry companies as fast as they could; the record labels, publishing companies, broadcast and print media outlets, as well as the live performance industry. The traditional businesses of promoting music (through commercial radio stations) and selling music (through brick-and-mortar record stores) have now evolved to the point where a cartel of about five or six media companies control everything you and I see, hear, and read. Recently, the live performance industry has been transformed the most. One Nation, a spin-off company of radio ownership group Clear Channel Communications, now controls almost 70% of the most important concert promotion companies, management firms, and large venues that showcase the most popular music acts in the United States. Clear Channel also owns over 1,200 radio stations in the U.S.

This consolidation process is far from over. The major media entertainment conglomerates are now positioning themselves to control as much of the digital music food chain as they can grab. The Sony/BMG merger is an example of this. Some of the other powerful companies are Disney, Rupert Murdoch's News Corporation, Viacom, and Universal. General Electric and Microsoft may not be far behind these companies with their ambitions to own more of the entertainment media.

Big Changes in Broadcasting

Radio station ownership rules were once quite restrictive in order to protect and encourage a free flow of information. In the late '70s, the number of radio and television stations that could be owned by one corporation in a particular market was very limited. Some of the restrictions were removed in the early '80s under the Reagan administration and the rules were loosened even more by the Communications Act of '96. The George W. Bush Administration has been quite vocal about doing away with the remaining restrictions on radio and television station ownership rules. This means, for example, that one city could have all their commercial radio stations owned by only six or fewer corporations. Our access to entertainment, news, and information about important political and social issues is increasingly limited to what a small group of companies choose to broadcast or print. Because of this situation, many points of view are silenced and our entertainment options are limited without our knowledge.

I'm a Musician. Why Should I Care?

Let me give you a short history lesson about the where area I live. In the mid 1990s Seattle, Washington was an example of a city that had about twenty-five commercial radio station general managers, who represented a variety of different owners. Today there are six general managers, who represent *six* dominant media ownership groups. Companies such as Entercom and Clear Channel each own several stations in the Seattle market. Those companies and others own dozens of radio stations in most U.S. radio markets.

The issue of radio station ownership affects musicians directly. When one company owns several stations that used to be in competition with each other, and the music and program directors at these stations work together to choose the songs for *all* their stations, that means that independent artists have almost no chance of getting their songs added to these stations. Prior to the mid 1990s, a record label could play one competing station off another. That's no longer the case. Today, when a station like Entercom owns all the significant rock stations in a market like Seattle, if you can't get onto one of their stations you probably won't get serious airplay anywhere in that market or others that are similarly controlled.

Live Performance Blues

The corporate merger syndrome has also infected the live performance industry. Toward the end of the last decade SFX Entertainment sold its radio station holdings to—that's right—Clear Channel Communications, who as I stated above, spun off that concert business in 2006 to a company known as One Nation, and whose board of directors happen to have several Clear Channel executives on their board.

As one industry pundit said: "We're now dealing with the Wal-Mart of the concert business." So, want to open up for a touring major act in your hometown? Or, how about getting a tour once you're signed to a label? Will your booking agent and manager be walking arm in arm with Clear Channel? If not, what could happen to that national tour you were hoping to get?

Music Retail Consolidation

The traditional brick-and-mortar music retailers have their concerns too, as small and large record stores continue to be bought out. Best Buy's purchase of the Sam Goody record store chain was an example of music retail consolidation. Any changes in the retail landscape should be of great concern to developing artists, bands, and record labels. The accounts you're used to dealing with could be gone tomorrow, putting in jeopardy your chances of getting paid due to the intricate legal makeup of these mergers and acquisitions. Sadly, in late 2006 after 46 years of supporting independent music, the venerable Tower Records chain folded up and is gone; bad news for aspiring artists and labels who benefited from Tower's commitment to carrying as much music as possible. There's no national record store chain left to replace them.

Traditional music retailers are also on the alert for competition for sales coming directly from the record labels. As it stands today and for a good while to come, record labels will continue to rely on music retailers to sell the bulk of their releases. But behind the scenes, record labels big and small are rapidly taking direct online sales to customers into their own hands. How will all this play out? Only time will tell.

Getting Signed: The Way it Was

Thirty years ago it seemed like a new generation of entrepreneurial musicians and labels had found a simple yet effective way to make and market their music. College radio was doing a great job of exposing alternative music. Independent labels and distributors had carved out a solid niche with the support of a thriving alternative press and live performance circuits. With the advent of MTV, many alternative acts of the '80s began to break through to a more mainstream audience.

Beginning in the latter half of the 1970s, the most effective way to grow a music-based career was to Do It Yourself. The DIY movement included alternative rock bands, acoustic singer songwriters, rap and hip-hop artists, experimental, and new age artists. They began putting out their music on their own, or on small independent labels. These enterprising musicians found a way to get their music to a niche fanbase through upstart record distributors and independent record stores. They got their records played on many college and non-commercial radio stations, got the music press to review their records, and found live performance venues to perform their music. Their reward for all this hard work was either a modest but steady income, or the attention of bigger labels who offered them contracts and a chance at greater glory. Even more rewarding was the realization that their work made them true contenders—if not with gold records, at least at the negotiation table—where they could barter with record labels for better deals and be less exploitable because of their business savvy.

Getting Signed Today

Today, the DIY method of establishing your career has become the strongest tool available to songwriters and musicians who want people to hear their music. A surprising number of artists and bands are enjoying the benefits of owning their own label these days. For me, the genius and hard work of the artist Ani DeFranco continues to be a model for what I call the FourFront marketing approach. She has sold millions of records over the last decade by first learning the basics of music marketing and then slowly growing her label, Righteous Babe Records, to the highly regarded place of honor she holds today.

Some good news for musicians and bands is the tremendous influence that the websites, www.myspace.com and www.youtube.com have had on new acts. It's now essential to have a presence on both of theses revolutionary sites.

In addition, thousands of musicians over the last decade have educated themselves about the economics of the music business. Once a musician examines the clauses in a major label contract and begins to connect the dots, a self-produced record or an independent label deal becomes more appealing.

Bigger Rewards for Developing Your Own Career

According to many entertainment law attorneys, the standard deals once given to new artists can change significantly when a label seeks out a band. The following recording contract issues are more negotiable than ever, if you have done some career development of your own:

- **Better Royalty Rates:** Artists are paid for their records from a percentage of the sales of that record, (based on the record's list price). A high rate just a few years ago for a new act was 14–16 points, whereas buzz acts (acts that are in demand by labels) can get up to several points higher.

- **Ownership of Masters:** Artists who can buy back the master recordings they made for a label after their contract has expired, or after the label drops them, have more control of their destinies than artists who can't do this. The more a label wants you, the easier it is to negotiate a reversal of master ownership. This is especially important in this digital era where there are so many new ways for your music to used and for you to be paid good money.

- **Creative Control Issues:** Many artists are concerned about the label's power to decide key issues such as selection of material, choice of a producer, graphic images, etc. If these issues are important to you, take the time to develop your career.

- **Non-recoupable Issues:** Buzz bands have more say in what a label can claim as "automatic" recoupable expenses (promotion costs, videos, percent of touring budgets, etc.)

- **Controlled Composition Clauses:** In a nutshell, this is a clause that labels insert into their contracts with most new artists. It reduces, to 75%, the amount of money due to the songwriter and publishers for the songs on the record from product sales (mechanical royalties—see page 108). The standard rate, (currently 9.1 cents per song, per record or unit sold) is more negotiable with buzz acts.

The more an act can build success on their own without a label's help, the more power they have when negotiating recording and publishing contract offers when they do come along.

New Technologies: Good News and Bad News for Developing Artists

Artists and bands getting into the recording industry today have many new tools to help them succeed. Change is everywhere, from the choices available to record music, to marketing and promoting it. Some of those changes are direct challenges to the old analog traditions that helped create the music business we know today. Others are new opportunities that await the enterprising artist/entrepreneur. Check out some of the most important new developments.

- The file sharing pioneer Napster may be long gone now, but the offspring of Napster live on; there are dozens of other illegal P2P sites all over the Internet. Because of the Pandora's box these web companies have opened up, the business of promoting and selling music will never be the same. Granted, many of these sites are in legal trouble with the RIAA, (Recording Industry Association of America, an industry advocacy association that represents the interests of the major record companies). Like it or not, enterprising computer hackers will continue to be a thorn in the side of all musicians who create and distribute music, since music can always be turned into bits and bytes (1's and 0's).

- Musicians who hope to make a living from their music must come to grips with the fact that music isn't valued by consumers the way it was even ten years ago. Music fans today think "Why should I pay for a CD when I can download almost anything ever recorded either for free or less than $1, and store it on my computer or burn my own CD?"

But just when things started to look quite hopeless, along came some very useful Internet promotional programs that allow you to spread the word about your music. As we have mentioned repeatedly throughout this book, anyone willing to learn a few technical skills in exchange for powerful exposure opportunities can visit sites like www.cdbaby.com and really take charge of selling their music online. The Internet is in a state of flux and will always have opportunities for musicians, but you must seek them out and stay current as things change.

- Artists who want to sell or promote their CDs over the Internet have many choices these days. One of the most innovative and effective methods is the amazon.com/advantage program. Other online retailers offer similar programs for independent labels, (see page 157, Selling Your Music Online). Artists can have a strong presence online by signing up for this free program and creating a selling page with their own graphics, CD information and sound samples. This doesn't mean that artists shouldn't consider selling their music from their own websites through a secure service. That's a valid alternative.

- In early 1999, a meeting of the major record labels resulted in the creation of the SDMI (Secure Digital Music Initiative). The initiative attempted to find ways to limit the threats to copyright ownership by using "encryption" and "watermarks" of downloadable music so that musicians and labels could prohibit unauthorized usage of their music, as well as trace where an illegally distributed song file came from. It has really faded away, but deserves credit for standing up to help musicians and copyright holders preserve some of their rights in this digital age. Digital Rights Management is with us; companies who deal with online downloads and have major label product are using DRM methods to protect the content on those CDs. The debate over how important DRM is will go on for some time to come. Developing realistic policies that protect the record labels, artists, distributors, and sellers of music is an ongoing challenge to all parties involved. (But remember, for every new protection device that is created, an enterprising computer hacker stands ready to unravel it.)

- In addition to MP3 and the file swapping phenomenon, other downloadable music technologies have been established over the Internet. Seemingly out of nowhere a few years ago, Apple Computer and Steve Jobs captured the minds and wallets of music lovers everywhere by introducing the iPod and later iTunes, which are the leaders in the downloadable music race. But watch out, companies like Creative, HP, and now Microsoft are hard on Mr. Jobs' trail. One thing is for sure…there will be many more choices coming to download and play music, video and video games.

- While it's getting harder for independent artists and bands to get commercial radio airplay for the reasons already mentioned, there are still hundreds of college radio stations and many new Internet radio stations playing a wide variety of music. Streaming audio software has made it possible for anyone and everyone interested in being a DJ to broadcast their favorite music as a web radio station. This is great news for developing acts that have a strong niche following of one kind or another. Stations like www.live365.com and www.pandora.com are making it easier and easier to create your own radio show to showcase your music. And don't forget you can post three or four songs on www.myspace.com and www.facebook.com as well.

- An agreement on how Internet radio stations will pay copyright holders for their streaming content has now been agreed upon. At the moment it looks like fan supported "hobbyist" Internet stations may be in trouble, as the Copyright Tribunal announced in the spring of '07 higher fees that may put this vital new web service in jeopardy. Stay tuned, as an appeal is in the works, as we go to press.

- Podcasts are here to stay. A year or so ago, these easily created mini-broadcasts that can be downloaded into your iPod or MP3 player were considered a joke….the joke is over. Get with it. Start finding ways to create and promote your music with your own podcasts. (Be sure to check out my free *Music Is Your Business* podcasts at www.fourfrontmusic.com)

- A digital music revolution *within* the current digital music revolution has to be the rapid growth of music going mobile. Nearly fourteen billion dollars in new revenue is expected to be generated in 2007 from consumer mobile music spending. You already know about ringtones, but how about ringbacks, alert tones, full-song downloads, mobile video and graphics, streaming radio, ticket purchases via cell phones, mobile games? And of course an increase in text messaging abilities will connect you with your fans. I suggest that you check out *Billboard* magazine's mobile phone news every week to help you keep up on this important new music marketing tool, www.billboard.com .

Grab the Future

Challenges and changes for the independent musician are here to stay. No one ever said being a successful musician would be easy. But any dedicated musician can benefit from the new ideas and opportunities that crop up almost daily. With every bad news report about the control of the media and the limited exposure opportunities for music, there's some good news for those curious enough to explore where few have gone before.

I hope that as you learn about the many changes surrounding you, you'll be motivated to keep up on them as part of your commitment to your career.

So, what unique ideas can you think of to get your music to a potential fan? Use your imagination. There are countless ways to expose, promote, play, and sell independently produced music, even in an era of major corporations and media control. The time is ripe for you to take advantage of some of these new marketing opportunities. Who knows, maybe your idea will be the one to spark a true revolution for getting music to the people.

Licensing Music for Films, TV, Commercials, and Computer Games

Whenever a producer of a film, television show, commercial, or computer game wants to use music in a project, there are two different kinds of licenses which normally come into play: a "Synchronization License" and a "Master Use License."

The terminology here can get confusing, so to make it simpler, let's take a situation where a song, (a "musical composition"), has been written by a songwriter named "Joe A." The music publisher for this song is "B Music Publishing Company." Let's also say that three different bands have each recorded their own separate versions of the song, and let's call those bands X, Y, and Z.

The Synchronization License

The producer of a film, television show, commercial, or computer game must obtain the written permission (which is called a "synchronization license") from B Music Publishing Company, the "music publisher" of the musical composition.

As a general rule, the term "music publisher" means the owner of the copyright of the musical composition. Assuming that the songwriter hasn't signed a music publishing agreement for the song with an established music publishing company, then the songwriter will be his/her own music publisher, and will affiliate with ASCAP or BMI as both a songwriter AND as a music publisher. However, if the songwriter has signed a music publishing agreement with an established music publishing company, then that company will be the "music publisher" of the song and will be the party issuing the synchronization license.

Just to be clear, we are not talking about the rights to use a particular *recorded version* of a song, but instead, only the right to use the *underlying song* itself. Permission to use a *specific recorded version* of a song is called a *"master use license"* and is discussed next.

The Master Use License

A *master use license* needs to be obtained by the producer for whichever *recorded version* is going to be used. So, if the producer of a film, television show, commercial, or computer game wants to use Band A's version, then the producer must obtain a *master use license* from the band (if the band is unsigned), or, if the band is *signed,* then from the band's *label.* (Bear in mind, though, that even when a band is signed, the band's recording contract may very well contain provisions requiring the *label* to obtain the *band's* approval before allowing the band's music to be used in a film, television show, commercial, or computer game. Also, there are certain union and guild rules that are applicable.)

The comments above, concerning the producer's obligation to obtain a master use license, assume that the producer wants to use an *already existing* recorded version of a song. However, there are situations in which the producer may want to have a *new* recording made, usually as a newly-recorded "work for hire." Sometimes this happens because the producer cannot obtain the necessary band and/or label approvals (as can be seen, for example, in some recent commercials using Beatles' songs), and sometimes it's because the already existing recorded version does not stylistically fit the project for one reason or another.

In this situation, i.e., when a producer is having a new version recorded as a "work for hire," the producer does not need to obtain a *master use* license, since the producer isn't going to be using a master recording owned by *someone else*. But, even then, the producer still needs to obtain a *synchronization license* from the music publisher of the *underlying song*.

Common "Synchronization Licensing" Issues

There are many issues which may arise whenever a synchronization license is being negotiated between a producer of a film, television show, commercial, or computer game, and the publisher which owns the underlying composition.

Some of the main issues are: the length of *"the term"* of the license (i.e., how long the license will be remain in effect for); the scope of the *territory* (i.e., the geographical area in which the producer can use the song in his or her production); and whether the producer will have *exclusive* rights to use the song, or instead, whether the publisher can give other producers the right to use the same song at the same time.

The Term

Theatrical Films: The term is generally for the "life of the copyright" (in other words, the license will last as long as the song is protected by copyright law, which, as a general rule of thumb, is today 95 years).

Television: Sometimes for 2, 3, 5, or 7 years, or, currently much more common, for the "life of copyright." (There's been a rapid trend toward "life of copyright" in recent years.)

Commercials: Typically an initial term of anywhere from 13 weeks to one year, often with the producer's right to renew for another equal term upon payment of an additional licensing fee (which might, for example, be 125% or more of the original fee).

Computer Games: The term is generally for the "life of the copyright," or for a 2,3, or 5 year term. As a practical matter, there are very few computer games which will have a life span of over a year or two, and so in most instances the producer won't consider it all that important to obtain a *long term* license.

The Territory

Theatrical Films: Typically the territory is "worldwide."

Television: It used to be that the territory was usually limited to certain countries. Today, most often, "worldwide."

Commercials: Local, regional, national, certain countries, or worldwide, i.e., depending on what the parties negotiate.

Computer Games: Worldwide.

It's important to mention that even though a license may say that it's a worldwide license, a producer has to be very careful here, especially if it's a large company doing business in other countries. This is because of the fact that in many foreign countries, licenses issued directly by publishers are not valid for those countries. Instead, a producer seeking to clear the rights for those countries must obtain a license from a rights organization or governmental agency in each of those countries, even if the producer has already obtained a purportedly "worldwide" license from the U.S. publisher.

Exclusivity Versus Non-Exclusivity

For Theatrical Films and Television Shows: Synchronization licenses are almost always non-exclusive in regards to films and television shows. If there is exclusivity, the producer will usually be paying dearly for it. Assuming there's no exclusivity, the owner of the song can license it to as many other companies as it likes.

For Commercials: There may be exclusivity for a limited period of time. When there is exclusivity, it's most often *limited* exclusivity, limited either to the territory of the license and/or to particular products or industries.

For Computer Games: Usually non-exclusive, though sometimes the license agreement will prohibit the music publisher from licensing the music to be used in other *computer games* for however long the license agreement will be in effect.

The Amount of the Synchronization License Fee

How big the synchronization fee will be in any given situation will depend on many factors, such as the degree of public recognition of the particular music involved (for example, whether it was a hit song in the past, and if so, how recently), the nature of usage (e.g., in a film versus a television show versus a commercial, etc.), and the term of the license. Depending on the nature of the production (film versus television, etc), there will be other considerations as well. For example, in the case of a film, there are such considerations as how many times the song will be used in the film (and for how long each time), and whether the music will be used in the foreground (versus the background), or in trailers.

Even when the up-front synchronization license fee is small, there can still be some very substantial public performance monies to be eventually received by the publisher and composer from their performance rights society (i.e., ASCAP, BMI, or SESAC), as discussed in more detail below.

Often the license agreement will contain a "most favored nations" (aka "MFN") clause, which says that if multiple songs are used in a film, computer game, etc., then if the producer pays another publisher a higher fee than you (as a publisher) have negotiated, then you'll get the same (higher) amount that the other publisher has negotiated for.

"Master Use" Licensing Issues

Many of the issues mentioned above in regards to *synchronization licenses* are also issues in negotiations over *master use licenses.*

The amount of the *master use fee* that is *charged* by the *record company* is often very similar in amount to, or identical to, the *synchronization fee* charged by the *publisher* in that same situation.

In some instances the record company negotiating the terms of a master use license may be more anxious (than the music publisher who is negotiating the *synchronization license*) to have the music used, in order to promote an artist who currently has a record out. So the record company may be willing to agree to a lower fee than the publisher is willing to accept. On the other hand, I've often seen instances in which the record company has required a higher fee than the publisher has.

Also, sometimes there's a large difference in the fees charged by a publisher and record company because there's a small publisher or record company involved which isn't experienced in the licensing area, and which unknowingly (and unnecessarily) quotes too low a fee to the producer.

Additional Income from ASCAP/BMI/SESAC for Publishers and Songwriters

When music is "publicly performed," (for example, music which is broadcast as part of a television show, or performed online in a computer game), the *publisher* of the underlying song and the *songwriter* will earn not only the synchronization fee which they received from the producer, but also the "public performance" income from the publisher's and composer's performance rights society (i.e., ASCAP, BMI, or SESAC). This "Public performance" income can be very substantial.

Sometimes, however, the public performance income can be very small; when music is used in a cable show, for example. This is because of the low rates that have been negotiated between ASCAP and BMI on the one hand, and cable networks on the other hand. The fact that these rates are so low has become a controversial issue among many members of ASCAP and BMI, particularly given the fact that many of the cable networks have become lucratively profitable for their owners.

In any event, there are still many situations in which public performance income can be quite substantial, and in those situations the publisher is often willing to accept a synchronization license fee significantly lower than it would otherwise be inclined to accept, rather than potentially losing the deal (thereby losing not only the synchronization license fee paid by the producer, but also the "public performance" income earned from ASCAP, BMI or SESAC by reason of the broadcasts of the television show). This is particularly true in certain instances, such as when a song is being used as the title song for a TV show, or when music is being used in infomercials which are being broadcast over and over for long periods of time, which can generate large amounts of "public performance" income.

Bear in mind here that we're only talking about the public performance income payable to *the publishers and songwriters* of the underlying song. The same considerations do *not* apply to the owner of *the master recording* of a particular recorded version of the song, i.e., a band or its label. Under U.S. copyright law, the owners of *master recordings*, unlike the owners of the *underlying songs*, are *not* entitled to public performance income for the broadcast of their recordings in the United States (except for certain Internet uses). The situation is different in many foreign countries, where labels can earn substantial sums from the "public performances" of their master recordings in those foreign countries.

In short, the owner of the master recording's only source of U.S. income from the master use license will be the up-front master use fee which it receives from the producer, since it will not be receiving any public performance income from ASCAP, BMI or SESAC. As a result, the owner of the master recording may feel more of a need (than the publisher) to negotiate to receive the highest possible up-front fee from the producer.

Licensing Your Masters Overseas

If you're an artist or indie label, one way to significantly expand your universe is to license your master recordings to record companies outside the United States.

There are advantages of doing so. Aside from the obvious advantage of generating additional record sales, there's also the advantage of creating a relationship with a record company outside the United States who will have music business relationships in that foreign country and who can connect you up with booking agencies, venues, festival organizers, music publishers, etc. in that territory. This may enable you to tour and build an audience in those countries where it otherwise might not be practical to try to do so.

The Basics of Licensing

When you enter into a music licensing agreement with a foreign record company, you're in essence authorizing them to duplicate and sell copies of existing masters, in exchange for paying you a royalty for each record sold. The label is responsible for paying all costs, such as the costs of manufacturing, promotion, and advertising, and it's up to the foreign label to manufacture CDs and to get those CDs distributed in their territory.

One alternative to a foreign licensing arrangement is to manufacture your CDs in the United States yourself, then export them to distributors in other counties. However, one big disadvantage in going the "export" route, at least if you do it legally, is that for most foreign countries, you'll usually be paying a government-imposed tariff in those countries of 20% to 40%. Also, a distributor gets a much smaller piece of the pie, and generally isn't going to do the level of proactive marketing and promotion that will need to be done to break you successfully into foreign markets.

As a result of these factors and others, the best alternative for the vast majority of U.S. indie artists and labels trying to break into foreign countries is going to be a licensing arrangement with labels based in those countries, rather than a distribution agreement in those countries.

Approval Rights

A U.S. label that wants to enter into licensing arrangements with one or more foreign labels must first make sure that it has the rights to do so under the terms of its recording contracts with its artists. If it doesn't already have such rights, then the label needs to get its artists' approval before entering into any such licensing arrangements with foreign labels.

Negotiating Clout

As a general rule, it's going to be much easier for a U.S. label or artist to get a foreign licensing deal, and especially a deal on very favorable terms, if its records are already selling well in the U.S. and the artists already have a significant reputation in the U.S.

Basic Deal Points

The basic deal points of the typical music licensing agreement are as follows:

Scope of License. The license may cover one or a few specified recordings, or may cover your entire catalog. It's sometimes a good idea to start out with less than your entire catalog, so that you can "test drive" the relationship first before committing your entire catalog.

Territory. If you're licensing masters to indie foreign labels, you'll normally be licensing only for a particular county or for a particular group of countries. Often the agreement will be for so-called "bundled countries," such as Benelux (standing for Belgium, the Netherlands and Luxembourg) and GAS (Germany, Austria, and Switzerland). On the other hand, if you were entering into a foreign licensing agreement with one of the major worldwide labels, such as WEA or BMG, you might be licensing your masters to one company for *all* countries outside the United States in one fell swoop. As a practical matter, though, a deal with one of the "majors" is normally not available to a U.S. artist or label unless you already have major sales in the U.S.

Incidentally, if the territory is defined in the licensing agreement as the "European Union" or similar terminology, the territory will in effect change over time as more countries join the European Union.

Term. Typically the term of the agreement will be for five years, though often such agreements are for three years or seven years. Generally, the smaller the advance, the less of a justification there is for entering into a longer term.

Normally, there's also a "sell off" period added to the end of the term of the agreement, which allows the label to sell off any existing inventory for an *additional* six months to a year after the end of the term. If there's a "sell off" period included in the agreement, it's wise to add a clause prohibiting the label from manufacturing more copies of a CD during the original three, five or seven year term than they can reasonably expect to sell during that three, five or seven year term.

A practical tip: As soon as the licensing agreement expires, it's a good idea to send the label a "Notice of Termination" even if the contract doesn't require it. (It usually doesn't.) Otherwise, there's a significant risk that the foreign label will, innocently or not so innocently, continue selling your records. The risk of that happening can be significantly reduced by sending them a "Notice of Termination." Be sure to send any such notice in such a way that you have proof that it was actually received.

Exclusivity. Normally the agreement is "exclusive," in which case you cannot later authorize any other company in that territory to sell your records during the term of the licensing agreement.

Royalty Rate. Unlike the United States, where royalty rates are usually based on the *retail price* of records, the royalty rates in most other countries are based on a price that's somewhere between the wholesale price and the retail price. For example, in some countries the

260

price is based on the "PPD" ("Published Price to Dealer") price. In other countries, like France, they often use the so-called "BIEM-IFPI" rate.

Typically, the royalty rate is in the 15% to 22% range (and sometimes more). This is higher than the typical rate in the U.S. because the foreign royalty rate isn't based on the *retail* price as in the U.S., but instead on a designated price that is significantly lower. Hence, in order for you to come out roughly the same in terms of dollars and cents, the foreign royalty rate has to be higher.

Here are a few random tips about evaluating the royalty rate:

- The best way to evaluate the royalty rate is to run the royalty calculations and figure out what you'll be earning for each record in dollars and cents, rather than getting fixated on percentage rates, etc. In order to do any useful number crunching, you'll need to find out the exact price that the label is currently using; then convert that amount to U.S. dollars, and then do your royalty calculations based on the royalty terms contained in the proposed licensing agreement.

- There's often a difference from one county to the next in regards to what are considered acceptable royalty provisions. What is customary in one country is often not customary in another country. So, if you're negotiating royalty provisions for particular foreign countries, you need to know what is customary in that country. For example, royalties in the U.S. are typically not paid on promotional free goods that the record company gives away, but in some other countries that isn't the case.

- If you're comparing offers from two or more companies, you need to investigate and compare the reputation and financial stability of each company. You can sometimes end up doing much better financially with an average deal from a relatively honest company than you'll do with a great royalty rate from a crooked or financially borderline company.

- If the licensing agreement contains any definitions of, for example, the "PPD" price, read the fine print very carefully.

- If you're licensing your masters for a country where the local currency is subject to frequent major fluctuations, you may want to have the licensing agreement provide that you'll be paid a specified amount *in U.S. dollars* for each record sold. That way, the amount that you get for each record sold will not be changing throughout the term of the licensing agreement as the value of the local currency fluctuates on the world currency market.

Advances. The amount of the advance that is paid, if any, will depend on the foreign label's forecast of how many records can be sold in their territory. Advances vary wildly and can be anywhere between $500 and $50,000 (but sometimes higher and sometimes lower).

In some cases, it will make sense for you to enter into the licensing agreement even if the advance is minimal, if there's a good chance that your relationship with the foreign record company will significantly help you to get established in their territory. By the same token, because of the difficulty of auditing foreign countries and trying to collect money from foreign companies, often times you have to assume that the advance is the only money that you'll ever see from the deal.

The advance is normally deemed "recoupable" (the label can reimburse itself for the advance from your future royalties), so if your advance is $5,000, and if the total royalties end up being $15,000, the label later will pay you only $10,000 (i.e., the $15,000 in royalties minus the $5,000 advance). By the way, the advance should also be described in the contract as being "non-refundable" (so that you won't have to ever pay it back).

Release Commitment. You should have a clause in the licensing agreement requiring the label to release the record by a certain date, and that if they don't do so, you have a right to terminate the agreement.

For masters that already exist at the time of the licensing agreement, you'll normally want to have a fixed calendar date by which time the record has to be released. For records not yet recorded, but that will be recorded and released during the term of the licensing agreement, the release commitment is usually 90–120 days within the date of your delivery of the master to the label.

You want to be careful that the contract language is very specific and precise, and you'll also want to be sure to ship the masters in such a way that you'll later be able to prove the exact date of delivery if necessary.

Sharing in Other Types of Income. Sometimes there's potential income from sources other than record sales. For example, a U.K. ad agency might want to use a track in a film, and so the licensing agreement needs to deal with this scenario. If at all possible, have the contract provide that the rights to enter into those kinds of deals stays with you and are outside the scope of the licensing agreement. By the same token it usually makes sense to give the label the piece of any such deal that they find for you, so that they have a motivation to make such deals happen.

Sometimes the contract will say that the foreign label has the rights to enter into such deals for your masters, but only for territory/countries covered by the agreement, and that in return, you'll receive a share of the income from such deals.

The bottom line: The main thing you absolutely want to avoid is a contract that gives a foreign label the right to enter into such deals, but doesn't spell out your rights to receive a certain specified share of the income from such deals.

Payment. Payments are usually made semi-annually. The agreement should provide for the royalties to be *wired* to your account at the label's expense (as opposed to the label mailing you a check, which can cause very long delays in your actual receipt of the money and the clearing of the check).

Foreign Taxes. You'll also normally want a clause requiring the foreign label to help you file the necessary paperwork with the foreign government(s) involved, so that the foreign label will not have to withhold foreign taxes from the royalties that are otherwise payable to you. If that's not possible, at the very least, you want some arrangement whereby the foreign label gives you a formal statement at the end of each year as to the amount of foreign taxes that were withheld that year, so that you can claim the appropriate tax credits on your United States tax returns.

Audits. There should be a clause allowing you to audit the foreign label's business records, and providing that if there's a discrepancy of more than 10%, they must pay your audit costs. It will probably not be practical for you to audit the foreign label's business records, but you still want to have that option if at all possible.

Mechanical Royalties for Foreign Sales

Mechanical royalties, i.e., the royalties that record companies pay to music publishers/songwriters based on how many records are sold, are handled differently almost everywhere outside the U.S. than they're handled in the U.S.

How to Find Music Licensing Opportunities

There are a various ways to find music licensing opportunities, for example:

- **Researching Foreign Labels.** You can obtain the necessary contact information from such directories as the *Billboard International Buyer's Guide*. (Check with the reference librarian at your local library to see if they might have a copy on hand that you can use, and if not, ask if they can borrow a copy for you through an inter-library loan from another library.) Also, an Internet search can help you locate foreign labels that are appropriate for you.

  Before submitting material to a foreign label, it's usually a good idea to send them a professional and non-hypey e-mail first, just to find out whether they're even interested in considering your material.

- **Tip Sheets.** Tip sheets such as "New on the Charts" allow subscribers (and sometimes non-subscribers) to post a listing of masters that they have available for licensing.

- **Referrals.** Check with any established artists and American labels that you know of, in case you think they might be able to turn you on to appropriate foreign labels.

- **MIDEM.** There is a large international music business conference in Cannes, France every year (in late January), called "MIDEM," where people negotiate music licensing deals. The practical side of it is that unless you are a well financed artist or label, it won't be affordable to attend that conference. One alternative is to buy the MIDEM conference directory, which you can use as another resource directory to locate appropriate labels.

  Incidentally, there are occasionally people who will advertise that, for a cash fee, they will shop your material at the MIDEM conference. Be very careful with any such arrangements and check those people and their track records out thoroughly. You obviously don't want to find out after the fact that you have just financed someone's vacation in the south of France and have nothing to show for it.

About the Authors

Christopher Knab is the owner of FourFront Media and Music, a Seattle-based consultation service dedicated to helping independent musicians promote, market, and sell their music. He has worked in the business side of independent music for over thirty years.

In the 1970s Christopher owned Aquarius Records in San Francisco. He co-hosted the first commercial alternative rock radio specialty show in the nation ("The Outcaste Hour"), and later "The Heretics" and "The Modern Humans" on stations KSAN and KSJO in the Bay area. Using his on-air name "Cosmo Topper," he gave dozens of now-legendary alternative bands their initial radio exposure.

He was the cofounder and Vice President of 415/Columbia Records (Romeo Void, Translator, Roky Erikson, et al). From 1985–1994 he was the Station Manager of Seattle alternative radio station KCMU (now KEXP 90.3 FM) during Seattle's grunge era. He was also the president of the Northwest Area Music Association. A member of the faculty of the Art Institute of Seattle for eighteen years, he taught music business courses in the Audio Production program.

His website www.fourfrontmusic.com, established in 1995, continues to be a highly regarded Internet resource, hosting dozens of useful articles and links for independent musicians. He's also a speaker and panelist at music industry conferences and is a voting member of NARAS.

Christopher offers music business workshops, classes, and private consultations. FourFront Media and Music, 1245 S. 128th St., Seattle, WA, 98168, (206) 282-6116, chris@knab.com.

Bartley F. Day is an entertainment attorney with over twenty years of music industry experience. He is a frequent speaker and panelist at music business conferences and entertainment law conferences in Vancouver, B.C., Austin, Texas, New York, and other cities throughout the US.

He divides his time between Los Angeles, where he is Vice-President of Legal and Business Affairs for Media Creature Music, (a music publishing company headed by Sharal Churchill, former head of music for MGM), and Portland, where he has an entertainment law practice focused on music law. He represents numerous nationally known recording artists, independent labels, distributors, music publishers, producers, managers, concert promoters, and merchandising companies.

Bart also represents film and television production companies, e-commerce and game companies, authors and visual artists, and clients seeking to register and protect trademarks. He is outside music counsel for Vivendi Universal Games, the computer game unit of Universal Studios.

From 1998 to 2002, Bart served as an elected member of the Board of Governors of the Pacific Northwest Chapter of The Recording Academy, the presenter of the Grammy Awards. His monthly column, "Legal Ease," ran from 1986 to 2005 in the music magazine *Two Louies.* Bart is a member of the Executive Committee of the Intellectual Property Section of the Oregon State Bar, a member of the California Copyright Conference, and has been admitted to practice before the U.S. Supreme Court.

Bart's email is bart@entertainmentlawwest, his website is www.entertainmentlawwest.com.

Christopher Knab and Bartley F. Day are also the co-authors of a chapter entitled "Contracts and Relationships Between Independent and Major Labels" in *The Musician's Business and Legal Guide,* a book compiled by the Beverly Hills Bar Association and published by Prentice-Hall.

Index

A&R Reps, 31–32, 91, 207
Add, 184
Airplay
    college radio, 184–85
    radio stations and record labels, 177–93
Arbitron, 181
Artist development, 12, 13–14
    checklist for, 66
    history of, 12
    major label, 88
Artist royalties, 108–10
    profit split deals and, 121
ASCAP (American Society of Composers, Authors, and Publishers), 13, 53–56, 57, 254
    additional income from, 258
    choice between ASCAP and BMI, 53
    music publishing income and, 122
    registering your original songs with, 82
    song indexing departments, 81
    writer's share, 58
A-side protection, 100
Band agreement, 13, 26, 80
    band name, 51
Band names
    choosing, 49
Bar code, 139, 169
    CD duplicators and, 82
    explained, 86
    monitoring record sales and, 129
    SoundScan and, 83
BDS (Broadcast Data Systems), 179, *See* Nielson BDS
Bidding wars, 126
Billboard Magazine, 134, 191
    mobile phone news, 253
Billboard's Radio Monitor, 192
Bio, 207–9
    how to write, 207
    sample band bio, 210
BMI, (Broadcast Music, Inc.). *See* ASCAP
Bogus compilation albums, 35
Booking agents, 228, 229
Breaker, 191
Brick-and-mortar independent record stores, 151–55
    retail consolidation, 249
Business structure, 24, 55
Buy-in, 134
Cassette demo tape, 28
Clear Channel Communications, 248–49
CMJ (College Music Journal), 184, 191
CMRRA (Canadian Musical Reproduction Rights Agency), 118
College radio, 184
    college rep, 184
    getting airplay, 194
Compilation albums, bogus, 35

Compulsory mechanical license, 114–19
    Harry Fox Agency, 116
Con jobs, 66
Contract periods, 113
Co-op advertising, 134, 148
Copyright, 45–47
    band agreement and, 24
    copyright notices, 81
    forms to file, 45, 46
    original material and, 82
    photographs and, 217
    poor man's, 47
    SoundExchange, 171
Cover letter:, 206
    sample of, 212
Cover versions, 114–19, *See* Compulsory mechanical license
Crossover hit, 176
Demo kit, 205
Demo listening session, 31
Demographic, 178
    Arbitron, 181
Design, 27
    design tips, 84
    quality of, 27
Digital aggregators, 170
Distribution, 8, 37, 69, 88
    distribution options chart, 136
    independent record labels and, 129
    major labels and, 128
Distributor one-sheet, 133
    description of, 144
    required by distributor, 133
Distributors, 131, 148
    instructions from, 147
    payment from, 133
    requirements of, 132
    shipping instructions for, 135
    store programs and, 133
    types of, 131
DIY (Do It Yourself), 28, 250
Domain name, 161
Drive time, 180–81
DRM (Digital Rights Management), 252
Early adopters, 70–72
E-music retail, 169–70
Entertainment attorney, 14, 23, 37, 51
Fact sheet, 208–9
    sample fact sheet, 211
Firm albums, 112
Four Fronts, 85
    explained, 4
    gatekeepers of, 208
    how they work together, chart of, 9
    marketing plan, 138–39

overview of, 5–8
  structure, chart of, 2
Free goods
  distributors and, 133
  royalties for, 109
FTP client software, 163
Gatekeepers, 18, 28–29, 207
  media and, 204
  radio stations and, 182
Getting signed
  DIY, 250
Harry Fox Agency, 114–19
  mechanical license and, 80
House concert, 71, 233–36
Independent distributors, 129, 131, 244
Independent record labels, 88, 87–89
  radio exposure and, 174
Independent record promoters, 36, 185
Independent record stores, 150
Internet
  downloadable music and, 252
  electronic press kit, 165
  good news and bad news, 251
  promotion opportunities, 71, 156
  radio stations, 253
  selling your music and, 164
  website, your own, 165
ISP (Internet Service Provider), 160
Late adopters, 73–74
Liability releases, 81
Licensing music, 254–58
  basics of, 259
Live performance, 35, 225–30
  band tour schedule, 237
  do's and don'ts for, 229
  performance contracts, 226
  revenues from, 231
  rip offs, 35
Major record labels, 87–88
  call-out research, 188
  radio airplay and, 177
Manager
  artist management deals, 63–65
  compensation, 64
MAP (Minimum Advertised Price, 151
Marketing plan, 138
  sample of major label, 140
Mass merchandisers, 151
Master recordings
  licensing overseas, 259
  ownership of, 96, 121
Master use license, 254
Mechanical license, 55, 80–81
  other terms for, 115
  outside the US, 118
Media
  tips for working with, 165
Mediabase, 180
Middle adopters, 72–73
MIDEM, 263

Money, 26
  band agreement and, 23
  for recording and promoting your music, 26
  investors, 80
Multinational corporations, 248
Music career
  being discovered, 28
  checklist for, 39
  commitment to, 23
Music industry contracts, 92–93
Music marketing, 76
  at major labels, 124
  changes in the last 30 years, 244
  early adopters, middle adopters and late adopters, 70
  house party, 77
  new challenges to, 248
  your fans and, 76
Musicianship, 29
  original ideas and, 31
MySpace, 71, 74, 167, 194, 204
Neilsen/SoundScan. See SoundScan
Net artist rate, 99, 101
Newton-John, Olivia, 111
Nielsen BDS, 182
Non-commercial radio, 184
  airplay, 194
Notice of termination, 260
One-stop distributor, 131
Option periods, 113
P.O.P.s (point of purchase items), 169
Parody, 117
Pass through clause, 99
Payola, 185
Performance, 224
  questions for venues, 242
Permission forms, 81
Podcasts, 253
PPD (Published Price to Dealer), 261
PPW (Plays Per Week), 179
Press clippings, 213
Press kit, 205
  folders and envelopes, 214
  ingredients of, 206
  photos, 215
Press release, 218
Producer agreement, 81
Product development, 4, 5, 12, 68, 69
  questions for music retailers, 172
Production companies
  deals, 94–96
  defined, 94
Production credits, 81
Profit split deals, 120–23
Promo kit, 205
Promo Rep, 124–27, 174, 178
Promotion, 178
  costs of, 27
  day by day summary of, 197
  strategy, need for, 80
Public performance income, 257

Publicist, 208
Publicity, 204, 219–20
    questions for magazines, newspapers, and e-zines, 221
Publishing
    music publishing company, 53
Publishing deals
    administration deals, 61
    catalog representation, 61
    co-publishing, 60
    income participation, 61
    overview of, 57
    single song agreement, 59
    step deals, 60
    sub-publishing, 62
    traditional, 58
Quote sheet, 213
Rack jobber, 131
Radio and Records (R&R), 175, 191
Radio promotion companies, 196
Radio station, 177
    consultants and, 182
    general managers, 179
    music directors, 179
    playlist, 179
    program directors, 179
    promotion department at, 183
    relationship between record labels and, 177
    the Internet and, 253
Radio station music formats, 175
    Arbitron reports, 181
Record label, 78
    radio airplay and, 177
    starting your own, 78
Record one, 99
Record producer agreements, 97
Record promotion, 178
Record release, 80
    expenditures for, 26
    legal checklist for, 80
    manufacturing tips for, 84
    priority releases, 124
    profit margin of, 151
Record sales, 129
Recording contract

advances, 102
    artist royalty rate, 108
    contract periods, 113
    options today, 112
    recoupables, 105
    red flag issues, 106
    term of, 111
    twenty years ago, 250
Retail
    music sales and, 150–55
Retail outlets
    in-store marketing programs, 150
Returns policies, 135
RIAA, 171
RIAA (Recording Industry Association of America), 251
Sampling, 81, 83
SDMI (Secure Digital Music Initiative), 252
Shopping a recording, 36
    scams, 36
Songwriting, 13, 32, 228
    issues to deal with, 39
    radio programming and, 182
    scams, 37
SoundExchange, 171
SoundScan, 86, 129–30
    registering with, 82
Synchronization license, 254–58
Tail-out commission, 64
Tip sheets, 192, 197, 263
Tracking, 182, 190, 197
    CMJ and, 192
    PPW (Plays Per Week), 179
Trade magazines, 191–92
Trademark
    Band names, 48
Trademark notice, 82
Trademark registration, 50
Unit, 169
UPC (Universal Product Code), 133
USNRC rate (United States Normal Retail Channels), 108
Work for hire agreements, 81
Working a record, 169
Writer's Share. *See* ASCAP, BMI

How to Promote Your Music Successfully on the Internet

Learn the promotion methods one musician uses to bring in over $5000 a month from the Internet!

A message from the author: The Internet is an amazing promotional tool for independent musicians. You can get radio play, grow a fan base, create a distribution channel, set up your own tour and sell your music all online. Wouldn't it be great if thousands of people from all over the world heard your music every day? What if you could use the Internet to sell hundreds of CDs and downloads every month? It doesn't take a brain surgeon to make it happen, but it does take hard work – and you need to know what you're doing.

Therein lies the problem. Most musicians just have no idea where to start when it comes to online promotion and distribution. Some get as far as putting up a web site, but stop there. They aren't sure what the next step should be. That's where I can help.

Who am I? I am an independent musician just like you, with one difference: In the last year, I've used the Internet to generate **over $60,000 in income**. Hard to believe, isn't it? But it's true. Today I'm doing the "music business" full-time from my home in Springfield, Oregon. I now invest my time working on my music rather than spending 40-60 hours a week working for someone else. I'm truly an *independent* musician.

My intent with this book is to give you the information you need to begin promoting, selling, and distributing your own music successfully online. I'll give you *proven* ideas you can put to use *immediately*. It doesn't take a ton of money to get started either – that's another great benefit of living in this digital age. Simply put, I'll take you step by step through the same marketing strategies I've used over the last ten years (since 1995) to promote my own music on the Internet and run my music business on my own terms.

I know you're skeptical. I too am a skeptic by nature. Here are just a few of my many testimonials from readers....

> *"How to Promote Your Music Successfully on the Internet"* is an incredible resource! It's not only the hundreds of techniques and tricks, it's how truly inspiring this book is. I sold more than 3000 copies of one of my CDs in 9 months as a result of reading this book." - Mihkel Raud

> "I bought your book and I just want to say a big thank you for inspiring me so much. Before downloading the book we were doing well online, but it took a lot of trial and error which in turn took time. After reading your book, things are beginning to skyrocket for us. We have huge interest in our debut album which is released soon and have built up a sizeable fan base which is growing by the day. If I'd have paid 5 times what I did for the book, I would still be absolutely delighted with the results I've got from implementing your methods." – Liam

> "I downloaded your book... initially I was skeptical (I am a fellow software type of guy & very analytical about things)... I just wanted to tell you that I LOVE it. Thanks a million—it's worth every penny."—Sheldon Schake

Want to know more? Visit my web site at www.promoteyourmusic.com . There you can read dozens of customer testimonials, get more detailed information, and even ask me questions if you like. LET ME TEACH YOU how to SUCCESSFULLY promote your music from my own life experience! Read all about it at....

www.promoteyourmusic.com

ORDER FORM

To order additional copies of
Music Is Your Business: *The Musician's FourFront Strategy for Success*

Your Name: _____

Address: _____

City: _____ State: _____ Zip: _____

Phone Number: _____ E-mail: _____

Please send _____ copy (or copies) of: ***Music Is Your Business*** at $39.95 US, each:

    Washington residents, add 8.8% sales tax to your subtotal: _____

    Shipping and handling, US & Canada, add $6.50 per book: _____

    Shipping and handling, international orders, add $12.00 per book: _____

    Total amount (US funds only): _____

Payment: Check ___   Money Order ___
Make check or money order out to FourFront Media and Music.

Credit card: Visa   Mastercard   **Sorry, ONLY VISA and MASTERCARD accepted!**

Credit Card number: _____

Name as it appears on card (please print): _____

Expiration date: _____

Mail to: FourFront Media and Music
               1245 S. 128th St.
               Seattle, WA, USA 98168

Questions about ordering? Call (206) 282-6116, or e-mail info@fourfrontmusic.com.

You may also order a downloadable PDF version for $29.95 from the FourFront website: www.fourfrontmusic.com